Margaret Dargelmaier

THE STATIONS
OF SOLITUDE

Also by Alice Koller

An Unknown Woman

THE STATIONS
OF SOLITUDE

Alice Koller

William Morrow and Company, Inc.
New York

Recognizing the importance of preserving what has been written, it is the policy of William Morrow and Company, Inc., and its imprints and affiliates to have the books it publishes printed on acid-free paper, and we exert our best efforts to that end.

Library of Congress Cataloging-in-Publication Data

Koller, Alice.
    The stations of solitude / Alice Koller.
      p.   cm.
    ISBN 0-688-07940-7
    1. Koller, Alice—Autobiography. 2. Philosophy.
    3. Solitude. I. Title.
    PS3561.0398Z477 1990
    818'.5409—dc20
    [B]   89-29899
                                                CIP

Printed in the United States of America

First Edition

1 2 3 4 5 6 7 8 9 10

BOOK DESIGN BY WILLIAM McCARTHY

To
JAMES LANDIS
Without Whom Not

PROLOGUE

A station is a stopping place.

Long ago, and in some far places even today, the geography of the land designed routes of travel. Midway through a mountain pass or at the entrance to a valley, an inn was a station and each was distant enough from the next to be welcomed by the traveler. If you walked or rode a horse or a donkey, you followed the line of inns if you could afford a dry bed, hot food, perhaps a bath. Otherwise, sleeping wherever you could, you were at the mercy of robbers or pneumonia or worse. And when the food you carried with you from wherever your journey began gave out or became too hard or moldy, you stole whatever would sustain you, or you knocked on doors and begged, or you exchanged your labor for a meal before you moved on. In one way or another, therefore, you paid at each stopping place until you arrived at your destination.

Today stations exist where those who own the vehicles of transportation decided that stopping is most profitable. The route that linked the stations around the hills and through the valleys and across the rivers was devised only afterward, after the economic decision was made. But the stopping place is only for the conveyance. You must transport yourself whatever distance remains when you disembark, a nuisance you tolerate because the station is near enough to where you really want to go. At that place, your destination, you expect to achieve the compelling purpose that uproots you from your daily round, lets you assign the inconveniences to some far corner of your memory.

The elements are the same now as they ever were, as they ever will be. A destination, some purpose sufficiently powerful, propels you into a journey. There are stopping places on routes designed by persons other than you for their economic profit. From the start of the journey to its end, you pay.

I am not Catholic. I am not religious in any sense of the word. Being religious requires a certain temperament, and I do not possess that temperament in any degree. No subject is too sacred for me to inquire into, and I ask too many questions. I could never consider "Believe!" to be an adequate reply.

So do not expect the stations of solitude to imitate those of the cross. They share common elements, but only because both are journeys.

Their destinations differ and the designer of the route differs: persons other than Jesus designed his destination and the route he took.

The profit differs, as is to be expected, since the designer of the route differs: profit accrues only to those who invest.

The price to be paid differs. The cost to Jesus was his suffering at twelve of the stations, presumably not at the thirteenth, where he was taken down from the cross, nor at the fourteenth, where he was placed in the sepulchre. Christianity emphasizes the voluntary nature of his acceptance of that price. That, and not alone the suffering, is the point of the devotional exercise that Catholics reenact within the walls of their churches and in their pilgrimages to the Holy City.

The kinds of stopping places differ. The route of the historical Jesus began on a specific date, followed a certain line of travel, and ended a certain number of hours later. But the stations of the cross became and remain a line of meditative travel that has been and will continue to be traversed by uncountable believers who reflect on Jesus' suffering at each of these stopping places, creating a repeatable route from what had initially been a singular series of events, as all temporal events are. In the eighteenth century the Franciscans reconstructed the route where it was first completed, providing Jerusalem with the now conventional number of fourteen stations (originally they were fewer), but the Way can exist in any sacred place. You have only to set foot on it and it will lead you to its terminus.

The only real similarities are that the stations of solitude, like those of the cross, mark out a journey that is a repeatable line of travel, and that anyone can choose to undertake it.

In circuiting the stations of solitude, your destination is the kind of person you wish to become. The line of travel is the process of shaping a human being, and the stations are stopping places in the process. Except perhaps for the early stations, the route is ad libitum: you move from one to another station at will, not because it is next in line. And there are circuits within the circuit: you will return to some of the stations many times because the person you yourself are designing is not completed the first time through.

The stations are recurring circumstances in which a certain kind of decision, and then acting on it, are required of you. The decision you're called on to make will have far-reaching consequences for the person you are, the person you wish to become. It is the price of the journey: that at this stopping place you must make a choice. At the early stations you throw out old choices and choose anew. At the other stations you reflect, you observe, you reassert an earlier choice or you revise it in the light of new observation, new reflection. At every station, therefore, you pay. But you also profit: you will learn, you will approach more closely who you want to be. Sometimes the choosing and the learning are painful; sometimes they are imbued with joy. Sometimes the choice is easy but the consequences are painful. Or the other way around: you suffer in choosing but the consequences are salutary.

I am not simply carried along by the hours of the day. My doings follow a distinctive pattern that is composed of and by my purposes. My purposes are the things I do that matter to me above all else. They are of my own making. I commit myself to them. I make choices in accordance with them, and my commitment to them commits me to other choices that are consonant with them, that are often the means for bringing them about.

My purposes are the geography that marks out my line of travel in circuiting the stations of solitude. Sometimes, just as I'm certain that I've arrived at my destination, I find a familiar station looming up before me, and I alight again. I have stopped here before, sometimes more than once. I return to these stopping places to carve more closely to my purposes the then-occurring events of my life, to consider some unpredicted consequence of my initial choice, or to somehow incorporate events over which I have no control: those precipitated by the actions of others or by nature itself.

The stations form a circuit that I chose to enter upon. My circuit will end when I do. But the stations of solitude will still be there to be traversed.

THE STATIONS

1

UNBINDING

THE ISLAND OF Nantucket lies thirty miles out to sea, south of Cape Cod in the Atlantic Ocean. For me it is a time as well as a place: I often say 'before Nantucket' or 'since Nantucket.'

During the winter of 1962 I spent three months there with the German shepherd puppy, new to me, whom I named 'Logos.' He had been observing and making sense of the world for four months before I wandered into his life. I was thirty-seven years ahead of him in sheer time on earth, but, unlike him, I did not comprehend the world we gazed at in common. From Boston I drove us south to Woods Hole, where we boarded the ferry, and then on Nantucket I drove six miles to the cottage I had rented in the village of Siasconset at the easternmost end of the island.

Every day, morning and afternoon, we walked to the ocean, sometimes by the roundabout route through the golf course, sometimes by the short way down the sloping road behind the post office. I quickly learned to time our arrival on the sands to coincide with low tide, although often I simply went there when I needed to be near the water, walking parallel with it, watching the line of its receding, its resurging, visible the entire length of the shore, a mile or more. Once a week I drove into Nantucket town for groceries, for a pile of books from the library, sometimes using the trip as an excuse to see other human beings on the streets, in the stores. My meals were nearly the same every day: eating was not a pressing concern. The mattress on my iron bedstead was thin, and it sagged into the ancient springs. But I was not on Nantucket to catch up on sleep or to meet new people. I was there to try to find out what I had been doing with my life up till then.

For a good part of each day, particularly when Logos and I were walking, most particularly when I stopped to sit on a certain log that had been washed up on the sand, I compelled myself to become aware of my ways of perceiving the contours of a situation, of responding to other persons, of recognizing the impact of others on me and mine on them, of gathering information, of selecting what would count as relevant, of deciding what to do and when and why. I did not rest from my questioning. And one day I came upon the purpose I had been pursuing all the preceding years. I had not known I had been doing that thing: I had believed I had been doing something quite different. So it was a huge thing to learn. Understandable, but ugly. Not palatable in any way.

I spent a night and a day deciding whether to continue living. During that night and that day I found that I knew how to call things by their right names, so that what was real stood out sharply from what was only phantom. I did not exactly decide to live. I only did not decide not to.

The price for opening my eyes each morning thereby became apparent. I had only to cast out the purpose I had allowed to reside in my heart since I was four years old. It did not deserve my pursuit, and anyway it was not of my deliberate choosing. With it, I could discard the beliefs and attitudes that had arisen from it, fed on it. I had no reason then to believe that I'd ever be able to replace that purpose with other purposes sprung from my genuine spontaneity (not understanding at the time what any of those words meant), but I set myself to chart a fresh life that I was unexpectedly eager to, unexpectedly uncertain I could, shape for myself.

The day after I left Nantucket I knew that I had never elsewhere done anything so important, even though I was then unable to say what, exactly, I had done. Only afterward, when I was joyously in the thick of the new life I was daily designing, tailoring ever more closely to my own contours, did I try to piece together the path that led me from Nantucket to where I then stood. To understand how I had gotten from there to here, I sat down to my typewriter and wrote my thinking. Long before I reached the end, I knew that the writing was a book, and I kept thinking of it that way during all the fourteen years publishers kept rejecting it until one published it as *An Unknown Woman*.

Less than a year after Nantucket, I talked for some hours with a man I knew well about what I had done there. He listened closely, watching me all the while I spoke, comparing, I think, the person he saw before him with the person he used to know. When I finished talking, finished answering his questions, finished refuting the statements he put to me by way of attempting to prove that I had not done what I said I had done, he was silent. Then:

"I can do that," he said.

"I have no corner on it," I replied.

"And I can do it right here." In that university town he was one of the golden boys.

We never spoke of it again.

A year ago, which is to say twenty-five years after our conversation, I learned that he has been in analysis for many years. Did he try to do the thing "here"? Perhaps not. Or perhaps he failed, too deeply embedded in "here" to be alone in the only way that would have led him to the first station of solitude.

You begin marking out your line of travel in the instant you recognize the extent to which you are alone: thoroughly, unremittingly, without other human beings. I call it 'being alone elementally': as an element, unconnected. It is the essential human condition.

Instead of calling it by its name, you perhaps flee from it. For you, being alone is being achingly aware of the absence of other human beings, and only the presence of another person can salve it. Yet that fearsome being alone is merely the starting point in an exhilarating process, the first step along a continuum whose end point is so far from terrifying that it is beyond price. The far point itself is accessible through a multiplicity of creative acts. It is your solitude, your unending creation of the life you can choose to live. By aborting the process at its early harrowing appearance, by rushing toward surcease through other human beings, no matter whom, no matter at what cost now or later, you deprive yourself of the one gift you can give yourself that no one else can ever deprive you of: the person you wish to be, the life you wish to live.

Being solitary is being alone well: being alone luxuriously immersed in doings of your own choice, aware of the fullness of your own presence rather than of the absence of others. Because solitude is an achievement. It is your distinctive way of embodying the purposes you have chosen for your life, deciding on these rather than others after deliberately observing and reflecting on your own doings and inclinings, then committing yourself to them for precisely these reasons.

During the more than two decades of my solitary life I have been at pains to point out that I am not alone in fear and trembling. I am only, have only been, without other human beings.

To become genuinely solitary, to be alone well, you must first have been alone elementally. For that, no "here" will do. An island is not necessary. Only be away from everything familiar: every person, every relationship, every circumstance. Friends, a mate, an analyst, a priest, a teacher, your family to take you in, even one person you can talk to, liquor, drugs, the occult, the divine: if you have any of these you are not ready to undertake the interior journey that will let you confront the person you are.

In that place, wherever it may be, where you will know no

one, have no obligations to other persons to deflect you from your unbinding, you will learn two things.

The first is that you are a ragtag assembly of relationships and of memories of events and hopes for the future, that their accretion is something you have more or less stumbled onto over the years, that you have patched together a life from the leavings of others. How you will go about discovering which parts of that ill-assorted collection to toss out, which to retain, if any of either, is a course of thinking, feeling, understanding, deciding, known only to you and that only you can devise.

The second thing you will learn in that place is that your life is entirely within your own hands: to shape to you, to make fit you, as only you know how best to do, how to do at all.

To lone (I am inventing the verb) is to become oneself and *thereby* to be able to spend one's time pursuing one's purposes independently of the presence or absence of other human beings. You lone in the process of becoming able to be alone well, but also in the practice of being alone well.

There is no "method" for doing the thing. Coming to understand who you are follows no easily delineated procedure. No one sudden illumination comes from you-know-not-where, after which everything falls immediately and perfectly into place. There are, instead, fleeting shafts of light, and it is you who prepares the groundwork for their appearance. They let you go forward a little way, but soon they disintegrate, and you fall back into the dark a greater distance than you had gained. But then you lure out another light, and follow it until it, too, slips away. So, winning and losing, in shreds and chunks rather than in a single unbruised whole, you find that the work is done.

That route toward yourself that you pursue by yourself is your reflective occupation at the first station of solitude. The journey is almost totally one of looking back. When you leave the station, you will probably never look back again. There will be no nostalgia for the life you used to live: it belongs to someone you no longer are.

The participants in the great drinking party Plato narrates in the *Symposium* decide very early in the evening that they will use their wine not to become drunk but only to refresh themselves while each of them has his say in praise of love. When the turn comes around to Aristophanes, he invents a tale about the origin of human beings.

In the beginning, he says, we were nothing like we are now. We were globular in shape, and we had one head with two identical faces, one looking back, the other forward. Each face had two ears, two eyes, one mouth, one nose. Our rounded bodies had two pairs of legs and of arms, and when we decided to change direction we simply used the set of legs pointing that way to take us there. Each body had two sets of genitalia, and there were three sexes. The men were those whose genitalia were both male; the women, those with two female genitalia; and the third sex had one male set, one female set.

In time, these round beings felt themselves to be so powerful that they tried to climb into heaven to dethrone Zeus. He, not wanting to destroy them totally, because that would end all their offerings to him, but wanting to teach them a lesson, arranged to have them sliced in half from top to toe. Under his direction, Apollo turned the face on each half from back to front, stretched the skin from the sides to cover the gash, and moved the genitalia around to the front. Thereafter, they walked around on only two legs.

From the moment of the bisection, each half ran throughout the world looking for its other half: the men for their man-half; the women for their woman-half; the man-half of the third sex searching for the woman-half, and she for him. And when they found one another they clung together and would not be parted.

And so we remain, said Aristophanes: we are all one or other of these three sexes. If Hephaestus, the great Joiner, were to come along to ask us what we want of one another, we would not be able to reply. But if he would offer to join us together again forever, we would realize that becoming the one whole being we had been before would exactly express our love for one another.

Just so will you rush throughout the world to evade being alone elementally, searching everywhere for the person or other being who will make you whole again. But you yourself are your own Hephaestus. What can be welded together is the gash at the place where you slice away the old self that you allowed to accumulate around a hollow center. You, not Apollo, can turn your face forward rather than back. And thereafter you will walk into new days of your own designing on only two legs.

2

STANDING OPEN

ON NANTUCKET I slashed away everything that was preventing my seeing, my hearing, my feeling, my understanding. When the thing I had been concealing from myself emerged, I raged, I screamed, I wept.

After a time I said, "So that's how it is."

Not too much later I said, "No longer."

By those words I moved onto terrain where almost everything that before had been familiar ceased to exist. I could more readily walk, uncertain, into the unfamiliar, because for all my preceding years, I had been paying an extortionate price for the familiar. I could not have guessed the profit in letting myself be uncertain of what I would do or become.

When I stepped off the Nantucket ferry onto the mainland on a cold February evening in 1963, any passing observer would have described me as a grown woman. From the inside, however, I looked out onto the world as an infant, confident of only three things:

Logos was of my heart.

I had to live near the sea or other wildness.

I possessed a passion and perfect eye for color.

You could pack it into a thimble, that tiny collection. But it was mine, freely chosen by me, once I was free to choose. Three things, where before I had not known there would be any! They had made themselves known to me when I slit my surface covering and wriggled free of it, as a snake its skin, a caterpillar its molt, walking away from everything that had hobbled me, everything that was not mine. They spoke clearly to me, those three things, and I, open to them, heard them. I moved toward them, smiling.

What it is to like, to want? Genuinely to like, to want? I raised these questions daily, hourly, on Nantucket. I could not answer. I had read and listened to the words of others pointing out the direction in which the answers lay, but I could not set my feet upon the path that would take me there.

Now I knew the answers, and the journey from there to here was short, all but instantaneous, once I removed the constraints on my spontaneity. To like is to incline naturally toward, to bend naturally toward. Some object or person inclines you to itself, bends you toward it, without promptings of any sort from any other person, from any "should," from any rule. You want something whenever you, trusting your own spontaneity, find yourself moving toward the thing, smiling. Liking, wanting, are pure, plain, direct, when you've unbound yourself from ancient longings.

I had come this far—three items!—by doing nothing more than standing open to what there was, right there before my eyes: all impinging events, ideas, people, objects. I *was* open. I therefore let myself *be* open. (I could have run for cover again.)

In the early days of the new life, I found myself saying, thinking, noticing, hearing, looking for, being drawn to: doing, being, without forethought. Nothing in me constrained me, restrained me. Having discarded all previous guides, I let myself be unguided. Having divested myself of familiar ways of behaving, I had no option but to be myself, whoever that would turn out to be. I was no longer behind the scenes manipulating the doll I, before Nantucket, had tried to make everyone believe I was. No one was behind the scenes at all, neither manipulating, nor feeding lines, nor applauding. There was only me: one, undivided.

Just there is the mark of being open: nothing intervened between me and doing, feeling, speaking. I *found* myself doing some new thing without having considered in advance the doing of it. I *found* myself being angry, interested, apprehensive in circumstances in which no one had told me that I ought to be angry, interested, apprehensive. I *found* myself affecting someone, affected by someone, without deciding in advance that he or she or I would respond to one another in just that way. I *found* myself speaking words I had not in advance planned to speak.

All these are gifts I still give myself. Not planning what to say, I find myself saying what I mean to say. That's surely worth discovering: what I mean to say. Not even in the early days was it an intellectual exercise: "Today I shall find out what I mean." Rather, unless I said what I meant, not trying to deceive anyone into believing anything except what I meant, I might take that slow easy glide down from fooling someone else to fooling myself again. Instead of wondering what others would think of what I might say, and for that reason abort the saying of it, I said what I meant and let them worry about what they thought.

At the memorial service preceding my father's burial, members of my family and of the congregation approached my mother to escort her toward the open casket. She sat sobbing loudly in the row in front of me, and as those people lifted her to her feet she struggled against them. Each step was a battle between her holding back and their half-carrying forward her nearly rooted body. Her wailing and half a dozen shoes scraping across the carpet were the only sounds to be heard.

In the quiet room I heard my voice say, "Let her be. Take her back."

Instantly they turned her around and led her, unresisting, to her seat. No one questioned the command I had not in advance considered uttering, even though the circumstance was one in which I had no authority to utter commands.

I spoke, not because I could not bear to have my mother be in such pain, or whatever it was she was voicing. She did not matter to me: I had disconnected myself from her on Nantucket, and it was my triumph that I had done so. I spoke in that silence because she was a human being who clearly, plainly, did not want to approach the casket, and I could not permit her to be forced to do something she so plainly, clearly, did not want to do. And although I returned to her house that day and spent an hour there among the mourners for whom she had prepared a meal, when I left I never saw her again.

This spontaneity, this sense of your own genuineness, is something you trust from the moment you come upon it. It is the serene fulcrum on which will turn all your choosing, thinking, believing, all the piecing together of your life from that time forward. Accompanying it, although perhaps no more than another face of the same coin, comes an omnipresent sense of newness.

This is the second station of solitude.

It is the end point you reach when you have thrown off everything foreign. It is the starting point for the new life you are now able to shape as you will. In my end is my beginning.

Still, I should not say 'your spontaneity.' The possessive pronoun with the noun misleads you into thinking it is a thing belonging to you, some part of you that you have somehow not discovered: a mind's eye, an inner ear, a still small voice. It is none of these, but this: you being yourself, acting and responding without planning in advance what you'll say or do, without considering whether or how you will or ought to act or respond but simply being as your newly freed inclination moves you. It is doing, seeking, feeling, liking, wanting, without a prepared exterior, varnished and perfect, between you and any person, any circumstance. It is you being a certain way: spontaneous, yourself. 'Your being spontaneous' is the properly grammatical phrase, but the gerund trims my leeway for saying these things.

It is being free. But it is only part of being free.

At least since Kant, philosophers have distinguished two aspects of the concept of freedom. Not duplicitous because of its two faces but rather whole, like the moon, all of whose sides we can at last see. Free: not only having no restraints but also being self-governing according to laws of your own choosing. And even though acting in accordance with those laws can carry consequences you might not choose for their own sakes, you acquiesce in those consequences because they are the price of the laws you *have* chosen. You mistake freedom when you focus only on the first, the being unhindered. A spoiled child governs herself only by the whim of the moment, having no conception of her most intimate purposes, and thus having no conception of the consequences that will ensue from her actions. Heedless of them, she will be at their mercy, for they will occur, will she, nil she. Because the second holds the key, clarifies the interrelationship of both. Not being bound by anything except what you choose, where your choices spring from a genuine sense of what your life is and can become: that's the connection between there being no constraints and your being self-determined.

You cannot reach this second station until you unbind yourself at the first. These two stations, alone among all the others, are inextricably connected, irreversibly ordered. You do not travel to it: it is no more than a doorway off the first. But, like Alice's doorway, you cannot enter it until you are the right size. In the moment you cast off your last fastening, you will be here: standing open, viewing the world and everything in it as though for the first time, each moment presenting itself as an occasion to be freshly sensed, perceived, conceived; saying, doing, wanting, seeing, understanding things you have not said, done, wanted, seen, understood before.

Only you can come upon your own spontaneity, only you can unloose it. I can't even tell you what it's like: by its very nature, it is ineffable. But I can point out for you a line of travel toward it, and I can say: "By this route you will arrive. At this place you will in time come to the thing."

You are not like someone who has been blind since birth. All the words in any language can't help me let a blind person imagine the color of a male cardinal, but neither can I lead her to the bird himself and say, "There. That's red." She cannot regenerate her optic nerve, but you cannot see only because of the encrustations you have let seal your eyes. You have only to rip them away. The cost is exceedingly high, but when you step through the doorway that you will then fit, where you will then stand open, you will know forever that no one could put enough gold into your hands to buy your unbinding back from you.

3
CONSTRUCTING

THE KNIFE THAT carves away the old is wielded by your hand, no other. After you discard the parts of yourself you no longer want to own and are being guided and impelled by your own spontaneity, you turn the knife to the flat of the blade and use it as a mason's tool, gathering up and cementing together the new parts of the new self you have freed yourself to construct according to your own design.

It is the third station of solitude: choosing the elements as well as the pattern in accordance with which you will thereafter construct the mosaic of the self, the life, that belongs to you.

From Nantucket I carried back to the mainland two categories of thing. Logos and wildness and color were in one category. The other held two principles for my journey to the strange land:

I would let myself be open to whatever else came along to join the three items I was already certain of.

I had to know what was true. *Had* to.

They're quite different, these categories. In the first, each item carries some mark on itself that lets me directly gather it in, without intervening steps, without stopping to question. Whatever I find myself going toward, smiling. Of inanimate objects that I brought into my household—an uncomfortable but crudely beautiful Spanish chair, a set of black and brown bowls and goblets and plates

14

from Italy, a lamp of Indian brass—I could say only that they spoke to me. All these are highly specific fragments, bits, units.

The other category consists of criteria for choosing, guides for action, principles of commitment. They take longer to acquire since I gather them in a different way. I accumulate a certain number of bits of the first sort, and then the "I" doing the piecing is caught by something in common among them, reflects on them, and elicits it from them. Or from some action of mine I lift out a principle that I find myself using. Or in anticipation of some future action I temporarily adopt some maxim that seems sensible to try out, perhaps to discard later if it proves unsuitable. Ways of proceeding that were habitual to other persons demanded extended periods of consideration from me. And even when I finally permitted some new precept to enter my repertoire ("Not all questions deserve a reply"), I often found myself relearning it when some situation in which I found myself didn't immediately call it forth. Only afterward, thinking over what I had done or said, would I see the new principle as one I could have used. Thus slowly did I join some new fragment to the collection, some new guide to the already functioning system of beliefs and habits, integrating the new with everything else I had chosen, no seams showing.

One principle served me as knife: I had to know what was true. It was one of the two with which I laid out my line of travel at the early stations, the one still in my portmanteau that touches all the rest.

'True' is a term applicable to statements, not to the world, philosophers of my stripe say. Reality, in this version of things, is that which true statements purport to be about. 'Purport' is crucial. It includes the eventuality that the statement is false, purporting to be true but failing. It excludes utterances that do not purport to be true at all: commands, exclamations, rules, promises, and so on.

In order to know whether the statement you utter or hear someone else utter is true, you must go and observe that which your statement purports to be true of. What exactly happened? Why this rather than that? In these circumstances, someone in this relation to me would naturally say (do) thus-and-so, yet he said (did) other-than-thus: how explain the discrepancy? Have I taken into account all the relevant matters? Is there evidence from some independent source that would tend to confirm my statements? If not, is my account of the matter one that some competent observer might agree is the most plausible (since we must often act on less than adequate evidence, and even be our own competent observers)? Is there evidence that might tend to disconfirm my account? If so, am I willing to start all over again to try to discern the hard outlines of a situation, a relationship, removing the muck under which it lies buried?

And yet, before you can know whether what you say is true, you must first know what you mean to say: you must first try to say as carefully as you can what it is exactly that you are looking to find.

Coming to understand what you mean to say and coming to know whether what you say is true both require you to ask questions. The questions are of different kinds but they nourish one another, and their answers give rise to fresh questions until, after a time, you're willing to accept the answers you reach. Provisionally, any-way, until they in turn, as they will, give rise to further questions.

By such ceaseless questioning, by not even entertaining re-sponses, mine or others', until they first met a standard of clarity I did not then know I possessed, by making myself see and hear what was there to be seen and heard regardless of what I might want to see and hear, I had discovered the truth about myself on Nantucket. I could do no less than pursue with the same tenacity the truth of every subsequent circumstance that mattered to me. It is difficult enough to decide what to do in most of the situations of your life. How to decide at all without the firmest foundation of carefully articulated true statements you can obtain? And when the consequences of your decision will endure for years, how to weigh them *in potentia* unless you learn as much as you can about each of them and about their bearing on everything else you do? It is the barest minimum requirement for acting rationally.

Through the unknowing tutelage of my mother, I became someone who has to know what's true. Not simply because she named me 'Alice.' Barely in command of an elementary school education, she did not know that 'Alice' derives from the Greek *alitheia*, truth. She couldn't know that she had selected the one word that would accurately name my occupation, my profession, my very being. The least surprising fact about me is that I am a philosopher, a person who seeks to understand. It is the prior condition for knowing what is true.

Nor did she choose the name because she had always loved it. When she was pregnant with me, she happened to see a woman wheeling a baby carriage, and the baby within seemed to her the most beautiful she had ever seen.

"What is your baby's name?" she asked the woman.

By that casual circumstance, just as moviegoer mothers a few years later named their daughters Shirley and Judy, my mother named her baby, me, with the name I detested as a child.

"So plain," I used to say, "like Grace. And Mary." Learning my first foreign language in the seventh grade, I discovered 'Alix' as one of its two French counterparts, and I proceeded to spell my name the new way on homework and test papers in all my classes, not just in French class, throughout one entire semester. One day my French teacher took me aside to explain that the English spelling of my name had a perfectly legitimate French pronunciation that she herself thought was rather nice, and thereafter I reverted to 'Alice.'

No, it was not just by naming me that my mother succeeded in laying her indelible stamp on me. She did it by not telling the truth herself.

If she had always exaggerated, always put a little spin on the facts, it would have been easy enough to catch on and to make the necessary correction, as a cook does when he knows his oven thermostat is off by fifteen degrees. But my mother lied just often enough to keep me off-balance: I never knew when she was telling the truth. And so I had to spend a good deal of time weighing her words against facts, against actions, against other people's words, against what I myself saw and later heard her describe, in order to sort out what was true from the ever-receding barrier she kept erecting between me and it.

Once she said, "We have no food in the house." Not three minutes earlier I had taken an apple from the refrigerator, leaving untouched dozens of eggs, butter in bulk, bottles of milk, fruits and vegetables packing their cooling compartments, roasts already cooked, other meats awaiting preparation, and an assortment of sauces and condiments in jars and bowls. I had been almost unable to close the bin from which I had drawn the apple, so tightly wedged in was it with its kind.

Never before in my fifteen years had so damning a piece of evidence come so swiftly to hand to measure against her words. I returned to the refrigerator, flung open the door, and read off its contents to her. Then I inventoried for her ears the freezing unit above: racks of wrapped and labeled meats, more butter, bags and cartons of vegetables, cylinders of juices.

She was sitting at the kitchen table preparing a shopping list for groceries, and she lifted her eyes only long enough to give me a dirty look. I knew that look very well. It had been directed at me more and more frequently in those days of my beginning to be old enough to make real the dream I had held so long: to leave her household at the earliest possible time.

Even so, even counting the days, it was two years later, a week before my eighteenth birthday, until I could walk out of her door and into the wide world where I ever after applied the lessons I had learned through her unintended instruction. Where I ever after, until Nantucket, looked for her, whom I thought I had left behind.

Long after I was able to free myself from the stranglehold she had on me, long after I had cut myself off from her so totally that she had been dead three months without my knowing it until an attorney wrote to notify me, I'd wonder in an idle moment why she had lied so often, so seemingly capriciously. But I never bothered to press the inquiry: it mattered so little.

I suppose the answer is simple enough.

In her family of three brothers and three sisters, she being the eldest daughter, her father was the dominant person. No one, not even her mother, ever laid a glove on him. The principle that a girl gets what she wants from a man only by guile, and even then, even after she tries all that, she's still at the mercy of the king's whim, was not confined to that working-class household in which she grew up at the turn of the century, but she certainly breathed it in. So when "No" is as equiprobable as "Yes" from absolute authority, and when you're not too intelligent in the first place, you learn a way of dealing with the person who holds all the reins, and later you transfer that procedure to everyone else.

My mother could not have made a poorer choice of husband, both for herself and for him, than my father. He was bright, perceptive, gentle, not ambitious but hardworking, far better educated with his law degree than she. He had no inclination to dominate her or anyone else, and she, who understood only how to be subordinate to someone in power, came to nurture an immense contempt for him that quickly became her determination to head the household. Whatever she had learned of coyness, of girlish ways, in being the daughter of her father turned inside out in being the wife of my father. If my father couldn't be the person in charge, as her father was, she'd have to be. And since her father ruled by no set of beliefs that she, with her limited wit, could discern, she would rule her own family the same way.

Still, there was that other power beyond her household: the whole rest of the world. And since the only way she knew how to deal with authority was to placate it by half-truths, that became her path toward achieving her purposes in relation to everyone else.

Over the years these two ways of behaving intermingled, and by the time I began trying to figure things out, she was telling lies within her home and outside of it too. During my growing up, I saw her as pure willfulness.

But I was her child as well as my father's: I had willfulness of my own, and I took her on. If she failed in shaping me toward some specific purpose, she'd instantly let out all the stops. She'd scream, I'd scream back. The difference between us was that I hated the loud fury whereas she saw it as the natural means for getting what you want. After one of those sessions, I'd run to my room and close the door, there to remain for an hour, trembling with horror and hatred, while she merely returned to her sewing.

When I finally rooted her out of my being, I had already lived thirty-seven years. I understood then the extent to which she had been pulling the strings of my every move as though I had been her marionette, even though I had removed myself from her geographically and economically. I had inhaled from the air surrounding her what she had inhaled from the air surrounding her father. Unlike her, I was able to rid my lungs of it, and to start all over again to understand: how to be, with myself and with other people.

So having to know what's true was not a principle I chose at random.

How to recognize what's true when you've spent a lifetime pretending? The stakes must be high enough.

And when are the stakes high? When not discovering what's true will leave you only two alternatives: to find some way to live, knowing that you've failed in the most important thing you can ever do for yourself; or to find some way not to live any longer.

So you try to shape your bewilderment and your terror into a sharp and clear understanding of the task and of the means for resolving it. Your perceptions of what you're up to take on an immensely keen edge when you are at the same time aware of the cost of failing. Because the only way you don't recognize what's true is by refusing to recognize it. And you do recognize it: you do know. Indeed: only you know. And here is why being away from everything and everyone familiar is the geography of the first station: familiar people and circumstances cushion you, make it easier to keep on pretending that you have no purchase on the matters you are trying (you tell yourself) to learn the truth about. So don't look for someone to hold your hand during the unbinding. And don't expect anyone at all to applaud when you've done.

Then how do you know whether what you're doing, what you've done, is what you set out to do?

Like gold, it will ring true for you: what you come to understand need satisfy only your sense of, your criterion for, what is true.

That's a difficult sentence for a philosopher to write. It was a difficult sentence for me to utter, alone with Logos in the living room of a house at the edge of a moor on an island thirty miles out to sea, knowing all the byways of all the arguments for and objections to all the theories of truth that appear on the philosophical agenda, two thousand years' worth. The received wisdom is that a statement can't be true just for you or just for me: it is not true unless the conditions in which the stated outcome occurred can be repeated and the outcome found to occur again by anyone knowledgeable enough to undertake the confirming experiment. My sentence, however, makes no claim for concurrence, explicitly denies that concurrence is relevant.

The small opening bears remarking: anyone knowledgeable enough. Because only you are knowledgeable enough when the matter at issue is who you are, what you want to do with your life.

□   □   □

When Hume bent his hard eye inward, he came upon only this bit of memory, that particular anger, this specific fondness, but no overarching Self gluing them all together. One's self, he concluded, was no more than this, that, or the other item of awareness present at any given instant. But in playing his game of hide-and-seek he seemed not to have noticed that he was It. So Hume could not have stated the problem properly. Because, in fashioning a new person, I confronted the paradox that I was both the self being pieced together and the "I" doing the piecing. What that "I" would turn out to be, viewed abstractly, was a question I could postpone until I was far enough along in the doing.

At a certain point I became aware that the making carried with it an imperative for making into a one. I was daily conscious, not simply of doing new things, of seeing in new ways, but of unifying into a single life the threads that were entering from, that I was sending out to, all directions.

Kant wins over Hume hands down: a self is not simply an assortment of thises and thats but a latent system, all of whose thises and thats can fit together. Can be made to fit together. Can, if you choose. Once you come to understand, or otherwise find, your purposes, you cannot evade ranking them in hierarchies. Once their order is chosen, they commit you to decisions that are for that very reason easy to make and yet prodigiously difficult to carry into action. By then, you are able to choose only between two sorrows: to give up the commitment, or to give up acting on it. If I have anything at all left to teach, it is what living this way is like.

On Nantucket I dismantled one self. Since Nantucket I have been designing, constructing, another. Some of the new assembling was intentional. Some of it went on, after I got the hang of it, without making myself deliberately aware that that's what I was doing. After a time I took the parts apart to study, to wonder at, reflecting upon and coming to understand how my self was built, what it consists of.

To this station I returned more frequently early in the undertaking than I do now. Particularly since the day I noticed a narrow path opening off my well-worn route and pursued it to its end. It led to another station that is rarely visited and that you may decide to pass up when you come upon it. But that is matter for a tale later on.

I surround myself with silence. The silence is within me, permeates my house, reaches beyond the surfaces of the outer walls and into the bordering woods. It is one silence, continuous from within me outward in all directions: above, beneath, forward, rearward, sideward. In the silence I listen, I watch, I sense, I attend, I observe. I require this silence. I search it out. The finely drawn treble song of a white-throated sparrow is part of it. Invasions of it by the noise of engines are torments to me.

This is my solitude.

I do not cloak it among other persons, and I know how it appears. No sign of submission, in the eyes of most men; too assured, in the view of most women; not properly respectful, to the gaze of all those in authority. I have become that third gender: a human person, the being one creates of oneself. I fell in love with my work, became fiercely protective of my freedom, started to make new rules. In this, Sartre is surely right: persons are not born but made. The choice lies escapably within ourselves: we may let it wither away, or we may take it and run.

4

AWAKENING

I AWAKEN IN darkness. The only sound I hear is the even flow of air being blown by the small rotating fan on the floor just beyond my open bedroom door. I lie without moving for the moments it takes me to fasten onto the day of the week. It is Sunday. The second of my own two days each week these weeks. The thought shifts me off the bed. I need no light. I know my way.

This morning the moisture in the air is already high, remains high from yesterday and the day before, is projected high for today, perhaps into the early days of the new week as well. If I lived less visibly than I do in the house where I abide this year, others equally small clustered too near mine, I would wear only shorts and thongs. But I cover the top half of my body as well. The lightest briefest shirt is almost tolerable.

These minutes have gone by without sound from me. I intrude neither into the darkness nor the silence. The early morning, before dawn, before first light, is my time. I take it in privacy. By not turning on lights, by inserting myself soundlessly into the day, I am simply one more natural entity. I do not need to announce my presence in order to be.

Footgear becomes an issue, a small one. Whatever shoes I find in my room to get me downstairs will come off in the kitchen where my boots stand ready for taking Kairos outdoors. Booted, even in summer, I can withstand the soaking dew on the morning grass where we wander or in the woods three miles away. I drive us there some mornings, once the dark recedes.

This morning as I start to descend I hear Kairos downstairs, feel him listening to my steps, watching at the bottom for me to appear. I slide my right hand along the wall at the first landing until I touch the banister's edge that will guide me downward in the dark. Kairos spends the night independently of me, now in this two-story house, as in houses we have inhabited with rooms all on one level. Some nights, in thunderstorms particularly, he climbs the stairs to my room where a thick foam rubber pad I made for Ousia long years ago rests in an alcove it almost fits. He never really awakens me when he reaches my bed, his head on the same plane with mine where I lie pillowless in imperfect sleep. I have already heard him taking leave of his mat downstairs or wandering into the kitchen for a stop at his water bowl. I have heard the faint clicking of his nails on the uncarpeted section of hardwood floor at the foot of the stairway, and I know he is deciding whether to ascend to be with me. During the past year his hindquarters have occasionally made climbing difficult. What is at the top of the stairs had better be worth the effort.

Have I heard him first? Or have I awakened him by moving my body just enough to reach his unimaginably sensitive ears, a sound where none had been until that instant? Have I awakened him by the least turning of my body on my bed, or by a new rhythm of breathing, or by some shade of a sound that is beyond my audible range? And he, hearing me, changes position on his own bed or leaves it, making the sounds I then hear?

Do I awaken my dogs—Logos for nearly thirteen years, Ousia overlapping nine of those and remaining with me six more, now Kairos, companion to Ousia for four years, until he and I were left alone these last eight—or do they awaken me?

The question is one for which I can never have the answer,

and yet, for the twenty-five years I have lived without other human beings in my household, lived in the country without other
human beings even nearby, I find myself recurring to it, puzzling over it.

My first country house, in Connecticut, was surrounded by
woods. There were no other houses on my side of the steeply curving
highway. Across the road one house stood uphill, another downhill,
of mine. Woods buffered us from the road and from one another.
Logos was only nine months old, too innocent to know the difference
between the sounds of human stealth and those of a careless raccoon
on his nightly stroll. Not yet trusting Logos to be my ears in the
new house, fresh from the three months just ended on Nantucket,
and before that, from a lifetime in cities, I set myself a task during
my early years of solitude: to immediately identify every sound in
the night. I taught myself to awaken, out of no matter how deep
a sleep, at any unaccustomed noise, until I understood that wild
creatures lived in the country too. I soon gave over the task to
Logos, who in time handed it on to Ousia, and now it belongs to
Kairos. But I have never lost my aural acuity or the trick that uses
it. And now that Kairos' hearing seems less keen than last year
(although from the living room he can hear me in the kitchen
opening the package that contains the graham crackers he knows
as 'cookies'), I have once again set myself to come awake instantly
at any sound that I in my sleep cannot account for.

In that house in Weston, while I was still learning the true
shape of my day, I awakened as late as seven in the morning. It is
the schedule of people whose livelihood requires them to appear in
an office somewhere by nine, as I then had to do during my first
year and a half in the country. The sun would have been up for
an hour in winter and for more hours than that in summer and yet
I would still sleep. I used to resent the light flooding my room,
assaulting my eyes, awakening me before I had finished sleeping.

I squandered part of my first paycheck buying special shades to lightproof the room where I slept, then closed my bedroom door each night as double insurance of darkness, light from the other rooms upstairs otherwise penetrating the shrouds of my sleep. The whole rest of the house was for Logos, and he, a fitful sleeper, patrolled the rooms, up and down the polished stairs half a dozen times in the night, more than that when the moon was full.

Had I left my door open, Logos, awakening just before dawn, would have wandered into my room, nails tapping on the floor, tongue tentatively exploring my face that rested unprotected on the level of his. With the door closed, the first morning sound I'd hear would be his muffled step approaching my door. He'd circle a few paces, then come back again to sniff half a dozen times at the narrow space between door and floor to assure himself that I was there behind the silent wood. I'd hear his body sliding down the door until the whole of him lay against it on the floor, and there he'd sleep again. An hour later when I'd open the door, he'd be on his feet, already bestowing on me his matchless morning greeting that had started my day every day since he and I lived alone together on Nantucket.

Within days of our moving into the Weston house, Logos chose the closet in the guest bedroom as his nighttime resting place. The closet was wide and shallow with a sliding door that I kept open for him. When I understood the permanence of his intention, I bought an inch-thick slab of foam rubber cut to the size of the closet's floor, and sewed a cotton cover for it, a mat for his retreat during the long night, or at any time.

But some nights, if Logos were sick or if the loneliness for my own kind were too cruel, I'd leave my door open. Logos would begin his sleep by lying beside my bed on our only rug, a blue-green-black hand-loomed wool extravagance, now vanished, while I, who sleep on my stomach, would dangle my left hand over the edge of my mattress until the tips of my fingers touched the fur of his back, and somehow that scant contiguity would bring sleep to me at once.

My connection to Logos opened me out to the whole of the natural world and taught me the intimacy of my interconnections with earth, air, water, with wild creatures, initiating me into a world I had inhabited for nearly forty years without living in it. I still enlarge that education, still draw on it, cannot now conceive being without it. Its beginnings lay in the barely noticeable first step of letting Logos outside as soon as I awakened each morning. That minimal commitment very quickly turned into my going outdoors with him, and then into leading him away from the immediate environs of our house and lawn. Where else but the woods? Where else but the lonely unpaved road nearby where cars coming along would be audible far in advance of their visibility and where the protruding rocks and the ruts of the road would deter most drivers from entering at all, would slow to nearly second-gear travel those whose reasons for choosing the route were as compelling to them as mine to me?

And this being outdoors was taking place very early in the morning, when few human beings had yet awakened. By their default I inherited the silence. After that I had only to look. To look and then to try to see and then to see. And all the while listening, at first hearing I knew-not-what. Because in the country seeing a wild creature directly is rare. Most of the time you have to be satisfied with the signs a creature leaves behind. Or the sounds it makes when it knows you're there or when it doesn't or when it knows but doesn't care. And sometimes you hear the sounds for years without identifying their maker. Until one day you see the creature in the instant he utters that pure three-note whistle that breaks briefly at its peak and then descends, and you can't believe that only this chickadee, among the tens of thousands you've seen, has finally in your presence made the sound you've heard only from hidden members of his species during all your years in the woods.

The early morning walks were only the first of the day. There were walks in the last of the daylight, no matter the time of year. The very long walk in the early afternoon. And the ten-minute gambols outside on weekends, morning and afternoon, no matter the weather, as much a respite from my work as a release into noisy activity for Logos after hours of lying quietly under the long desk where I worked, his chosen place.

To work at home, my schedule my own to fashion, emerged as the first clearly defined goal of my new life. Grants from a federal agency supported some research the government considered valuable, and Connecticut College affiliated me with itself to administer the funds. Thus did I come to be daily at my own desk and in the woods with Logos beside me. There could have been no happier woman in the world than I.

Awakening on your own schedule teaches you in an extraordinarily short time the contours of your day, its sleekest fit to your most intimate rhythms. My permeatingly important discovery was that I had a primitive need to be outdoors at dawn, immersed in and observer of the day's beginning. With Logos I'd walk in the woods or stroll down the old gravel turnpike a mile away, be back in my kitchen for breakfast at sunrise, and be at my desk working before six of a summer morning, and only a little later in the depths of winter. Mornings are mine: I came to know it forever in the first few weeks of my grant, as the hours of my day became ever more surely bent to purposes I was at the same time exploring. Not before noon did I allow any person, any event, to trespass into the reading and thinking about the new topic that had already begun to interest me, stirring up connections to the philosophy I had done in graduate school. But there I had worked under duress that was external and in time became convoluted into pressures I laid upon myself. Here I was able to let the problem itself direct me, rapping at doorways into the knowledge that I had acquired under those impossible circumstances, knowledge that emerged in forms I had not consciously designed and yet that seemed to be waiting for me to pluck them out, as Excalibur for Arthur, to bring them to light, to my light.

When Ousia joined us the following year she let me know that where I was was where she wanted to be. From the moment I closed my door at night, she settled against it on the other side, no matter that the floor was hardwood and that downstairs she had a rug-covered closet of her own. She did not move from that place until Logos came looking for me when he awakened at dawn, nudged her aside from occupying the place he knew to be his, then inhaled my scent at floor level, where he settled himself for the last stretch of my sleep.

When Ousia's estrous cycle began six months later, I absented her to the vet's protection for the necessary ten days because, although I wanted her to bear Logos' son, she would be too young until another year had passed. The day I retrieved her, the vet cautioned me that Logos might still find her exceedingly attractive even though she would not be receptive. Rarely do medical people make statements of such sheer accuracy. For the rest of the day I ran interference between Logos' amorousness and Ousia's snapping rejection. At bedtime I scooped Ousia into my room along with the foam rubber mat I had bought and the new cotton cover I had sewed in her absence for her closet bed downstairs. She spent that night and the next with me, the door firmly closed, Logos patient on the other side. By the third afternoon she lost her lure, and the two resumed their former relationship: she adoring the king, he ignoring the intruder. But from then on and for the rest of her life Ousia, who never budged through the night until I flung back my covers each morning, slept in my room on her own bed at the foot of mine.

After six years in Weston, we moved to Canada, a former Harvard classmate having arranged a faculty appointment for me in a university with a name prophetic of a time that I try never to think about. Logos, ever ahead of me in taking the measure of our surroundings and unfailingly aware of whatever I was feeling, became sick the very first night we arrived. At seven the next morning I found a vet to examine him. I could probably prevent surgery, he told me, if I'd nurse Logos according to his exact directions. I unpacked my bed and the dogs', opening only enough cartons from our move to find a few spoons and plates, and spent unbroken hours with Logos during our first ten days in that house. No bedroom door closed him out at night. When he passed through the crisis he elected to sleep in one of the other rooms by himself, but my door remained open ever after.

In our next house in the country, in Connecticut again, awakening became the first game of the day.

Unpillowed, my head rests flat on the surface of my bed, twenty-odd inches from the floor. It is exactly the height of the pair of cool noses that graze lightly against my forehead, then wander into my hair to stay briefly for a deep sniff; of the warm tongues that explore my eyelids and the tips of my fingers that I have carelessly allowed to lie exposed.

"Is she awake yet? Let's see who can get her up first." If they were whispering to each other, Logos and Ousia could not be saying these things to me more plainly. If I betray the faintest hint of a shade of movement, I lose the game.

Do they really interrupt my sleep? No doubt I shift and roll and slide and breathe a little differently in the shallow sleep that preludes my full awakening. Logos promptly construes any of these changes as an invitation to begin the day, not only because he himself awakens quickly, getting to his feet in the same moment he opens his eyes, but also because, having three years' head start on Ousia, he knows better than she which are the true and which the misleading indications that I can be lured off my bed.

In my awakening I am not alone: I am merely without other human beings. The friends who greet me consider each day a new one to be tied off only when it ends: not before, not later. What matters is only this: we are together, all of us, here, this morning, and nothing could be more extraordinarily felicitous than that.

I raise my head: Logos' forceful tongue lathers my face. Ousia thrusts her nose between us, growling softly that he would dare to think the privilege exclusively his. Logos gives way in recognition of my incomprehensible liking for Ousia, so that, by gracefully ending his share of the morning loving, he's doing something for me rather than for her.

Touch alone tells me who has petitioned me awake. Ousia's face is sleek and silky; she is content to lay her muzzle against my face for long minutes while I stroke her head and rub her ears. Logos' fur is shorter: not stubbly but almost bristling with the vitality that makes him impatient of any contact lasting longer than five seconds.

I roll out of bed, go to the door, and hold it open.

"Do you want to go out?" I ask.

Two pairs of eyes regard me solemnly; sometimes Ousia blinks once. Both dogs stand or sit as though frozen wherever they happen to be: even the most hard-nosed experimenter will understand that they are saying "No." Only when I close the door again do they move, each to some comfortable place within eyeshot, while I dress. They want to go out, but *with* me. Yet I always give them the choice.

In silence they watch me. I get as far as putting one foot into a leg of my jeans: Logos immediately takes up his station next to the door. I reach for a shoe: Ousia places her forepaws flat on the floor, lowering the whole front half of her body in an immense stretch that raises her back almost in an arch. She shudders slightly from the effort, utters one big sound that I know is only a yawn, and strolls over to Logos, there to wait out the last minutes of my levée.

One shoe on, two dogs holding their breaths to go out, I sit on the edge of my bed.

"Okay, Logos: where's my other shoe?" It is the second game of the day.

Logos can guess, and is almost never wrong, which pair of footwear I am about to use. Slippers, sneakers, sandals, pumps, boots: morning or any time, I find only one of them, no matter how neatly I may have laid them ready. Logos, sauntering past while I am elsewise occupied, lifts the shoe with his mouth, flips it slightly to get a better hold, then finds some corner where he lies with his chin resting on it: it is his guarantee that I will not be able to leave the house unless I first make arrangements with him. But sometimes in his hurry to get to the door ahead of me he leaves the shoe behind; or I dawdle too long over choosing a sweater; or I receive an early phone call. Unexpected minutes thus intervene between his having the swag and my needing it. When I watch the way he goes about trying to remember where he left the shoe, I swear he deliberately looks in the wrong places for the sheer joy of keeping the game going. His tail moves faster in proportion as his glances under the bed or bureau become more cursory.

I try to raise the ante. "Don't you want to go for a walk?"

He rushes to the door, barking that I have misunderstood him if I think he doesn't. No good: I am still without my shoe.

"Logos. My shoe."

He stays at the door, sitting as alertly as though I had put him under an obedience command, brazening me out. Our eyes lock.

"My shoe."

He breaks then, going straight to a place where I have already looked three times, and drops the shoe at my feet on his way back to the door. The toss of his head conveys his belief that only my blackmail lets me win.

We are outside so early that heavy dew bathes the grass. Rubber boots keep my feet dry and let me follow the dogs through brush of any height. This morning walk is first before everything: before breakfast, even before coffee. It is my way of thanking Logos, then Ousia, for their nightlong continence. But what started as my gift to them has become theirs to me: I *must* be outside in the young morning. It is a need of mine to see the unsurpassable New England light on the leaves or on the snow, to gauge the clarity of the sky, to smell the coming of summer or the edge of autumn in the air, to locate the branch from which stanzas of birdsong pour. And if from time to time my first inhalation outdoors tells me that someone surprised a skunk nearby, or that the humidity will be unendurable by midday, even these bits of intelligence are superior to what I breathe and hear and see on the rare occasions that I awaken in a city.

This Newtown house is the tamest of the four Logos and I have shared, of the three in which Ousia has joined us. Granted, there are two acres of grass, which I myself mow; two ponds; a brook in constant motion except late in summer; and another two acres of wooded steep hills directly behind our house. A combination of natural and fabricated fencing runs around the entire circumference: I saw to that, with the help of a man I hired during the first three days we moved in. Yet, even with these four or five acres in which Logos and Ousia can run free or climb or swim, I am aware of constraints. At least half a dozen other houses are visible from the curving expanse of our lawn, and we are within audible range of householders who probably mutter in their beds at Logos' first salute in the morning light. I miss the deep woods of our house in Weston, where Logos could bark his fill to persuade me to throw a stick for him and not easily be heard by any other human ear. Most of all I miss the miles of beauty, never to be had again, along the winter sands of Nantucket where Logos and I, before Ousia, walked without seeing another human being. I promise myself that our next house will border wildness again.

From New England I transported us to Washington for what would become nearly a ten-year exile. Washington, because the federal government would not run out of money, and I, whom the academic world would not hire, could be clever enough to find some opening into the honeypot. I offered my pen educated for other purposes to anyone who would pay me for my words on paper: to write, to edit, to analyze policy, the latter being a task that I think may exist only in the federal government, which is nothing if it is not policy.

We did not live in Washington but across the Potomac in northern Virginia. Our house was at the end of a thousand-foot-long gravel lane that was my driveway and that ended at the doors of my garage. Woods covered my side of the lane, marched beyond the lawn I was letting grow wild, and cut my dwelling off so casually from the respectable houses and carefully trimmed grass on the other side of the lane that I saw only one of those neighbors once during the more than three years we lived there, and that only because of some emergency he had. We wandered along paths in the woods that differed for different times of day or different weather or different moods, and fewer than a handful of times did we encounter other human beings, they having entered from the far side, from the turnpike to the east nearly a mile away.

From my civilized house at the edge of wildness I made forays into the world of power, returned home clutching an assignment like a squirrel an acorn in autumn, and worked in my study, occasionally in libraries, on a schedule of my own making. When I exhausted the printed materials in books and reports that my project needed, I'd tap into the immense amount of information stored in the heads of an astounding number of extremely knowledgeable and competent people. You find the people by getting on the phone.

During one of these calls I stumbled upon a new idea about awakening. On a certain day the person at the other end of the phone turned out to be a writer, and we traded notes about our shared problem of saving out enough time and energy for our own writing after the day of scrambling for our living had claimed most of both.

"There are weekends and evenings, of course," one of us said.

"But evening has never been my time for working." This from me.

"About six months ago I started getting up at four-thirty. It gives me three hours before I even have to think about the office."

A plain idea, fortuitously voiced. Even though it sprang from someone other than me, I recognized it as belonging to me. I never laid eyes on the man, but he changed my life.

That night I set the alarm for four-thirty, and the next, and the next. Working alone at my desk with only my lamp for company was unspeakably exhilarating. When I'd sense the room beginning to lighten, I'd scrunch more closely over my work, my pen hurrying to finish the last sentences before Logos and Ousia, stretching from the sleep I had interrupted by stealing out of bed at the new hour, came to tell me it was time for our walk. After a few days I yearned for more of that dark silence, and so I set the alarm for four o'clock. Within a week I no longer needed an external prompt to awaken me because, unknown to me until then, I had touched my well-spring: I was awakening at my own time. From then on, I simply awakened at that hour, or close to it, as I still awaken now, to the beat of my own internal rhythms, thereby tripping the pattern in accordance with which my whole day unfolds.

At that hour I have two joys, or three, or twelve, depending on how you count. My work in the absolute silence. The silence itself, almost palpable for the sense it gives me of being part of it, of making what I wish of it. And being outdoors in the darkness, the stars overhead, the air fresh, the silence nourishing.

The time is mine. No one else is about. As fancy moves me, I write at my desk until, in the long minutes of dawn, the upper sky becomes exactly the same shade of blue that it held the evening before at dusk. I roll back my chair, and Kairos and I wander this path or that in some woods nearby. One blue October dawn we were crossing an abandoned pasture when I looked eastward and up into the sky. High above the horizon at which the sun would not appear for another quarter-hour I saw three things arranged along so perfect a vertical that I did not have to move my eyes to take them all in. At the base, the waning crescent moon, risen not three hours before, halfway toward its highest point in the sky. Midway, five Canada geese in wedge formation flying south. At the peak, moving with illusory slowness in the opposite direction, a supersonic jet gleaming from the brilliance below it, laying down its vapor trail that superscribed the flight of the geese with a white path in the rapidly paling sky.

Two houses before last, a shapely hemlock stood ten feet tall a few yards beyond the kitchen door. It was the home of a flock of slate-colored juncos, a fact handed to me when I stepped out into the darkness with Kairos the first morning I awakened there. Half the hemlock erupted in juncos flying in all directions to evade the unexpected threat. Within a week they became accustomed to us. Thereafter, only if I carelessly brushed too close to the hemlock's slender drooping branches would a single junco startle and fly off.

Another October in another town a red fox and I stared at one another in the dawn light at a distance of something less than twelve feet. He was more visible to me than I to him, a half-ton of shiny blue steel concealing me as I drove slowly along that country road, scouting out new routes for me to run and for Kai and me to walk. The three of us were the only creatures awake and doing on that day's reach toward sunrise, and the glimpse I caught of the fox's tail as I passed made me forget to throw in my clutch when I stopped. The car stalled, but its gift was silence. The fox emerged from the shrubbery at the end of a driveway, then stood quietly, hearing Kairos shouting at him from the backseat, trying to locate the source of the sound, looking straight at Kai but unable to see him behind the closed glass windows. I drank my fill of him until he turned back into the bushes, retracing the route that had brought him to me.

Some mornings I work only an hour, and then, in the dark, drive Kai to the woods a few miles north. By the time we arrive, we will have outraced first light. Thousands of mornings I've been outside in the darkness before the cutting edge of dawn that is the trailing edge of night. In woods, on trails meandering along hillsides, in the midst of broad meadows, I've cleared my mind of all distraction, doing nothing other than looking around me, all my senses primed to mark what surely ought to be the unmistakable difference between darkness and the light. I'm not sure I've ever succeeded. You'd think there'd be a moment at which you could say, "Now, right now, it's no longer dark. Now, this instant, the light begins." Yet I stand wondering whether my night vision is becoming more acute, or whether in these swiftly moving moments first light is already growing around me.

If I ever come upon it, I know I'll lose it by merely standing there and marveling at it. Because while I'll be trying to decide whether I'm finally seeing first light plain and simple, it will be melting into the minutes of early dawn, when everything is clearly visible but the sun has not yet risen. If you are not yet aware that time slides along, carrying you with it moment by moment, go outside any morning into the silent dark and look for the very beginning of first light.

The morning after Christmas a few years ago, near half past six, I walked out of my door into streaming moonlight. An immense full moon lingered above the western horizon, not ready to set for another hour. From below the eastern horizon a coppery red suffused the sky. I headed due north on the flat country road, shorn fields on either side, Kairos' and my morning footsteps the only sounds in the silence. To my left the old ivory of the full moon idled against the royal blue of the western sky. To my right the sunrise yet to come was lightening the eastern sky toward daylight blue. Twenty minutes later when I turned homeward, south, the reddening edge at the eastern horizon extended higher, and now the huge moon wore a faint flush of palest orange. West the setting moon, east the rising sun, their concert lighted me inside and out all the way home.

There is a price to this early rising, but I pay it without reluctance: I am tired by half past eight in the evening. By then I've been awake, thinking, working, in motion, for sixteen hours. It is the length of anyone's day. Sometimes, not often, I want to attend an evening meeting or a lecture that begins at the usual eight o'clock. But soon, sitting quietly, I find myself sinking into sleep, and I lose the thread of the talk in battling to stay awake. I do not win. At the first polite moment I leave. If I can participate—having dinner with a friend, say, or reading from my work in front of an audience—the extra adrenaline always surges to keep me awake. But once at home I pay a double price: stimulated by the interchange, I have passed the point at which I naturally fall asleep. I lie wakeful for long hours, sleeping only a short hour or two until my body's clock, still set for the early hour, awakens me. The following day I know by midafternoon that I'm tired, and I touch my bed that night earlier than early.

And what of films? Concerts? Ah, they cost money I don't have. Parties? They cost money to give and even to attend, but primarily they require knowing enough people who are more or less accessible geographically and who touch, even though it be on the periphery, one or another aspect of my life and I of theirs. And I do not have that: I am not part of any community. But that is less a consequence of my awakening at four o'clock in the morning than of my knowing why I awaken at all each day.

Consider: unless the very time at which you awaken is set only by your own body's clock and not by some foreign sound that, although you may have chosen it, is timed so that you'll arrive somewhere on someone else's schedule, then all the other events and actions that enter your day are functions of some continuous compromise you're engaged in with other persons, not all of which or whom may be to your liking. Not that compromise is bad. But if you're uncertain at the very core of your being why you awaken each day, the compromises in which you're engaged all day long will rarely be skewed in your favor. Once you know why you awaken, the hours of the day become subservient to that purpose, those purposes. It is an inherent consequence of a purpose: that it shapes your time. The question is only: whose shaping will you permit? Either you know your own purposes, or you will in your ignorance allow your life to be carved away, slice by fine slice, pursuing the purposes of others. You may be aware, acutely or with hazy vision, that your life is being lived for someone else's purpose. It is your life, to live as you wish. When will you start?

5

WORKING

I WRITE MY thinking. I think by writing. I persist in the belief that I can articulate whatever I think about. Because I persist, I can. Because I know how, I can. By the words I choose, by their sound and sequence and significance, I shape for you new eyes, new ears, a new mind, so that you, reading, listening, say, "Yes, that's what I mean (or see, or think, or hear)." I write what I mean, what I understand, what I know. This is my work.

It is a peculiar kind of work, writing one's thinking. It is not writing fiction, or poetry, or criticism, or history, or plays. It is not even autobiography. It is not reportage, or commentary on current events. It is not instruction in some economically useful skill. It is not homily. Several philosophers, all men, all secure in their tenured positions at major universities, tell me (indeed, they insist) that it is not philosophy, but they are the same people who let me hang in the wind. Members of English departments are uncomfortable (because it is not fiction or poetry or . . .). Essays, perhaps? Yes, I essay to write my thinking. I am a philosopher studying my own mind. And when I look outward at the natural world, I essay to write my seeing and hearing and touching.

Ah, you say, do people get paid for doing that?

You are raising a different question.

Getting paid is the reason for having a job. A job is doing

something other people want done, and so they have to pay someone to do it.

Work is a world apart from jobs. Work is the way you occupy your mind and hand and eye and whole body when they're informed by your imagination and wit, by your keenest perceptions, by your most profound reflections on everything you've read and seen and heard and been part of. You may or may not be paid to do your work.

Getting paid to do your work, being given money so that you'll simply continue doing whatever your work is, is the only worldly success worth remarking.

People who know what their work is but haven't found a way to get paid for doing it confront a problem that pervades all aspects of their lives, a problem jobholders never encounter. They must figure out how to keep for themselves the portion of their day in which they do their best work while at the same time giving over enough of the rest of their day doing someone else's work, having a job. People who work do two things, not one. Like jobholders, they have to support themselves. Unlike jobholders, they must support their work, too.

On the wall near my desk hangs a diploma, inscribed on parchment and in Latin, signed by the presidents of Radcliffe College and Harvard University, admitting me to the rank of Doctor of Philosophy. In philosophy. A Ph.D. squared, a friend observed.

Lawyers need courtrooms and offices for the exercise of their skills; surgeons, scalpels and special rooms and sterile clothing; carpenters need tools and ladders; conductors, the instruments of the orchestra. But philosophers need only a chair to sit in (we can even stand) to do what we do: explore a vagrant thought to see where it will lead, uncover the assumptions lying hidden in a stated belief, pursue the consequences of a proposed course of action to their bitter or felicitous end, untangle concepts that don't belong

together, bring together ideas commonly believed to have no connection to one another. It can sound like simply talking. And any
conversation, any event, can prompt it: the questions of philosophy
lie in wait in the ordinary as well as the unusual circumstances of
daily life. Sometimes, socially anyway, I have had to clench my
jaws to keep from speaking. Still, these head-splitting efforts to
understand can't be closed off until tomorrow or after the weekend.
Some philosophers, I among them, must understand everything all
day every day. And no wonder: understanding is what philosophers
do. A dozen years ago, during my lawsuit against the two veterinarians who let Logos die, I had occasion to say that over and over:
"I *must* understand." But the persons to whom I said it mocked it
as an explanation.

Yet, two years after receiving that diploma, I was not being
paid to do philosophy. I had held six other jobs: publisher's reader;
secretary to a city planner; freelance writer of encyclopedia articles;
scientist at a contract research company; assistant to a magazine
editor; one semester of a university's nonrenewable teaching appointment at its lowest rank and salary, obtained only after writing
two hundred letters of application and only because the philosophy
department had a last-minute vacancy. I had lived in New York,
Cambridge, Santa Barbara, Boston, then New York again, where
one autumn morning I awakened in terror and despair to stare into
a mirror at the ruin that was my life.

I fled to Nantucket to try in that isolated place to make sense
out of everything that had gone before. I walked the miles of winter
beach twice, three times, each day, alone except for my new shepherd puppy. Remembering, discovering, analyzing, doubting,
weeping, screaming, cursing, I tore away all the beliefs and attitudes
that had hobbled me up till then. After three months I left Nantucket
having neither place to live nor job but knowing for the first time
the difference between telling myself the truth and telling myself
lies. To retain that hard-won criterion, I had only to say what I

meant from then on: having undeceived myself, never to deceive myself again.

Without having gone to the near-wilderness that was Nantucket in winter, I could not have done it. There I learned what the shape and texture and locus of my daily life had to be. By having removed all socially imposed regulation of my activities, I began to uncover the intimate rhythms of my being. The imperceptible changes I was making in the ways I moved through my day would suddenly coalesce into something wholly new. Although I could not have said so at the time, I was providing myself with the context in which I most naturally flourish. But being on Nantucket was a happy accident.

Without having had my back up against the wall, I could not have done it. I had run out of alternatives. I had nothing and no one to fall back on if I failed. Some small part of that may have been accident, but no part of it was happy.

Without Logos, I might not after a while have bothered to get out of bed. Some part of finding just him, no other dog, was accident. But all of having him was happy.

Without my philosophical training, I could not have done it. I knew how to ask questions, and I knew what counts as an adequate answer. I knew how to open my beliefs out to merciless study. I knew how to take the role of my own worst enemy attempting to refute me. I knew how to carve away vagueness so that only clarity remains. I knew how to start thinking and never stop, but who besides philosophers knows what thinking and never stopping is? No part of that was accident. No part was happy.

These four, but without my being a philosopher I might merely have found Nantucket the most congenial shore from which to walk into the water.

I did not understand any of this, nor what my work was, for some years.

□ □ □

In the first few weeks of my raw new life after leaving Nantucket, I took the only job available. It was just a job, a source of income. Rather good income then, for a woman, and sufficient for me to pay off two-year-old debts, buy clothes, many of which I still wear, and furnish my house, while I came to learn the nature of my days. While I kept my freshly opened eyes sharpened for the work I'd want to do if I ever came upon it.

The company that hired me was a contract research organization. Its business was to conduct research, under contract, for people who had money to spend for solutions to their problems, usually the federal government. The company could either wait for the feds to announce their needs through public channels, write proposals to perform the research requested, and hope theirs was the lowest bid; or they themselves could propose research and hope thereby to tap some as yet unnoticed government need.

Into my second year I found a federal agency willing to sponsor a research project that I conceived. I gave my company the opportunity to make good on its promise of a raise six months earlier.

"Not yet, Alice. You know, there are men here who are earning less than you."

"And do they have their Ph.D.'s? And can they do what I do?"

"No, but they have families to support."

"So do I."

"But you don't want to incur their resentment when you have to work with them. Let's wait a little longer. Spring, say."

"Last spring you said six months."

"Not yet, Alice, not yet."

It was all the justification I needed for leaving and taking my project with me. To receive the research funds I didn't need the company. Statutes forbade my receiving the federal money as an individual, but any respectable institution could be an appropriate conduit. Connecticut College administered the funds for me, complete with most of the perquisites of faculty status, and left me in peace.

To work at home. In the country. With Logos. Startle me awake in the night and ask me to talk of happiness: I'll tell you of the long minutes of exultation on the day I knew that I had guaranteed our freedom and joy, Logos' and mine, for two full years.

The Air Force Office of Scientific Research was the federal agency sponsoring my studies in the foundations of linguistic theory. AFOSR's interest in a philosopher rested on the insightfulness of Harold Wooster, director of its information sciences branch, who saw the value of my proposal to clarify some of the issues in linguistic meaning that were bedeviling everybody's work in what was then called 'mechanical translation.'

Mechanical translation, a.k.a. 'machine translation' or MT, was a plan, more like a hope, for translating natural languages into one another using only computers. The initial idea was Warren Weaver's, conceived in 1948 when Russian scientific literature was so voluminous and proliferating so rapidly that there weren't enough human translators in the United States to do the job. Fluent Russian and English weren't sufficient qualifications: translators also had to be familiar with subject matter—physics mainly, biology some, much technology—so that they could provide American scientists and engineers with readable and accurate translations while the research was still current.

Attempts to program the computers started at what ought to have been the beginning. English and Russian vocabulary, English and Russian technical terms, English and Russian grammatical rules were stored in computer memory. But what came out was unintelligible. Human translators still had to spend almost as much time repairing the garbage as they would have spent doing the entire translation themselves. If you had no preconceptions about what ought to be happening, it was easy to see what was missing:

the tough-minded MT people had no way of accommodating linguistic meaning. I proposed to point that out to them in a way they'd find palatable.

The project was one I had invented. It would proceed along lines that I alone could explore, modifying them as I worked, choosing what to read and when to read it, choosing whether to work in the libraries at Yale or Connecticut College or whether to carry the books and journals to my own study so that I might from time to time lay them aside to go outdoors and play with Logos, choosing which days to work and which not, choosing my own hours, responsible only to one single deadline: October 31, 1965, when I was to deliver to Washington a final report that would throw significant light on a problem of far-reaching importance that had not, until I outlined it, been adequately addressed.

Each morning when I sat down to my desk I could immediately pick up the tendrils of the thought I had come upon the afternoon before. Each afternoon I pushed back my chair, still riding the growing excitement of what kept happening before my eyes: on the paper on which I wrote and on the page from which ideas sprang out at me. Each day at my desk something grew a little taller, broader, deeper, and it was all my own doing.

But Logos needed a companion of his own kind during the hours I was spending on the research that was buying us the life I was shaping to fit me. And so I brought into our household a female shepherd puppy, and I prepared for her arrival as I had not known how to prepare for Logos'. I named her 'Ousia,' the truly real. In time she joined Logos at the concentering point of my life.

By December of Ousia's first year with us, the book about Nantucket I had then barely started, a few pages at a time on weekends, began to intrude into my weekday thinking about the linguistics research. I wasted days trying to fight off its demand but it refused to be confined to only Saturdays and Sundays. I capitulated to its call. To begin writing it, I borrowed a few months from the research the American people were supporting. (I later repaid the debt by finishing the final months of the project without receiving funds.)

I was, you see, living in joy. A life of days in which my freedom was palpable; a life without other persons but also without constant longing for them; a life in which the motives of human beings were accessible for the asking or through patient observation; a life in which I weighed my small but obtainable goals and found them worth pursuing or else to be discarded; a life in which, secure at its very center, I looked out onto a world that was comprehensible, so that it was either malleable to my purposes, or else I was able to stop wanting the thing I could not have.

How had I come to such a life from one so unlike it? A life over which I had no control and yet over which no one else had any control, either; a life in which the purposes of other persons were as baffling to me as were my own; a life filled with days trembling on the edge of terror and tears.

An inward journey lasting three months had altered the entire vision of the world that thirty-seven years had heaped over me. That journey was an unguided one between two unknown points: what I was when I undertook it, and what I could become. I wanted to reconstruct for myself alone how, exactly, that journey took me from there to here. Writing of that journey became another journey, this time a directed one between two known points: what I had become and that other life that suddenly, as I began writing of it, seemed to belong to a woman unknown to me. I wanted to retrieve the path between before it dimmed. The journey that was the writing would lay before me the journey that was the doing, and then I would know, in all its particularity, the precise path by which the woman I am now, who was once unknown to me, came into being.

That was my subject.

To understand what had happened, what I had done, three years earlier, I needed to write it. Not that I understood it and then wrote it, but that the understanding came in the course of the writing.

I had to find the beginning, and the ending, and then fill in all the gaps, in an otherwise imperfectly connected series of events. Imperfectly connected, because connected merely by temporal next-ness: this, then this, then that. I needed to organize, lay a grid on, the unrefined data of memories and wantings and despairings that I stumbled upon, that I deliberately dredged up, that I forced myself to examine, when I undertook the process of coming to know myself.

Purposes constituted the ordering principle, the thread that strung together events seeming to have occurred at random, connecting them perfectly: I was making my own purposes clear to myself. And although, before Nantucket, comprehending another person's purposes was all but impossible for me, I now grasped with equal perspicuity the purposes of other persons. By the time you comprehend your own, the purposes of other persons become so transparent that they may as well be written on their owners' foreheads. Not that you project your purposes onto someone else, but rather, knowing what you intend, you don't get in your own way when you observe others, listen to them, talk to them, to see what they intend. And you must understand the purposes of others: if you understood only your own, you'd continually collide with theirs.

Understanding, clarifying my purposes, I could reconstruct the series of events on and preceding Nantucket as though they were being recorded while they happened.

("Ah," said a philosopher I know, "so *An Unknown Woman* is fiction!" No. The fiction is the belief that human beings can record, set forth the details of, an event while it's happening. The fact is that no one ever really records an event. The only sort of "recording" that ever takes place is of events that are already half-told through customs or rules that implicitly organize them before our very eyes. For the extended series of events we call 'processes,' customs and rules can't give us a beginning, a middle, and an end that will let us prepare a record. Where to find something that will serve the organizing function? For the process of coming to know oneself, the tool that lends structure is understanding: we can, we must, make our purposes clear to ourselves.)

If a journal is a congeries of unedited reports of encounters, doings, regrets, delights, hopes, written for one's own eyes, written so that the day will not be forever lost, so that at least the feeling of its passage will be present to memory, all the more reason for my book about Nantucket not to be construed as a journal. It is a reconstruction, a consciously crafted record, something I could do only afterward, after I succeeded in coming to know myself, after I grasped the beginning, middle, and end, and all the steps between. I did not describe the process by which I came to understand myself. I don't believe it can be described. But I set it forth, I displayed it, and in that sense I gave an account of it. *An Unknown Woman* delineates the process by which one comes to understand oneself.

In six weeks I wrote ninety-three pages. Then I remembered my obligation to Washington. But not conscience alone impelled me to return to the project: I had to set the Nantucket pages aside to salt.

Ink from pens and typewriter ribbons bites into the surface layer of paper, altering it in some way that a chemist could explain to me if I were to ask. I think of that ink as carrying my words into the page and, just as salt draws the bitterness out of eggplant and the excess water out of yellow squash and green, so ink draws off whatever cloudiness may have entered the paper with my words when I first incised it. When I go back to the page after a time of letting the inked words soak, the unclarities become visible to me by their contrast with the lean bones of the sentences and their joins, one to another. I take up my pen again, and then only the sharpened lines and their clear connections remain.

After my working holiday, I returned to my research and found myself drawn to the concept of a rule.

The problem of rules had been circling at the periphery of my project from the start. Not just because philosophers, following Wittgenstein's lead, had found in it unexplored ground, but also because linguists, under Zellig Harris' guidance and later Chomsky's, had come to realize that the presence of rules may be the distinctive characteristic of human language.

The whole of linguistics can be thought of as divided among three kinds of rules: syntactical rules that order the grammatical elements; phonological rules that distinguish and classify the speech sounds of a given language; and semantical rules that set forth the meanings of words or phrases.

The difficulty about rules from a logical standpoint is that by their very nature they cannot be true or false. Their nature is to direct us to do something, or how or when to do it. Only statements—sentences claiming that something is or is not so—can be true or false, and only empirical evidence of one kind or another can let us discover whether they *are* true or false. But since rules make no claim to be true or false, empirical evidence can neither confirm nor disconfirm them. The hallmark of an empirical science, however, is that experimental investigation is necessary (although not sufficient) to confirm or disconfirm its hypotheses and thus lend weight to or weaken its laws. Research can of course uncover whether certain persons on certain occasions of speaking or writing do or don't *use* certain rules, but empirical research cannot confirm what many linguists wanted to say: "These are *the* rules, all these and only these, for English [or French, or . . .]." Those persons saw linguistics as a formal, not an empirical, science, and their goal was to lay it out as a system of unbreakable rules.

Now, linguistics may be about rules without the rules being unbreakable, and it may be about a set of rules without being about a system of rules (which is a connected set of a certain sort). Linguists who believed their science to be formal had drawn an improper lesson from logic.

In logic, a conclusion is true if a certain relation (implication) holds between premisses and conclusion. The relation holds if the rules of valid inference were followed, and the rules of valid inference *are* unbreakable rules. The price of logical truth, however, is that it is purely formal: it is totally independent of empirical stuffings, the everyday kind of truth we're after when we want to know whether in fact Joseph arrived at the airport in time to catch his plane. For logical truth, the nub of the matter is that it's possible to reason correctly (which means: in accordance with certain patterns of reasoning) while at the same time uttering falsehoods, stupidities, and literal nonsense. But it's also possible to reason incorrectly (that is, to fail to be in accordance with certain patterns of reasoning) even while your statements are quite accurately garden-variety true. Because logic is concerned only with certain *relations between* utterances, not with the truth of individual utterances, nor with their structure.

Linguistics, on the other hand, is centrally concerned with the structure of individual utterances. In whatever sense linguistics is formal, it's not the glamorous pure formality of mathematics and logic. The rules that many linguists are seeking might be only homely formulas, some of which are simply less frequently breakable than others. And those rules might form only a collection, the way a disassembled combustion engine is a collection of engine parts, instead of forming a system, where the parts cohere tightly with one another, the way all the parts fit and function together in a working engine.

But if linguistics is neither formal nor empirical, its concern with rules—which everyone acknowledges to be a genuine concern—raises the question of the kind of science it is, a question falling straight into the laps of philosophers.

I was pursuing only one aspect of this larger topic, and I had no idea that it would become a full-fledged paper when I began. I was merely scribbling notes to myself in that internal dialogue that Socrates first drew to our attention. Thinking up the strongest possible arguments against my own position is the ostensibly difficult but floodingly easy way to be certain I'll find the flaws in my reasoning, the blunt edges of the ideas I'm trying to sharpen. By that device, dialectic, I covered pages. Then I scissored parts that didn't belong together and stapled together parts that did. One day I came to the end: the matter that had sent me to paper and pen to think out lay clarified before me. I had grappled to the mat a topic that had taunted me, and although I had had glimpses of the contours of that kind of triumph, its full face had never shone on me before. Not even the writing of my dissertation, undertaken as it was through my own relentless commitment to be done with it, carried such a sense of high accomplishment.

Then, like a boxer who has just won a prizefight, even though my opponents weren't other bodies but unclear ideas, I looked around for my next match. I was unwilling to let go of the intellectual intoxication that still clung to me. Out of the blue I remembered my unfinished struggle five years earlier to understand one laughably small segment of a Platonic dialogue.

The lecturer in the introductory course in which I taught sections at the University of California at Santa Barbara had included the *Euthyphro* on his reading list because he, like most philosophers who teach first-year students, believed it was Plato at his easiest. Well, the *Euthyphro* does exhibit the Socratic search for a definition, it does conclude without having achieved the definition while showing all the false starts people commonly make toward the goal, and it does display the tough pursuit of a question that is Socrates' eternal contribution to philosophy. It is also about religion. The reason most students used to (probably still do) take a beginning philosophy course was that the religious beliefs they had grown up with were being challenged by the new life they were then entering, and they expected that philosophy could straighten them out. So when Socrates says to Euthyphro, "I am glad to meet someone who really knows what holiness is. Please tell me, so that I may know too," students eagerly keep turning pages to find the answer, not understanding that Socrates' gift to them is the complex dissecting of the question.

Two evenings before the *Euthyphro* was scheduled for discussion in my sections, I set aside a couple of hours after dinner to refresh my memory of it. Outlining the dialogue, I discovered a tangle I had never noticed before in the second of Euthyphro's five attempts to define the nature of holiness under Socrates' close questioning. By midnight I still hadn't straightened out the line of reasoning, nor, after the day's teaching in a different course intervened, was another evening more fruitful. Faced with teaching the dialogue the following afternoon, I outlined the rest of it and tossed my unsorted notes into a folder to await a time without deadlines when I could finally clear up the problem to my satisfaction. I was uneasy at having to gloss over what I myself didn't understand, but for the next day's class it mattered more that philosophically unsophisticated students grasp the shape of the dialogue as a whole, and particularly that they gain some sense of what Socrates was up to.

The deadline-free time showed up fresh on the heels of my victory over rules. I spent a maddeningly delicious two weeks with the old impasse, leaving it only for a couple of days when I knew I had to put some distance between me and it, but I untangled it finally from beginning to end.

The paper on rules had been prompted by my research into semantic theories for linguistics. It was paid for by my Air Force grants, and it served some purpose for others beyond letting me clarify certain ideas. The *Euthyphro* paper, however, had no purpose other than the sheer doing of it. An intellectual problem had been nattering at me for five years. I had to resolve it. "Reasons and Loving in *Euthyphro*" was pure philosophy. Doing it, and completing it, marked for me the turning point from which thereafter I thought of myself as a philosopher.

During graduate school, and even after receiving my degree, it did not occur to me to identify myself by my field. Plato and Socrates were philosophers. So were Hume and Kant. Russell, certainly, and Peirce. How could I possibly consider myself to be among that company? True: I knew what they knew, and I knew how to do what they knew how to do. But being a philosopher wasn't simply being employed in a certain way, as being a carpenter was: it was thinking at a certain level of excellence at the peak of human intellectual achievement. I was unwilling to elect myself to membership in that group.

But that was before Nantucket, where I jettisoned all unexamined beliefs and attitudes. Now, three years after Nantucket, finishing my paper on *Euthyphro*, I knew that I was a philosopher and would be one ever after. I didn't need an academic rank next to my name to confirm externally what I understood from within. Writing the *Euthyphro* paper was the first time I had used my philosophical knowledge and skill to do something philosophical for its own sake. My unremitting absorption in it for all those days without being paid to do it, without even the promise that it would be published, gave me the exemplar for doing something for its own sake in my work, in my professional life. It matched the exemplar I already had at hand in my personal life.

That preoccupation with work, which had stretched over nearly three months of beginning to write the book I then called "Map of an Inward Journey," of completing the "Rules" paper and the paper on *Euthyphro*, hurled me into a state of exhilaration that I had never known before. That I have never forgotten, can never forget, perpetually tried through years of poverty and irrelevance to reinstate. That I once again find myself in as I write these words. Not all ecstasy is sexual. Or religious. And yet not *ekstasis*: standing outside oneself, out of control. I hereby invent *instasis*: standing inside oneself, in full and rapturous control begotten in doing one's work.

Instatic, I turned back to the linguistics project and quickly became immersed in writing the final report for AFOSR. I called it *A Hornbook Of Hazards For Linguists*. Considering that it was my first piece of full-scale research and writing since my dissertation, there were no easy straight lines between that and it. The route lay, instead, along the road that led south from Boston to Woods Hole, where the trip by ferry crossed thirty miles of water to Nantucket and to three months of walks on Siasconset beaches with Logos.

The form of my dissertation followed a centuries-old pattern prescribed as much by its traditional purpose of being a new contribution to knowledge as by my field of philosophy. The form of the *Hornbook*, however, could be whatever would most effectively serve its purpose. But the purpose was mine to choose as well. And since the content too was of my choosing, an extent as wide as my imagination cared to range along opened up before me.

The style of my dissertation was also laid down by academic custom. "We see that . . ."; "We must therefore conclude that . . ."; "One might suppose, however, that . . ."; "If we assume that . . . , then it becomes obvious that . . ." These constantly repeated phrases allow the trained eye to quickly pick out the structure of the overall reasoning. But their job at the same time is to conceal any hint of the scholar's individuality. Even that promotes the dissertation's purpose: the contribution is to be so soundly based that anyone can retrace your steps and arrive at your very same conclusions. If your own personality were to intrude, the impartiality you're aiming for might be tainted. Your ability to persuade might be charged, not to the strength of your argument, but to the power of your big blue eyes.

But there were only three people to persuade with my dissertation: the men on my thesis committee, most of whose leanings, quirks, blind spots, acuities, beneficences and malevolences I knew too well. Since their decision would be acceded to by the rest of the philosophy department, who would thereupon recommend my candidacy to the Faculty of Arts and Sciences, anyone with a clear eye on the purpose to be achieved would write a thesis that these very three men would approve with minimal fuss.

By contrast, the *Hornbook* would be sent to people of diverse backgrounds, only a handful of whom I had met personally. To reach that almost faceless audience of engineers, academic linguists, and administrators in nonprofit and for-profit research organizations, I had to convert their frequently voiced mistrust of and contempt for philosophy into their recognition that they were themselves trying to *do* philosophy without understanding what it is.

And where my thesis committee *had* to read what I wrote, this audience was at liberty to pitch it into the wastebasket even before reading a word.

It was in the course of chomping on that indigestible fact that the idea for the *Hornbook* came to me in one unified whole, its style inextricably tied to its form. Not another scholarly dissertation, one chapter unfolding after another, marching toward a conclusion that my readers, if they got that far, would never acknowledge, but my own *Philosophical Dictionary*, an alphabetic series of cross-referenced articles. Like Voltaire, I'd reach my audience by short swift forays into the thicket of problems my research had laid bare. By making one little point at a time, each article could let my reader concentrate only on it, to find it answerable or, with surprise, acceptable, before going on to the next. A reader could also move from one cross-reference to another. And so, piecemeal, the whole argument would get itself made. I'd get my readers' attention bit by bit, rather than by the sheer consecutivity of the reasoning, which, I had been astonished to notice in my early reading of their work, many of them simply ignore.

My readers would be educated, but they were not philosophers. So I'd have to lure them in by any means I thought might work. I was in good company. Leibniz wasn't above insisting on spectacle and amusement. Late in the seventeenth century the inventor of the calculus envisaged a public fair of scientific and technological exhibits. In his essay, "An Odd Thought Concerning a New Sort of Exhibition," he described the ways he'd draw the multitudes in. "Magic lanterns," he writes, "artificial meteors, fireworks, ballets of horses, instruments that play by themselves." The list runs to pages and is dazzling. During exams at Harvard, graduate students kept up one another's spirits by quoting this: "We will bring the man from England who eats fire, if he is still alive."

What rule said my *Hornbook* couldn't be light and fast while remaining transparently clear? What rule forbade readers to smile even as they found themselves drawn to agree with a conclusion they might not otherwise, without the honey, entertain? I was writing under the handicap (as they saw it) of being a philosopher, but it was in my hands to turn that to my own account.

Still, how to do it? I had promised to write ninety-two essays in philosophy for linguists, most of whom didn't know what philosophy is. They regularly denounced it, then calmly sat back and reinvented old philosophical theories, unknowingly hindering the progress of their own work by involving themselves in philosophical problems as though twenty-five hundred years of philosophy hadn't preceded them. They didn't realize that the alternative to doing philosophy in the matters that concerned them wasn't not-doing-philosophy but merely doing-philosophy-badly.

I had to say that plainly somewhere. Not just criticizing: that loses its punch very fast. And besides, why would anyone listen to me? Not only was I a philosopher: I had never published anything before. So first I had to get their attention.

Since they didn't know philosophy, I'd have to teach them. And I certainly knew how to teach. First I had to locate exactly where they were. Then I'd clear a path from there to where I wanted them to be. To where they should properly be in order to grasp each problem in its clearest outline.

I was smiling. I was very close to my solution.

I stopped reading new material, having learned when I wrote my dissertation that there is always new material to read. When I began writing again, the scholarly 'we' practically vanished. *I* was the one who did not undervalue a difficulty, who stated alternative versions of a question, who suggested a simpler criterion for deciding hard cases. When 'we' appeared, it included me among the members of a group I didn't hesitate to name: philosophers, persons knowledgeable about logic, all of us as children learning the mother tongue. Even so, skimming the pages today, I see that I put the scholarly 'we' to work more often than I'd use it today. But I hadn't yet broken all the rules: just the ones that snapped most easily when I, a mere slip of a girl, landed on them asking: "Why are they here?" and hearing only silence.

Because there are reasons for rules.

And here's a principle that, beginning its life in me as a seedling, has since Nantucket grown its branches into every aspect of my being.

There are reasons for rules. And if you can't find the reason, if the people who insist on the rule can't give you the reason, there may be none. When you ask, "Why do you do thus-and-so?" or "Why this way?" and someone answers: "That's how we've always done it," or "That's how we do things," you're not talking to a human being but only to a little round machine that moves. Or to someone who has reasons for not telling you the reason. Because the first time the thing was done, or done that way, there *was* a reason, now obviously lost in the mists of history, sometimes as long ago as a year and a half. And the reason could be good or bad, sound or groundless. Who is to know which, until you bring it up to the light to look at?

I have appointed myself as disturber of the placidity of persons who don't know that rules have reasons. Because human beings make rules, and we do it to achieve some purpose. Because something else can almost always achieve the same purpose. Because following the rule may even *not* achieve the purpose. Because sometimes the person making the rule knows that only a scattering of people will inquire after the purpose, and so he or she is able to bring about the most obscene of purposes: that people will follow a rule without questioning it. The obscenity lies in this: human beings can ask questions. 'Can': are able to. Not 'may': are permitted to. And being able to ask but not asking, people abdicate, tissue by tissue, their chief difference from stones. Stones move in whatever direction you shove them because they can—are able to—obey only the laws of gravity and friction, laws they did not make. We obey those same laws when we fall. But our lives aren't only falling, or being eroded by wind and water.

Three years earlier I had been sitting on Nantucket, examining and discarding all the rules I lived by that were not of my making. In the time since, I had flung overboard a hundred more. Nothing like standing there rule-less to tempt you into making your own. No, not 'tempt,' but 'allow.' Yet, not 'allow,' either, but this: to let you know yourself to be free to make your own rules.

And so in the *Hornbook* I danced and sang and did somersaults and played hopscotch and hung upside down from the branches of trees. The project I had begun, not for its own sake but mainly as a source of income that would free me from the daily nonsense of a job in someone else's office doing someone else's idea of what was important, had insinuated itself into my ardent custody.

In this unanticipated guise, the lesson about the course of loving that I had stumbled onto on Nantucket reappeared in Connecticut: that taking-care-of turns into caring-for, and that loving is caring-for. But where on Nantucket I learned it about coming to love a living being, Logos, here in Weston I learned it about coming to love my work.

Writing the *Hornbook*, particularly the stolen months of beginning to write the "Journey," taught me that working permeates my day. No sooner would I leave my desk to play with Logos, repaying him for his long patience during my hours of (to him) silence, when three more items about the philosophical problems lying buried in the linguistic discussions would stream into my head. Walking in the woods I'd suddenly think of another topic and I'd cut short our stroll to go back to my desk to add it to the growing lists of shorthand notations to myself. I started carrying a notebook on our walks, stopping to write in it while I leaned against one of the stone walls Logos and I ordinarily crossed by jumping. Eating, driving, shopping for groceries: my list kept growing. I was writing articles for the *Hornbook* wherever I was, no matter that I could not give them their full head on paper until I reached my desk.

Some days an article would all but flow out of my fingertips onto the typewriter keys. I'd pull the page out of the typewriter, and it would read just as I wanted it: fresh, pointed, clear. Other times the writing would start swiftly, then stop. I'd limp along for another sentence, two, three. The idea I was after was making its presence known to me as far more complex than when I first took hold of it. I'd roll back my chair and sit thinking until Logos would awaken, stretch, and let me know it was time to stop. I would have been sitting, unmoving, for nearly two hours. I'd follow Logos out the door, and for half an hour I'd let him distract me. When we went back into the house I'd head for my desk, picking up what had earlier been a knot of ideas. Unexpectedly it would fall into single disentangled strands, and I could begin to write again. By dinnertime I would have two articles on my desk where that morning there had been none. Throughout the evening my thoughts would keep racing, exploring the breathtaking scope of what I had begun to do.

The April day I packed off the manuscript of my *Hornbook* to Washington, I was sending out into the world the creature that had sprung from my head and my fingertips. Now separated from the nourishment and protection of my pen, my desk, my study, its life would be only as long as the eyes and minds of others, unknown to me, would find in it whatever light I had found in myself and then poured out onto each page.

On a bright September morning the postman knocked on my door to deliver thirty copies of my first book. They weren't printed on high-quality paper, nor were they bound between hard covers. They weren't really printed at all. They were simply clean photocopies of the pages that had been typed on bond with a special ribbon. The cover, designed by my sponsor, was a pale grey-green stock, just slightly heavier than the pages themselves.

But they were mine, and I was ravished by them.

I burst through the back door into the yard to hug Logos and Ousia, and then I led a race through the orange gate into our woods. I skipped along our paths, made a running jump over the low stone wall and would not, could not, stop a dance that carried us to the clearing that was our usual turnaround. Logos knew the place as one we never left unless he could chase sticks that it was my job to find and throw.

And when all of us had exhausted our bodies we returned to the house, smiles on all our faces.

Those copies of my first book arrived midway through the matchless gift I was giving myself: twelve months in which to write "Map of an Inward Journey," a purchase I had earned by saving half the income I received from the Air Force during the final year and a half of my project. Tax laws were different then. Gas cost

22 cents a gallon; home heating oil, 14. Some old notes I've just come upon run through a month's expenses; they total under $450. The day the project ended my bank account held $8,000. Two alternatives lay open to me. I could have bought a house (and I dearly wanted, still even more dearly want, a house). Or I could buy the time that would let me write the book I had to write. Had to. There weren't really two alternatives.

To begin the "Journey" I first stole time from the *Hornbook*, then later paid it back. To finish the "Journey" I used the money I had saved to buy free, loose, wide-open time. To buy my immersion in my work.

Finding the right form for my subject, the form that will let it reach its full and sweet growth, is always a time of discomfort. Not like an open wound that rivets your attention until you can get to the surgeon who will suture it, bandage it, allow the healing to begin. More like an aching back: you do whatever will ameliorate it while trying not to focus on it. Otherwise, you tense up, aggravating the thing that's preventing you from doing everything else. Because it's always there: a brake on your pen, a muted noise when you want silence.

The subject arrives first: wispy, amorphous. Two words, perhaps eight. Only finding the form will let the subject settle in, will let me write. Rarely does the form come to me all at once, a perfectly worked-out idea. In lieu of that, I've learned to seize upon whatever will get me started. In the course of writing, minor modifications, sometimes telling ones, may emerge. Occasionally the form changes drastically: from one day to the next the small-scale encyclopedia that the *Hornbook* became totally evicted the form of the standard report that I first proposed to Washington. Some ideas about women and power would not come out of my fingertips until I began writing them in the form of a lecture (that no one ever wanted to hear).

The form that opened the gates for the "Journey" was the present tense. It alone would let me exhibit the course of my discovery, prohibit the sort of excuses that second sight encourages. From the standpoint of the faithful reconstruction I wanted to write, concealing nothing, making myself say everything I could remember, I did not have to (I could not) begin by explaining what I was like before I went to Nantucket because that's what I went there to find out. The only part of that other life I needed to describe as I began was the state of mind that drove me to the island. After that I needed to say only what I came to understand of the life before Nantucket while I was in the process of understanding it. Flashbacks became, not a covert way of informing the reader, but an overt way of informing myself.

But the immediacy the present tense offered confronted me with an almost insuperable problem.

On Nantucket the central thing I learned about myself was that I didn't know what my feelings were. It took another whole year after leaving Nantucket for me to learn how to recognize, and then trust, the spontaneity of my feelings, and, with the light they shed, to learn what wanting is. At least one more year passed before I understood what I wanted. But the form in which I had chosen to write the "Journey" demanded that I reproduce a time during which my insight into my feelings was not part of my sense of myself. There are many ways to say it: I didn't know whether I had any feelings; I didn't know how to identify them; I didn't know when I was feeling something; I didn't know whether whatever I did feel was genuine; I was out of touch with my feelings. I don't mean that I used to be puzzled about whether an incident amused or irritated me: I mean that I didn't know *that* I was angry or sad; and worse, I didn't know that I didn't know it. (A philosopher to whom I said these things all but snorted: "That's nonsense!" But he has lived thirty years of his life not knowing how angry he is with the man whose protégé he was, unwilling to publish his now divergent thinking while the older man still lives.)

How, then, to set forth such blindness? Not to explain why I was like that, not to say that I was like that, but only to show it, and using only the present tense.

The problem had two parts. First I had to remember how the world looked to me before Nantucket, and up to the time I discovered the nature of my ignorance. I was calling on myself to show what my world felt like at a time when I did not feel my world. The wonder to me, as I began to re-create it, was how I had lived through thirty-seven years as the very embodiment of a sense of oppression that was relieved only at irregular intervals by some passionate involvement that regularly ended too soon for reasons unintelligible to me. The difficulty wasn't that I couldn't remember that burden: it was that that life was now so foreign that it was almost impossible for me to inhabit it even temporarily as I wrote.

And second, I had to present that unbelievable world in a believable way. Trying to remember some pre-Nantucket situation that had bewildered me while I lived it, I would suddenly grasp all its outlines. Writing, I could see what I had been doing then and what others had been doing to me; I could hear what I had been saying then and what others had said to me. Not that the sounds of past voices filled my room, or that wraiths of absent persons sat in my chairs, but rather that what had lain obscured emerged illuminated. Yet even though I knew, rehearsing now some eight-year-old incident, that I was furious then and didn't know it then, I had to write now as I had in fact felt then. I had to make my long-ago response to an affront look now like what it had felt like then, when the very existence of the affront was something I was then incapable of naming. Too late, I glimpsed the awful extent of the problem I had set myself: I had to conceal, not facts or names or dates or places, but my own understanding; I had to rein in my understanding in order to display the route my understanding pursued.

□ □ □

From a peak of clarity long afterward, I wrote my "Journey," elucidating the events external and internal that I still abbreviate with the one word 'Nantucket.' Writing the "Journey" let me grasp the nature of the gift I can offer my contemporaries, now as I live, and later, as readers enable one to spring to life again from a page: I am in intimate touch with my own feelings; I am not deluded by them, at least not for very long; and I know how to set them forth so that others recognize theirs in my words.

Peirce, greatest of American philosophers, taught us that philosophy is making clear what was not clear before. The gratifying compliment people unknowingly pay you for doing that is that they use your clarification to flood with light some matter the outlines of which they could not even discern before. Thereafter able to see the terrain through your clarification, they believe you have merely cleaned the window for them, whereas you have given them new eyes.

You may know my "Journey" as *An Unknown Woman.* Many who read it understand that it is not a novel, not a journal, not ultimately about me, but that in tandem with the narrative about my coming to understand myself it is an account of the *process* of coming to understand oneself: both tale and explication. Those readers have let themselves do philosophy along with me, even though some of them did not know to call it by that name.

During the fourteen years between writing my "Journey" and having it published, thirty publishers rejected it. "Too personal" was their almost unanimous reason. It took me nearly all that time to understand those words. They meant (I finally decided) that the matters I wrote of are of a sort one ought in decency to keep to oneself. Perhaps, if my "Journey" were autobiography. It is, rather, something else: the tangle of my thoughts and feelings and plans and hopes and despairs. A mind unraveling itself. An enterprise that can be presented to others only afterward, from the vantage point of the skeins untangled, the knots removed, the fabric an unbroken whole.

By the time I have written something, the words on the paper exactly as I wish them to be, I understand the matter they crystallize. Once written about, those ideas in those words have the same relation to me that an essay on the kinds of grasses has to the botanist who wrote it. Understanding some matter, I have in effect detached it from envy, anger, pride, shame, dismay, perhaps even grief. Writing of it is a mark of the distance from which I can ever after view it.

I write these chapters about solitude as I wrote those about Nantucket: primarily for myself. To learn what I think, to understand certain things I've done, certain things that have happened to me. To discover the path from there to here.

In writing of solitude, I'm writing about minds and selves, but not in the highly familiar way philosophers have discussed that set of problems for centuries and discuss them still. I write instead my own highly personal account of the way I have chosen to live, and of the consequences, only some of which were predictable, of my choices.

In a sense, this whole book is a philosophical inquiry into what it is to be a person: how one becomes a person, and what it is that one has become. I am teaching, not by telling, but by displaying the process. By writing of what it is for me to be solitary, I am sketching the outlines of the life of solitude everyone else lives. Can live, if you choose.

6
HOMING

IN SPITE OF social changes almost too swift to absorb, some aspects of human life still count as ordinary. Family, by marriage or by condominium; some more or less continuously known community of human beings, as friends or co-workers; a job or career that, by stabilizing one's economic circumstances, also carves out one's geographic location; a house, a home, some address through which one can be traced, with few gaps, over a more or less extended period of time; and cities and their environs, perhaps most of all, as the context in which all these continuities, these connections to persons and places over time, occur.

But my life has been extraordinary: outside of, beyond the boundaries of, the ordinary. The continuities touching me were, are, other than these.

Not marriage, not family, not a community of colleagues instituted and sustained for me a connection to living beings, but Logos. For twelve and a half years, all day every day, wherever I was, he was with me. Within three years of that beginning, Ousia touched our connections to one another, Logos' and mine, and multiplied them in ways I did not know that three can differ from two. And when that fullness ended, when Logos unwillingly left me, the threads connecting me to him floated free, still float free, and those connecting me to Ousia placed us in a different pattern

68

of two than either Logos and I had had or that she and I had had
when he was alive. Then came the time for Kairos, who made us
three again, but a three unlike that other, as did the pairs of us
differ from one another and from the pairs of that other. For fifteen
years the minutes of Ousia's day were tied to mine, and for ten of
those years to Logos', so that the five years she remained with me
after he was gone carried echoes every day of those first pairs, that
first three. And when Ousia left me, also unwillingly, Kairos and
she and I had been regrouping ourselves into new pairs, our new
triple, for four years. My connection to her still exists in the
moments of my day, separate from and yet in the thick of the pair
Kairos and I are, have been for the nine years that she is gone.
This twenty-five-year-long overlapping of friendships, of carings
and doings, is a continuity woven as tightly and intricately as a
tapestry. I could not have imagined its existence the day I held the
puppy Logos on my lap in the backseat of a car driven by the friend
from whose house I would leave the next day for Nantucket.

The second continuity I have, replacing the teaching job that
should have provided my economic continuity, is the profession I
invented, writing my thinking, that I can only erratically support.

Last month I had lunch with a man who has held the same
teaching job for twenty-five years. He is busy, productive, writes
books and articles, and he has lived with his family in only two
houses since they arrived at the university.

During the same twenty-five years, I have moved sixteen times.
Friends who have been tracking me tear up one page after another
in their address books, and when they dial long distance to call me
they're never sure that the phone number they have is my most
recent. Sometimes, letting my thoughts wander while I drive, I
suddenly focus on my route to make myself remember what town
I live in now.

Like other nondomestic mammals of moderate size, I forage
for my living where the food supply is. My migration has been

largely confined to the northeastern United States. The farthest north I ranged was Maine; the farthest south, Virginia; both within the same year, driving back and forth between them three times. I moved to Maine because it was as far away as I could go from Logos' death in Virginia four months earlier. But you never leave behind a death so huge. And anyway, the truth about his death was back there in Washington, where I was pursuing it through my lawsuit against the two veterinarians who had let him die. Eight months after I moved to Maine, I was back in northern Virginia again to stay for six more years.

Those two moves were for reasons other than earning my living. As was my reason for leaving Washington forever: royalties from the publication of *An Unknown Woman* let me end my ten-year exile from New England. Another time I left a house because a neighbor turned into a crazy lady who thrust hysterical notes under my door, rang the bell, ran away, then assured herself that I had received her scrawlings by calling to yell incoherent speeches, hanging up on me before I, astonished, could grasp her intent.

Apart from its ending, the stay in that house was surprisingly pleasant. The surprise derived from the fact that the house was in the center of a suburban town, and never before in the twenty years since Nantucket had I considered living with other houses surrounding mine. There have been other recent stays among near neighbors: three years ago Kairos and I lived in a house near a railroad station, the rooms empty for two months except for a borrowed folding cot and a kettle and a spoon and a bowl until I could piece together the dollars that would move my belongings out of storage.

But all the rest of the time I lived in the country, and it is the country that has provided the only other continuity I know.

The country was first. Even before I knew what my work is, I knew that I had to live in the country. I knew it that dark February evening when I drove down the ramp that the Nantucket ferry unrolled, clanking from its hold, to secure its passengers' transition from water to land, to the pier at Woods Hole. Somehow, somewhere, I would transpose to new ground the pure isolation of the Nantucket beaches where, during the three winter months just passed, Logos and I had been free to wander two or three miles in either direction without seeing other human beings. From the house we occupied in the tiny village on Nantucket's eastern shore, miles of heather and scrub stretched beyond our back lawn. Within fifty yards of setting foot on the unpaved road fronting our house we could step onto one of the fairways of Siasconset's golf course, further miles of unpeopled land on which to stroll, to look, to sit, to think. On Nantucket I became accustomed to, learned that I require, space without barriers.

The distance from Woods Hole to my first country house in Connecticut is less than two hundred miles. Had I driven straight to Weston from our point of disembarkation, we'd have arrived in about three hours. The actual trip lasted six weeks and led from Marblehead to Cleveland to Toronto to New York to New Haven to northern Ohio (twice) before I could at last assure, in Stamford, the source of income that permitted me to search for a house where I could reinstate the setting of silence and beauty that would from then on be essential to my days.

The stone fences of Connecticut border narrow country roads. Driveways wind back to white houses gleaming in the sun. In summer, the houses hide behind deciduous trees that ravish passing motorists, and only the bare boughs of autumn give the secret away. Such houses are lived in by the persons who own them. What chance had I, driving the roads of Weston on a March Sunday looking for a place to live, of finding such a house unoccupied, waiting for me to move in?

The FOR RENT sign in front of the house on the other side of the road snapped my head to. In the seconds of passing I took in the whole setting: woods all around, evergreens whose names I did not then know screening the house from the road, no other house in sight up the hill or down. By the time I had the wit to look for a safe place to get off the highway, to turn around and drive back, I came to believe that the house had been rented in the interval since I had passed. My soon-to-be landlord arrived within minutes of my phoning the number on the sign, and when he saw how enthralled I was by the wildness he showed me the paths through his woods before he showed me the rooms of his house. We struck a deal. He drove away in his yellow pickup truck, Tommy Phillips, iconoclast, in whose house I was to live for more than six years and who, with his wife, Olive, became friends unspeakably dear.

What do you do with a six-room house when your belongings consist only of books and clothes and a few sticks of furniture? Books and file folders fitted on the shelves and in the drawers built into the wall of one room that I marked for my study, its windows looking onto woods. Clothes were hung in closets, one with a built-in bureau. But once closets and drawers were closed, only my bedroom contained any furniture: my bed, a dressing table and chair that I had bought used in Boston, and a woven wool rug that daily pronounced its own uselessness. In the whole rest of the house, downstairs and up, there was only one other piece of furniture: a low table of indeterminate wood, its eighteen-inch-square top inlaid with ceramic tiles in a range of tans and white with four tiny orange tiles set at random among them. I used to be mad about orange. In the evening or when rain kept us indoors, Logos and I played catch through all those empty rooms for more than a year, until I gradually installed, piece by carefully chosen piece, the furniture that made the house mine.

What mattered about that little house was that if Logos awakened in the night I could open the back door and walk in the yard with him until he was ready to return indoors, and during those minutes I would not see a car or other persons or other dogs but only the stars, I would not hear the radios of neighbors or their laughter but only the wind in the trees. What mattered was that Logos' and my habit of awakening early in the morning did not intrude on anyone else's activities nor theirs on ours. What mattered was that at any time of day I could step into the woods that began at the edge of our lawn, standing still in the fall on a certain path to listen to the thunder of the male ruffed grouse, although I did not then know that that was the sound I was hearing.

Living only with Logos in that little house set back from the highway, I had access to my landlord's eleven wild acres, even to all the wooded acres belonging to the abutting landowner, whom I never encountered during my walks in the woods. As best I could, I kept within the boundaries of Tommy's land. But when you're standing in the midst of trees and you can see only other trees in whatever direction you look, you become aware of the arbitrariness of the lines that demarcate human ownership of one segment but not another of what lies before you as unbroken landscape. Standing in those woods I knew that if I had some accident from which I couldn't extricate myself, no one would hear me if I were to shout for help, so I'd stay aware of potential jeopardies without letting them preempt the center of my attention. Part of the pleasure was just that: that no one else would come along, that Logos and I could play, he barking, I laughing at his delight in clearing one of the wide stone fences in a single try, without having to curtail our sounds.

After two years of unimpeded access to that privacy I came to feel that the outer boundaries of my self approached that unmarked perimeter of Tommy's woods, that my being had indeterminate margins extending far beyond the surface of the epidermal layer that the eyes of other human beings saw when they looked at me.

In less time than that, I became aware of a sense of oppression, of physical discomfort, when I had to go to any city larger than the nearby towns. Not just because in cities the noise level was so high or the air pollution so omnipresent or the crowds so dense.

Even if these factors were to be lowered to some tolerance level acceptable to most people, I would not be accommodated. I was, I remain, uncomfortable in a city longer than a few hours because I am out of my habitat. Crisp air and silence and solitariness had become powerful needs of mine, not in any sense peripheral. New York was only an hour away by train, but during my six years in Weston I traveled there no more than three times.

My job in Stamford was buying me that place to live: that silence, that beauty, that joy. It is what I buy with all the jobs I have had since. That job differed from the others only in this: I did not then know what work I wanted to do. By the time I knew, living in the country had become so intimate a part of the life I was designing that I could not conceive of living any other way. Each time I packed up to move to another source of income, my first task was always to find a house in the country.

"How did you find a place like this?" new guests always ask.

"I looked for it."

And sometimes the looking would seem so fruitless, would consume so much time, so many miles of driving, so many long distance phone calls, that I'd wonder whether I'd finally have to give it up, live in cities near other people. But I had only to imagine hearing their sounds beyond my walls, the polite conversation each time we came upon one another in hallways or at the mailbox, the having to leash Logos whenever we went outside. And then I'd get into my car again, and drive and phone again, and somehow I'd always find the next place where Logos and I, Logos and Ousia and I, Ousia and I, Ousia and Kairos and I, Kairos and I, could live.

In my little house in Weston my education in practicalities began.

Take household water.

In the country a well lying sixty, a hundred, two hundred feet deep in the earth is your source of water. Yours: no one else's. It waits on the other side of the closed faucets in your kitchen and bathroom only because an electric pump, working silently away while you go about the business of your day, brings it up to you from that vast depth; piping carries it to a holding tank in your basement that stores water sufficient for your normal needs; and valves regulate the pressure under which it flows both into and out of that tank, ready for your pleasure. The low concrete box rising a foot or so above the ground beyond your kitchen window is the well's housing, and the flat piece of wood, perhaps four feet square, that roofs it over, is the pump-house cover. When you lift and lay aside that roof, you can jump down into the housing where rests your electric pump, the single most important item in country life.

You learn to listen for the sound of the pump. If you hear it churning away for a minute or two once or twice a day, all is well. If it turns on and runs without stopping, or if it turns off and on every few minutes, you're in trouble. The water table could be low, a line or even the tank could be leaking somewhere, or the pump could be on its last legs. You call an electrician or plumber at once, if for no other reason than that your electric bill will be staggering until the problem is corrected.

No one teaches you any of this in graduate school.

The Rural Electrification Administration, bringing power to country households in the 1930s, revolutionized life there less by enabling people to read at night than by giving them uninterrupted access to water, and then to water that could be heated. Even today the major consequence of a power outage for country life is that the pump shuts off. You can be ready for outages: candles, matches, flashlights, a few gallons of water in the refrigerator for drinking and minimal cleanliness, even a filled bucket of water in the basement for flushing toilets by gravity. But these are crude measures, carrying you only a few hours or overnight. Longer than that, you learn forever that almost every activity you engage in relies on electricity.

You acquire a healthy respect for plumbers. No matter how much you know about Hume, the person who can make a toilet work again has knowledge at least as valuable as your own. So you learn how all the parts inside the vitreous porcelain closet fit together and what they do, because most of its malfunctions occur on Saturday evenings.

And building fences.

During the nearly thirteen years of Logos' life, we lived in five different houses, and I built a fence at every one of them, even though, until the age of thirty-seven, I hadn't hammered together anything more substantial than a pair of ideas. Three of my fences went up new; two required me only to extend and mend fences already standing.

Building a fence demands two pairs of hands. If you own or can borrow a peculiar-looking tool called a fence stretcher and are strong enough to manipulate it, you can work alone. Otherwise, fence building needs one person to hold the fencing erect and taut while the other person secures it to wooden or steel posts. The five different fence builders with whom I worked every foot of the way were initially irritated by my questions about what they were doing and why that way rather than some other and about how some tool is used (and would they let me try it?). But no one can resist teaching something he knows to someone who wants to learn, so I became proficient in a collection of manual skills that women are not normally taught. Morning after morning I've held a claw hammer in one hand and a bucket of staples in the other, a round of wire slung over one shoulder, pliers and wire cutters stuck in my back pocket, returning to the area I stumbled away from the evening before, weary to the teeth, slivers of wood or thorns still buried in my flesh, palms and forearms cut, fingernails broken, shirts torn, jeans muddy, and clothes soaked with sweat that had already dried on me twice in the course of the day.

The fences were to keep Logos safe outdoors while I was twenty

miles away from him all day at my office. Outdoors, but also free
to move. Tying him to a stake in the yard or attaching his leash to
a pulley running along a clothesline stretched between two posts,
no matter how far apart, would have been versions of cruelty. A
fenced-in run was the only solution.

John did odd jobs to supplement his income as a mason. He
agreed to be hired, and he and I worked throughout an overcast
April Saturday. When he left, Logos had an area of freedom with
a circumference measuring 165 feet, a hinged gate closing him
safely within. It took me most of Sunday to finish off the tedious
details that security relies on, to clean up bits of wire and nails, to
fill with straw and fresh-smelling cedar chips Tommy's doghouse
that I had painted orange and that another neighbor had helped me
roof. I lured Logos into the run, closed the gate between us, and
went up to my bedroom window to see whether, in my absence,
he could possibly find a way out. He tried to vault the top, he
considered crawling through the bottom, and then he gave up. It
was a sad victory.

Monday morning I padlocked the gate in the run, leaving Logos
with a bowl of water and some of my old clothes to convince him
that I'd come back again. I left work a little early that day, but the
moment I turned into my driveway I slammed my foot against the
brake pedal so fast that the engine stalled. Outside our front door
sat Logos, as free of constraints as though I hadn't given over the
entire weekend to the opposite purpose. He rose happily to his feet
and raced down the driveway toward me. When he stood I saw
that he had been lying on my grey shorts. Not only had he gotten
out of the run: he had gone back in to bring them out again.

I received his noisy greeting grimly. How long had he been
loose? He could have escaped five minutes after I left that morning;
could have been trotting up and down the highway in puppy ignorance of its danger; could have been wandering along other roads
looking for me. Then I examined the run. Logos had dug a tunnel

beneath the fence: John and I had simply not buried enough of it in the ground. I changed into my jeans and, with what was left of the daylight, found long lengths of logs in the woods, used one foot to roll them up to the outside base of the fence, then stapled the wire to them. Logos never slipped out of the run again.

The other consequence of my first fence was a two-week siege of poison ivy. Neither John nor I had ever been affected by it, so we had worked in it all that Saturday, cutting it away to take advantage of a rock or a tree as unexpected support, yanking it out with bare hands. Overnight I lost my immunity. My eyes still swell shut at the merest brush with it, no matter how promptly I try to soap it off. It's one of the country matters I've become expert in: using minimal clues to avoid poison ivy, poison oak, poison sumac. Sometimes all you have to go on in spring is a slight reddish edge gleaming on young leaves in the sunlight. Sometimes in late November you see only the hairy rootlets after you've grubbed a thick bare runner out of the ground, telltale but too late.

My last fence was in McLean, in northern Virginia. I wasn't even considering building one. Logos was ten by then, Ousia seven, and the full-time job I held as speechwriter to a member of Congress allowed me to work at home most of the time. Not that the congressman went out of his way to please me: there simply was no space for me in his Washington office. To the congressman's top aide, however, my lack of interest in being in the midst of the Washington hullabaloo was incomprehensible. Worse: the congressman actually liked the speeches I wrote for him. So, from one day to the next, I was ordered to appear in Washington all day every day. I could have refused: I was supposed to refuse so that the congressman could fire the rival his aide saw me to be. But the next job I was lining up would not open for two more months. I pleaded for three days' postponement and scrambled to hire a man to help me build a fence: I would not leave the dogs indoors for the twelve-hour days the congressman often demanded. We fenced in a grassy area already enclosed on two sides by the house itself. Logos and Ousia could step into the screened porch at their pleasure, or they could lounge in the sun to observe the passing cardinals or the wood turtle we often encountered on our walks through the wild acres beyond the house. I used the fence for only a month. That's how long it took the aide to figure out another more reliable way to get me fired.

It was in that house that, at eight minutes past eight o'clock in the morning on March 10, 1975, the telephone rang announcing Logos' death. Fifteen years later I can still hear the phone ringing in that house of many empty rooms. The sound signaled the end of one life and the beginning of another that laid on me a necessity to write of that death, a bidding I have been unable to carry out until now.

That was the last fence because, with only Ousia, there was no need for fences. From Ousia's point of view, no place in the world was better than wherever I was, a version of things Kairos learned from her. Or perhaps he came upon it himself.

When the dogwood beyond the kitchen window in my Weston house started to come into flower the first spring I lived there, the soft green, then greening pink, then pinking white, then flat-out white were sufficient as sheer play of color to absorb my attention. But after its sepals fell late in May, the only colors visible through the window were the black-green of the Japanese yew on the far side of the dogwood and the undifferentiated green of the juniper woods beyond. An occasional bird (they were all indifferently "birds" to my ignorance) would perch on the dogwood on its way elsewhere, but briefly only, there being little enough on those branches to detain its journey. The dogwood was an ideal feeding station for birds, although two years would pass before I strung up my first piece of suet, not then being a vegetarian. I was not so much looking through that window in order to see what was there as I was offering some casual view to my eye while my thoughts went freewheeling around the knot of ideas that had sent me away from my desk for not being able to undo strands that wrongly and obstinately stuck together.

For the blessings of that window above the kitchen's electric range I was grateful to Olive, who had had Tommy place the window there when they built the house, the two of them working almost totally alone. In time I forgave myself for not knowing all the things Olive knew. She had been born less than half a mile away in the house where she and Tommy still live, had been born in the country while I had lived the first thirty-seven years of my life in cities. Olive grew up lying beneath tall shade trees in summer; mowing the fields behind the wheel of her father's tractor before she was ten, ignoring the heat of noon. She knew as a child the bitterness of pig-hickory nuts, knew that not they but shagbark hickories are to be gathered in the fall; knew how to find the nests of bantams, who lay their eggs in every which place on different days; had since girlhood the knack of making an independent pony come to her from the far end of its corral. I could at least benefit from what Olive had bequeathed to this house when she and Tommy returned to her first home, which she had inherited a few years before.

At the end of my first winter there, I saw from that window the crocuses she had planted against the low concrete wall of the pump-housing, where they collected the first warmth of the rising sun and were sheltered from the strong weather blowing from the west. Each early spring thereafter, as soon as the frozen ground began to soften I cleared away the twigs and dead leaves that had accumulated there since the spring before, watching for the first tips of their leaves to penetrate the hard earth, the darkness of their green distinguishing them from the bright green of grasses that would rob them of nourishment from sun and soil unless I meticulously, blade by blade, rooted them out.

At each new house I begin my search for the first thrusting

green in February. I am outdoors so often every day examining
the lay of earth and sky, no matter the weather, that any new item
on the land's profile all but shouts at me to take notice. It is in part
a game of hide-and-seek I play with whoever lived in the house
before me. Where would that gardener want to see the first brave
bloom of crocus after a long winter? Sometimes a few feet beyond
a living-room window, or against rock walls, or adorning the
house's stark foundation. Sometimes a grey squirrel will have upset
the householder's scheme, unearthing a bulb or two, burying them
in places perfect for a squirrel's cache, except that he or she forgets,
and anyway the nutrition jammed into that tiny globe is poisonous
to living creatures.

In one of my houses in northern Virginia there was a spot in
the woods that the sun lighted up from the east at six of an April
morning and again from the west at four in the afternoon. The
light in that part of the world is so often hazed over that a brilliant
clear day, so common in New England, is an occasion to be marveled
at, and only for a few hours, before the humid mist moves in again.
The area that the father of our country chose for our capital long
bore the name 'Foggy Bottom,' but even across the river in Virginia
miasma is the recurring hygrological note. And so, since it is
pointless to return daily to a place that was fresh and clear the day
before, I was startled to see two daffodils nodding in that sharply
lighted place in the gaunt March woods, the gift not of a visionary
householder but of a provident squirrel. For three days I feasted
on that square foot of gold against the grey trunks of bare trees,
and then abruptly an icy rain poured from the heavens. For an
hour I thought about the daffodils each time I looked up from my
writing, and then I flung on my raincoat and boots and ran into
the woods, scissors in hand, to bring the now recumbent flowers
into the house where for nearly a week they made luminous a corner
of my desk. (But the following spring I knew where to find daffodils
again.)

In Canada Logos and Ousia and I lived in a century-old brick farmhouse surrounded by a hundred acres of meadows that my landlord rented to a Mennonite farmer. We arrived during the first week in August, and the oats were waist-high. There were paths along the hedgerows of each of the meadows, but walking there in the early morning was like wading through surf, so soaked with dew were my jeans and Logos and Ousia, plunging through greenery that rose above their heads.

The Mennonite planted his oats and cut his hay without benefit of electrical equipment or rubber tires; he owned no automobile, although he permitted himself to be driven in one; no phone was connected to his farmhouse, but he frequently asked for the use of mine. The first day we ever talked he sat on his buckboard high above me, holding the reins of his team of horses, looking intently at Logos and Ousia.

"Do you send them after woodchucks?" he asked me.

"No." I was as surprised by his question as he by my answer.

"Do you have them hunt anything else?"

"Nothing at all. I don't want them to harm any creature."

"Then what do you have them for?"

He was not teasing me.

"They're my friends." Was I replying to him? "They're my companions. They protect me." It had never occurred to me that I'd be called on to explain to another human being why I had Logos and Ousia, nor that that explanation would be received with something approaching disbelief.

In the middle of September the farmer mowed his fields, his enormous draft horse hitched to an ancient scythe, he with the reins in hand, walking behind. From the window next to my desk I watched them, step by slow step under the blazing sun, until I could stand it no longer. I filled a bucket with water and walked into the field, hailing the farmer to stop. The horse drank the water as though he were inhaling it. I went back into the house again, working until the next time I couldn't bear to watch the pair of them. By the third bucketful, the horse saw me coming and stopped without waiting to be reined in. This time I brought along a jar of water for the farmer.

"He knows you already," the farmer said to me pleasantly, after drinking. From his point of view, both he and the horse could have worked half the day, the full day, without water. The horse would have had his fill back at the farmer's barn. No matter that when they finished the day's mowing, the horse would still have three or four miles of work hitched to the wagon, carrying the farmer home.

The year in Canada was so bad that the only good thing that happened was that two bad things that were supposed to happen didn't. For ten months before I went to bed each night I drew a heavy black X through the date on a calendar, and when my obligation ended in May, I fled to the United States. The instant I crossed the border I parked my car so that I could walk with Logos and Ousia on my own land again, smiling, waving at all the cars that passed us, and, for those few minutes, understanding something about the meaning of 'home.'

Our house in Newton had two ponds on its three acres of lawn. Who is to say that I didn't choose that house to provide Logos his summertime sport? He'd stroke off into the center of the main pond, send up shoots of water while he treaded, paddle after a ball I'd throw, do lazy laps. Ousia, however, did not swim. She circled the pond at its grassy edge, barking at Logos, and yet each day she was allowing herself to step a little farther into the water. She made her limits very plain: solid ground had to be beneath her feet. The moment she felt the pond bottom begin to drop off, her whole body became a braking system that enabled her to maneuver herself out of the water in any direction she chose. I, who had not learned how to swim until I was over thirty, decided to teach Ousia.

Both Logos and Ousia understood economic theory very well:

any object to which I added my labor was by those actions increased in value. If I merely reached down to pick up a stick to throw, neither of them might chase it. But if I worked the stick over, removing leaves from a cracked branch, snapping off the remaining twigs, banging the branch against a tree to remove loose bark, then finally breaking the branch into manageable size, by the time I raised my arm to throw the stick, both dogs were in a frenzy. I had only to pretend to do something to the stick—run my hand over it several times, slap it against a boot, inspect it closely—to get the same effect.

One morning I stood on the bank of Logos' pond and turned my full attention to a stick I had just picked up. Logos was not prepared to abandon the certain ball in his mouth for the uncertain stick in my hand, but Ousia came to me immediately. I tossed the stick into the water no more than two feet from the bank, well within her reach. She plunged into the pond, brought it to me, and laid it at my feet.

"Good girl!"

Her face broke into her huge smile, and her soggy tail dipped low back and forth.

I threw the stick again, this time far across the pond, making it land near the opposite bank. I wanted her to understand that entering the water was a possibility from any point along its border. We spent a good part of the afternoon and the next several days that way.

Came the day when, in six deliberately contrived tosses, I had the stick floating two strokes beyond Ousia's reach. She trotted happily into the water and thrust her strong neck out for it, but it was outside the farthest stretch of her mouth. She started to move forward but she was already at one of the places where the pond bottom dropped off, and I watched her struggle to keep her feet on something solid.

For a long moment she gazed at the stick. She directed two or three barks at it, a special baby bark she kept for important things like games. A breeze appeared, sending up ripples on the pond, and slowly the stick bobbed away from her in their wake. It was too much for her. Under the water's surface her front paw reached out for the receding toy. The gesture took her off her safe haven, and in that stroke she was swimming. Three more strokes delivered her to the stick, and the look of utter astonishment on her face as she swam back to where she could touch bottom made me start laughing. She climbed onto the bank, dropped the stick, and shook herself free of accumulated water and of the never-before-had feeling of being borne up by it.

"Ooss!" I threw my arms around her, soaking my already wet clothes against her fur. "You were swimming!"

She cocked her head. She knew that word. But that was a Logos-word. And then the half-smile opened her mouth all the way.

"Come on: swim some more!" I shouted. I picked up the stick and tossed it into the pond: it didn't matter any longer where it landed.

Ousia watched it hit and was in the water before the splash settled. She walked quickly along the bottom, felt the drop-off, hesitated a tenth of a second, and then she pushed off. Thereafter she dived into the pond each day as eagerly as Logos did.

Between laps, Logos was often content idly treading water. But Ousia looked for something constructive to do. Winds were always blowing stray branches onto the water, and the brook was always carrying odds and ends of sticks from all the overhanging trees into the pond that was its terminal. Ousia took it upon herself to be the pondkeeper, picking up one stick after another until her mouth could hold no more, then depositing the bundle on the bank. Each time she entered the pond she surveyed what still had to be done to clear the surface of debris, and she went about her task with high seriousness. Logos plainly regarded her as interfering with his more leisurely practices, but his real difficulty arose when she finished her day's cleaning and turned her attention to him and his red rubber ball. Then the battle lines between them were drawn as surely in the water as they ever were on land.

Our house in the hills of western Massachusetts was too near the road but its backyard melted into a hundred acres of woodland. We trailed paths, Logos and Ousia and I, finding red trillium in spring and larch turning golden in fall. Once, walking in the rain, I saw a striped maple, its green stripes running lengthwise down its bark, shining in the wet. When the rain stopped next day, I visited the tree again, and the stripes still gleamed as greenly in the sunlight.

At that house I fell in love with roses.

"Can you take care of them?" my landlord asked. He had bought the property only a few weeks earlier from the widow of the man whose sudden death transferred to me his rose garden.

What is there to taking care of roses in June except being ravished by them? Each morning I went slowly up and down every row in the garden, stopping to trace the contours of some breath-taking hybrid tea. Later in the day I'd make another tour of the profusion of color and line and fragrance. Logos had no interest in the peculiar way I was spending time instead of playing with him, but Ousia came along. The rows were too narrow for her to follow behind me, and anyway, one sidewise slice of her tail, and half a dozen blooms could become a scattering of petals on the ground. She sat or lay in one of the outer paths, her eye on my every movement, and from time to time I'd look up from my absorption in the yellow and pink and white and red beauty that had fallen to my care to see the black and silver beauty of Ousia.

"Oosie among the roses," I said to her one day, and thereafter it became one of her names.

The year was one of birds, surpassing in number and variety those who had come to any previous feeder of mine. From October, through nesting, through the time for fledglings in June, I stocked at least three feeding stations. A red string bag that began life packed with onions became my holder of suet. I sealed it closed with a piece of wire I had to twist and untwist for refilling, very tough on the fingers, especially on bitter days. A washtub I found in the basement was up-ended in another part of the yard for the blue jays, the rim around its bottom keeping the cracked corn from spilling to the ground. The only store-bought feeder hung from a maple branch outside my kitchen window, until the day a sharp-shinned hawk swooped out of nowhere into the flock of evening grosbeaks feeding on the ground. I saw him in the instant he seized one male, and I slammed my hands against the window, beating at the frame and shouting. The hawk changed course and flew off, low, the gorgeous yellow of the grosbeak dangling suspended in his claws. Hawks must eat too, but I did not see it my business to offer up meals to them. I moved the feeder to the front porch, hanging it from a hook in the ceiling, but when I returned to the kitchen, two male grosbeaks were perched on the branches of the red maple looking baffled, some chickadees sat in wonder, and a jay kept flying to the place in the air where the feeder had hung.

By late February the chickadees were coming to my hand to feed. I'd stand near the feeder unmoving, bare hands wide apart, palms up, one or two sunflower seeds on each. The first time a chickadee lighted on my hand, I was aware of a distinct presence that far outweighed the bird's actual ounce or less. The claws of its toes rested so lightly on my skin as to momentarily make me question my sense of my own body, but this creature could mate, build nests, rear young. I regarded him gravely and remained motionless while he stayed. It was not long. He looked at me, and I, trying not to blink because the motion of my lashes would be sufficient to end our encounter, stared back. Assured, he bent his head, lifted a seed with his beak, and was gone, leaving me with a slight tingling at the edge of my palm where he had briefly thrust his legs downward on my flesh for the boost he needed to be airborne.

One March afternoon, cleaning up the area of the dogs' run that lay in the woods, I straightened abruptly to ease an aching muscle. Something flew directly at me and I ducked. I looked around for my assailant and saw a chickadee on a branch not three feet from my head, gazing straight into my eyes. I suddenly understood that, from wherever he was when he saw me working in the woods, he had recognized me, coming to me there as naturally as he came to my hand at the feeder. I, not just the feeder, was a source of food; I was essential in the whole situation. And so I acknowledged his demand: I went into the house for a handful of seed and returned to that spot in the woods. I called, "dee-dee-DEE," and he and his fellows came to my gloved hand, took the seed, and flew to a branch to work on it. Would they trust me without a safe retreat nearby? I moved into the center of the yard where no protective trees could shield them. They came, perching first on the uprights of the fence to give themselves a clear view of potential dangers, then arriving from all directions, bringing their gift to me and leaving with mine.

Yet in April, when deep snow no longer prevented our walking in the woods again, I called to the chickadees as Logos and Ousia and I strolled our old paths, and although they called back in the trees above me, they did not come to my hand.

In that house, too, the day came when I had thirty-five dollars in the world. Sunflower seed cost $6.75 for fifty pounds. For three days I battled with myself and then I bought it, unable to watch the birds' bewilderment when they kept coming to the feeders, looking for food and not finding it. To feed the rest of us, I sold almost every possession I had so carefully chosen or been chosen by nearly ten years earlier. Each object carried for my eye or hand a special color or shape or line or surface along with and augmenting its function. Each was the beginning or ending of a story.

But I closed myself off from all that and drove to the office of the local newspaper to insert my ad offering almost everything for sale. On the front seat next to me rested a lampshade I had had made to my custom long ago: the woman in the classified department whom I had phoned for rates wanted to buy it before anyone else saw it. I had not finished parking the car when a dog wandered past, and Ousia and Logos in the backseat began barking at him. Then Ousia, angered by the dog's indifference to her, surged into the space between the two front bucket seats and reached across the lampshade toward the window. She missed. But on the lampshade four deeply etched lines from her claws curved from top to bottom. I yelled at her, I yelled for the loss of forty dollars' worth of object, and I yelled because I had to sell it at all. Then we all sat quietly for long minutes. I switched on the ignition, shifted gears, and returned home. I have the lampshade still, sixteen years later, and sometimes I let my fingers trace the markings Ousia left for me.

One by one, objects went out the door, and cash and checks stayed behind in my hands. I would not sell the desk and chair at which I first found my work, and the price I placed on the elegance of my couch made all potential buyers shake their heads longingly. Two men bought the maple butcher block table, seven feet long by three feet wide, that I had had made in Canada to be big enough to prepare food on, to dine from with eight others, to spread out all the versions of a piece of writing on. When the two men carried it down the back stairs they temporarily removed the outside door to be sure of slipping the table through the opening without hazard. But as the final eighteen inches slid outside in their cautious hands, a screw protruding from the hardware remaining in the door jamb gouged a long scar on the beautifully sanded and oiled surface of the table before the men could stop it, and I exulted.

For more than six months we had no house. I boarded Logos and Ousia with a vet in Connecticut, trucked what remained of my things to a friend's garage in Ohio, and drove to and from the couches of friends and acquaintances looking for jobs. For a few weeks I was a guest in a house only an hour from the vet. On Saturdays I'd pick up Logos and Ousia, and we'd go for long walks in woods new to us, then stay the night in a motel, I delaying returning them on Sunday as late as I could.

After two months without them I said, "Enough," and retrieved them from the vet. I bought a quilt for me and food for all of us, and for a week we lived in my car in a state forest. There was supposed to be a two-dollar fee for camping each night, but, although the ranger knew we were there, he never collected it from me. During the night, raccoons would bang the trash cans looking for food, and Logos and Ousia would roar at them from within the car. At dawn I'd let the dogs out to explore the events of the night just passed, and I'd stand brushing my teeth, looking down at the Connecticut River while the sun rose and set it to shining.

Water was at the bottom of a deep well, brought up after a minimum of eight pulls and releases of the heavy pump handle. But something had to be ready to receive the splashing icy cold freshness. I'd put the dogs' waterbowl on the ground beneath the wide-mouthed spigot, collecting only half the water that rushed out. To the dogs went the first drink each morning. The next filling was for my ablutions. The third through tenth got themselves transferred to the gallon jug I kept in the car so that, wherever we were during the day, the dogs always had water. For breakfast I chewed a roll saved from the evening meal. In a few hours I'd drive into town, read in the public library, buy a sandwich for lunch, then spend the afternoon in the library again, interspersed with short walks with the dogs. Late in the afternoon I'd find shady trees on some public lawn and feed the dogs from the bag of their dry food I carried in the car. My hot meal of the day was dinner in a restaurant, early so that I could find my way back into the forest before dark. The fifth or sixth night I rented a motel room for the luxury of a hot shower and a bed that would let me stretch my whole body in any direction. But the next night we were back in the forest again.

By the end of the week the writing assignment I had been hustling came through, and I moved us into a motel with woods beyond our door. We stayed for two months, saving money by paying the weekly rate, but when the assignment came to an end I packed our things into the car and we moved on.

In western Massachusetts I enrolled for welfare and food stamps. Looking for work one day through the women's center at one of the five colleges nearby I sat talking with the director. Unaccountably I burst into tears, then fled. Years later, when *An Unknown Woman* was published, a young woman came to speak to me after my reading at the *Boston Globe* Book Festival. In the middle of a sentence she began to weep. I took her arm and, talking to her all the while, walked her to the area where I had been asked to sign copies of my book. She quieted soon and left. When I finished all the autographing, the young woman appeared again, this time with her mother, who introduced herself as the former director of that women's center. The young woman started to apologize for her tears.

"Ah, but I cried in front of your mother once," I said.

The mother curved her arm around her incredulous daughter and said to me, "I wondered whether you'd remember that."

I tell her now that that was not the only time.

Nearly seven months passed before I rented with borrowed money a five-bedroom house in northern Virginia. I used only two of the bedrooms, but the house bordered ten acres of woods and was carpeted throughout, including the stairs, so that Logos, then ten and limping with arthritis, could easily climb up to the room that became my study whenever he wanted to occupy his old place under my desk, his chin resting on my feet as I wrote.

It was daring of me to sign that lease because I was only negotiating for, had not yet been hired for, the job of writing speeches for the congressman. We lived in those empty rooms for a week, exploring the woods, waiting for the son of my Ohio friend to load a rented truck with my belongings stored in the family garage and drive it down to me.

Scotty and his friend arrived late at night and slept in their choice of my bedrooms. That afternoon while I was guiding their transport of my desk up the stairs into my study, the phone call that my apprehensive ear was peeled for arrived. When I hung up I shouted: "I have a job!" and I whooped and danced and clapped my hands. The boys watched me, grinning, winking at each other.

In only one of all these houses did I ever say:

I am at home now.

Through the north windows of my study I could see the great pines that edged the meadows. Stone walls disappeared into the forest beyond. The brook tumbled down a low rocky dam, moving beneath its icy shell.

Early in the century someone must have stood near where I placed my desk and said, "In this perfect setting I will build a perfect house." He could not have known that he was preparing a dwelling place for me. When my future landlord bought the property sixty years later, knocked out walls and installed glass doors, added a broad deck to overlook the marsh that dominates the view from the east, rewired the interior and painted it white, exposed and darkened the ceiling beams, thus imparting an unmistakable quality of the Elizabethan, he, Gary, could not have known that he was redesigning the house for me.

But I, from the moment I first turned my car into the attenuated lane bisecting unmowed fields and bordered by stone walls and ancient trees, knew that this house on this land had been waiting for me during the nearly twenty-two years I had been looking for it. And when I moved in two weeks later, my belongings settled into all the corners and up against all the walls, looking quiet and finally at rest after the long journey here from everywhere else that began the February evening when I shifted into first gear and drove my car off the ferry from Nantucket.

That house did not belong to me, no matter that it fitted me, belonged to me in spirit. Worse: Gary would not guarantee my stay beyond early summer, and it was then only October. That did not prevent my savoring every day of living there, playing with Kairos on the dry fields in late autumn, tracking through knee-deep snow on our way into the thousand-acre state forest surrounding us, sitting in the darkened house to watch the full moon rise over the trees to illuminate the marsh where the water reflected it, listening at dusk to the hooting of the great horned owl, the sound moving across the open fields to reverberate in me as though I were the strings of a harp being plucked.

On a February day Gary came by to say that he had decided not to live in the house himself, that I could have it as long as I wanted it. I fell asleep that night wondering how I had deserved this house, this home. But a nightmare awakened me: men I did not know were breaking into the house through the basement door. In the morning I went downstairs to test the heavy steel door with its deadbolt barring even the possibility of intruders. And yet the dream was prophetic. A group of men, not Gary, compelled me to move from that house. I understood the dream only afterward, living in other quarters in the country, when I heard myself tell someone how the men had undermined my joy, breaking in on it, no matter that Gary had secured it for me.

This habitat, this home, has been very costly to sustain.

To live in the country, you must have income from elsewhere. And if the elsewhere is not within a driving distance you can tolerate, you must find an elsewhere that is. And it is always on someone else's sufferance.

To have my own house today, country or anywhere, I would need for a down payment a sum of money that I'll never possess as savings. To accumulate savings, you must first have money for current expenses, and then you must have an emergency fund to cover three or four months' expenses in the event of a major interruption of your income. But, apart from the two years bestowed on me by readers of *An Unknown Woman*, nearly the whole of these twenty-five years has been income-interrupted.

Soon there will be another place to live, another house to find. And another. Each moving on disconnects me further, loosens me link by link, from the continuities I still seek.

I stand cleft between the country and the university.

If I could have given up the university, given up the hope of contributing to and being benefited by the world of ideas as the center of each day, if I had wanted only to live in the country, I could have found some way to support myself, my household, so that lonely roads and upland woods were available to me with Logos and Ousia early mornings before nine, evenings after five, weekends. An office. Some suburban shop. Perhaps in time even having my own business, selling real estate, say. But those would have been jobs. What I had in mind was work.

If I could have given up the country, given up as daily sustenance the natural world I came to inhabit so intimately, if I had wanted only the university, I could have been part of the academic community, accepting an appointment no matter where, even in a city, simply to be teaching. Teaching would have let me do philosophy all day every day, would have placed me among my peers, would have let me circumambulate in an atmosphere of intellectual stimulation extending far beyond the one I was creating for myself alone in my study.

Or so the parallel reasoning should have run.

It happened that, Harvard Ph.D. or no, I was not considered part of the university. At first they wouldn't let me in. Later, they wouldn't let me in because I hadn't been in.

And so my desk became the bridge between these worlds of university and country. Writing my thinking, I could live in the country and be of the university even though not in it. I did not anticipate that so vast a portion of my energies, of my creativity, would go into barely surviving.

It was not part of my plan to become solitary. In the beginning I made myself seek ways to endure it for the time (I was certain it would not be forever) because it grew out of my choices. Yet not out of these alone but also out of the decisions of others and out of chance events. In time its benisons made themselves known to me, and finally I came to love it.

But I did not have in mind to become an anchorite. I wanted only to write my thinking, to teach and to learn. In a house of my own in the country.

Last week a new friend brought me a gift when she returned from her native Turkey. I unwrapped the small package at once, but the overall shape of the shiny globes and curving cylinders of blue glass puzzled me.

I looked up at her. "What is it, Sumru?"

"It's a common talisman in Turkey," she answered, and she, the holder of a Ph.D., began to smile. "It's seven elephants for someone who hopes for a house. This bead on the bottom wards off the evil eye."

They hang now from a hook in the southeasterly-facing window of my dining room, the seven elephants, graduated from small to large and strung together on a golden thread. In the morning the sun sets them to sparkling. Late in the afternoon the western sun lights up the laurel outside the window, but the blue glass elephants barely reflect their shine, and the bead on the bottom not at all.

For a house of my own I'll take all the help I can get.

7

LOVING

MORE THAN A year went by after I left Nantucket until I first started to think of writing about it. I believed then that there were two books I could write: one, about what I had intentionally gone to Nantucket to do; the other, about what I encountered there, outside of my intention. What I went there to do was to find out who I was and what I wanted. What I encountered there were the empty streets, the unoccupied houses, the caressing presence of the silence, the sea at low tide and high, the winter setting of the sun, the whole repertoire of changes in wind, sun, sky, and stars that constitute sea weather. Another half-year passed before I realized that there weren't two books to write, but one only. Because the space and the silence and the loneliness were not simply the background against which my interior learning took place: they were some of its crucial teachers.

And Logos was foremost among them.

A man with whom I had no other connection placed an apprehensive German shepherd puppy into my own uncertain hands. Into that man's hands I placed money. That's buying, in any language. But the word carries an overbearingly arrogant assumption. To buy something implies not only that one thereby owns the thing but also that one has a right to own it. Having a right to own it, one may thereby do what one wishes with the thing. A chair for which I exchange money is mine. If I enclose the chair in a glass case, people will think me dotty. If I take an ax to it and use it for firewood, people will think me extravagant. If I sit on it at my dining table, people will think me sensible. Actually, people will not bother to think me anything, because sitting is the usual thing one does with a chair. But I *may* do any of these things: both custom and the law permit them. They are consequences of owning, of having the right to own.

Even when Logos was new to me, when I had not yet made sense of my own value, let alone his, I never once considered him to be mine in the way a chair is mine. Rather, he was mine the way another human being is my friend or my student. Having a friend, having a student, are relationships into which human beings can enter. Having a dog is another. And just as friendships between human beings rely on some special quality elicited from both persons, who thereupon treasure the unique connection between them, let it develop along lines that neither can or wants to predict, enforcing no conditions on one another except those that might destroy their total and unending commitment to one another, so did this human being and that German shepherd have a certain relationship that will at first seem anomalous to you because owning—my being able to do whatever I wished with him—was not part of it.

I did not regard Logos as my child, or as a toy, or as a charming creature who endeared himself to me by being less intelligent than I and who thus needed me to take care of him. Nor did I think of him as a slave to do my bidding, once trained, but at other times to be chained or locked away. Nor, never, as my "pet," that term of amused contempt for another creature, implying that his or her whole life lies at the mercy of a human hand that can either stroke or strike, feed or withhold food, mold or otherwise shape the creature to that hand's purposes totally independently of what the creature might be or want.

Initially, Logos was in my life to serve a purpose for me: he was to protect me, since I would be alone and in an unfamiliar place, an island. But that isolated land where I had never before been was nearly untenanted: there was no one to protect me from. And even if the handful of people who inhabited the village of Siasconset that winter of 1962 had all been criminals, Logos was then only four months old. I had very little good sense during our early days in that house on the edge of a moor, but even I could recognize how foolish was my purpose within the first days of our being there.

Thus did I find myself with a living creature for whom I had no purpose other than the one I had just discarded. I could have discarded him along with it. I could have invented another purpose. Instead, he caught my attention as himself. At first, trying to see the world from his point of view was one of my entertainments. He was extraordinarily responsive to me, and almost from the start I saw that he was too smart for his own good. Coming to understand him therefore became an intellectual challenge. And there were offshoots of the aesthetic because of my sheer delight in looking at him, his color, the way the light fell on him. From there, it was an easy step, a quiet and natural step, to see him as a being in his own right, as an individual. If you are startled by the idea that a dog can be an individual, taken as seriously as any human being, then I ask you to consider that while it was I who started it, started treating him with the same respect and courtesy I extend to most human beings, he did in fact respond with whatever there was in him that wanted to connect with me at the point where I was reaching toward him. I was simply opening out to him an opportunity to explore his own freedom, as I was then exploring mine. In this way of freely moving toward one another, we each became ourselves.

None of this happened overnight. Perhaps half a year passed after leaving Nantucket until my breath caught up with me, and by then we were installed in our house in Weston, where only Logos could place a demand on me that did not spring from my own purposes or from the means necessary to attain them. Yet even that was of my choosing, because my commitment to him was unconditional, making its appearance in practicalities of every sort.

His food bowl was a matter for study. Plastic and aluminum were easy to clean, inexpensive, unbreakable. But they left my kitchen almost as quickly as they entered because, even filled with food, they traveled across the floor a jerky inch or two each time Logos bent his head for the next mouthful. I wouldn't like having to slide my chair alongside a sliding table with every forkful, nor should Logos have to. A weighted aluminum bowl that stayed in place while it was being emptied was therefore next: easy to clean but not so modest in price. It was surpassed, years later, by a heavy flat-bottomed glass bowl, come upon unexpectedly in a dime store where it was being sold as a container for punch: cheap, safely scaldable by the dishwater, breakable only by my own carelessness (but immediately replaceable).

And his outdoor shelter while I was away at my job. A few days before I built Logos' first run, Tommy arrived with a doghouse he had made years earlier for a long line of Phillips dogs and was letting me borrow. Together we hauled it down from his pickup truck.

"It seems small to me," I said, ungratefully.

"You don't want a lot of room for a dog," Tommy said. "A dog wants to curl up in something he fits right into. A barrel: that's what a dog likes. But you can't buy barrels anymore." Tommy drove off.

I examined the house with an eye peeled for safety. Paint was flaking, probably leaded. Nails were protruding into the interior. From inside you looked up at the sky through holes in the roof, out to the trees through slits in the walls.

Bunny Keene sometimes did odd jobs in his free time after

work in the wire factory five miles away. He showed me how to hammer back together the tongue-and-groove boards that had come loose from one another in the walls and roof of the house. He pulled old nails, pounded in new shorter ones, gave me some sheets of sandpaper with a short lesson on how to use the varying grades of it, and told me where to buy shingles and brushes and outdoor paint, including a primer. ("What's a primer, Bunny?") When I completed all the preparatory work, he came by on a Saturday afternoon to lay the roofing, overlapping the shingles just so, doubling them over the ridge, extending the lowest shingles a couple of inches beyond the bottom edges of the roof so that rain wouldn't run into the top edges of the walls I had just undercoated.

Bunny also built a platform to my specifications. It would be a dry clean place for Logos to lie on when the ground was muddy or too wet. To keep its underside from direct contact with the soil I bought cement blocks and lugged them, one by deadweight one, from my car and into the run. They had to be leveled, of course: another trick I mastered with another tool. I painted the platform and the house the same day: deep orange. The paint was lead-free.

And no matter what Tommy said about dogs liking to curl up into barrels, wood had to feel hard to Logos without some sort of cushioning material. Thick layers of straw went into the house as its first bedding, but they packed down too quickly, absorbing the mud Logos tracked in. Questions to knowledgeable people led me to cedar shavings, which also kept fleas away, stayed resilient longer, and scented Logos' coat to remind me of winter all year long.

When I left Weston I returned the doghouse to Tommy. Visiting him and Olive last month, which is to say eighteen years later, I saw it standing unused next to a fence. The roof still looked serviceable, only a tear or two visible, not enough to let water leak through. It's white now: Tommy hadn't liked the color that even now punctuates the items of my household. It still looks small to me, and I wonder now how Logos could have slept in it during all those weekdays for the year and more that I had to drive away and leave him behind.

Logos' food, his rest, his safety, his health, his dignity, his general well-being: each of these matters received the same thought and concern from me as though I were dealing with them for myself. As I saw it then, as I saw it later for Ousia, as I still see it for Kairos, since human society didn't permit him to do these things for himself, he no longer being a wild creature, the responsibility was mine to do them for him. And, just as I was daily aware of becoming free myself, so was I determined that he be as free as possible, albeit within some of the very limits that I myself acknowledged and, indeed, relied on.

All this was caring about Logos for his own sake rather than repaying him for what he was doing for me. Once I stopped thinking of him as being with me for my purposes, for my sake, the only other way to think of him was as being there for his own sake. In ethical theory, this is very elementary reasoning.

As is the concept of doing something for its own sake. It means that you act without thought for, without prospect of, benefit of any sort to yourself. Human beings being what we are, there are precious few things we do that fall under this heading. Most non-philosophers find the concept incomprehensible, even comical, on first hearing, not recognizing it among the job lot of principles they long ago accepted on the authority of someone else and still carry around. Yet there are circumstances that can unearth it where it lies buried in the deepest coverts of themselves as a Good to be sought above all others.

You are handsome or beautiful. Or rich. Or you occupy or have a secure connection with someone who occupies some position of power. You can discount people at the periphery and most of those midway between that and the center: you know why they're around you. But of those closest to you, you need to know that you they love *you* rather than your beauty or wealth or power. That's loving you for your own sake. In point of logic, it's exceedingly difficult to maintain that people love one another only for the pleasure they bring one another in face of the fact that all persons seek to be loved no matter what they do or are. You seek to be loved for your own sake. And if to be loved for your own sake, then how avoid loving another not for the pleasure the other brings but because the person is who he or she is? Loving the person for the person's sake.

You are a parent. To prevent harm great or small from befalling your child, you will take the harm upon yourself, and without thought of the consequences to yourself. In point of logic, you cannot then maintain that people act only to benefit themselves. You yourself will have acted otherwise: you will have acted for your child's sake.

You are a painter, a poet, a cabinetmaker, you repair clocks. The work uses all your imagination, intellect, wit, and energy. When you're doing it, you're all but unaware of time's passing. You know you'd do that work somewhere, somehow, even if no one paid you to do it. You are doing your work for its own sake. In point of logic, you cannot then believe that people work only for money or power or prestige.

Loving my work for the work's sake, loving another person for the person's sake: each of these facets of my life germinated and flourished, starting with the seed that was my commitment to Logos.

And even though I did not feed, shelter, exercise, keep safe, and take close care of Logos as part of an exchange of services we performed for one another, I was receiving benefactions from him that were so intricately tied into, so thoroughly integrated with, the whole course of my day, the whole pattern of future days I was in process of designing, that it would have been difficult then for me to lift out to the light those gifts and say, "This, this, and that would not be part of my life if Logos were not with me." It was only years later when those circumstances I had so perfectly tailored

to suit me no longer existed that I could comb through the threads
I had woven together and thereby distinguish the elements that had
been available to me.

For one thing, I was daily in the presence of a living creature
of exceptional beauty.

Logos had golden eyes. Patches of black fur, almost triangles,
circumscribed them. The eyebrows themselves were small triangles
that narrowed to a fine line toward the outside corner of each eye,
then vanished. His forehead and the middle plane of his face were
golden tan, soft contrast with the sooty shadowing around his eyes.
The blackness of his muzzle rose up to and merged with that tan
at the midpoint of his nose, then flowed backward nearly to the end
of his jaw. A tiny circle of black fur marked his left cheek. When
he'd turn to look back at me, his head in three-quarters profile, the
black of his muzzle outlining his face against the creamy background of his throat and chest, the whole aspect of him was so
astonishingly beautiful that I'd catch my breath, no matter that I
had seen it a thousand times before. At that special angle, he held
himself with a dignity that was almost imperious. One midnight a
friend walked me back to my car in which Logos had been waiting
for me all evening. I opened the door to let him jump out for a
quick tour of the trees and switched on my headlights so that I
could track his movements. Mike and I watched him as we finished
off our talk, and then Logos turned his head to look back at us.

"Why, he's a prince!" Mike said, and his voice carried the
same wonder that inhabited me up to the very day I saw the beautiful
face for the last time, unmoving for the first time.

Logos' mere presence let me live alone in country houses, having
only woods and wild creatures for close neighbors. 'Alone' is not
the correct word. It is a short way of saying something else. The
long way, the accurate thing to say, is that I lived with no other
human beings in my household. But I was not alone. As aware as
I was of myself throughout each day in that first house after Nan-

tucket, so was I equivalently aware of Logos. When he had to stay at the vet's for a few hours or overnight, his absence became the leading edge on whatever else I was doing until he was back with me again. When I left him at home while I spent the day in a library or kept a city appointment in the heat of summer, I was as aware of his not being with me as of his presence when he was; and on the drive away from the house without him I kept having the feeling that I had forgotten something I should have brought with me. That sense of his absence was itself a presence, as though a draft were blowing into a window that someone had left open but that I could not shut.

So 'alone' is the wrong word. 'Without other human beings' is precise.

From time to time some friend from New York or Cambridge would come to visit me, and we'd go for a stroll along my wandering paths in the woods that were now as much a part of my dwelling place as the house that was my legal residence.

"But aren't you afraid out here in the woods alone?"

It was to become one of the two questions most frequently asked me through the whole course of my life, but it startled me the first time I heard it. (The other was: "What have you been doing since you left Nantucket?")

"I'm not alone," I answered. Logos as always was in the lead by twenty paces.

My friend's tone of voice was impatient. "You know what I mean."

I was not afraid. More: I went into the woods as a child to a playground. I, who had grown up a coward, had shaken off the last clinging carryover from my rearing. But it was Logos' fearlessness that let me venture so far out of my old fearful self. Not that I was equally fearless. I aimed only to occupy that mean, not too much, not too little, that Aristotle tells us is worth aiming for when we're after what he calls the virtues. Neither cowardice nor foolhardiness, he says, but rather that intermediate disposition that inclines a man (he spoke only of men) to face and fear the right things from the right motives in the right way at the right time. According to Aristotle, the confidence such a man feels in these circumstances is courage, bravery. I never applied the terms to myself. 'Courage' is a word for the use of other people, for the view from outside. From inside me, I was doing what I did every day.

Another evening a friend drove up from Philadelphia on his way to Boston. Zeno arrived late in the afternoon, we took a rambling tour of my woods, and then we spent long hours over dinner. Logos was present the whole time. Zeno had tossed a ball for him to chase outside, had stroked his head, had, without making a deliberate effort to do so, made it clear to Logos that he, Zeno, was a friend of mine.

After dinner we wandered into the living room to continue our talk. Zeno raised the now familiar question.

"I'm not alone, Zeno."

My guest considered Logos, lying nearly asleep in a corner of the room. "What would he do if I were to try to harm you?" he asked.

"I don't know. Are you willing to try it and see?"

Zeno nodded. We rose from our chairs and stood side by side. From his distant vantage Logos raised his head a few inches, no more than faintly curious. Standing next to me on my right and without threatening me by voice or gesture, Zeno slowly placed his left hand around my right wrist.

No moment elapsed for us to anticipate Logos' movement. He was simply there in front of us, his nose at the place on my wrist where Zeno's fingers encircled it. His nose hovered an eighth of an inch above that join, waiting. His eyes sought mine.

"Don't move, Zeno," I said, stooping to tousle Logos' head with my free hand, nuzzling my face into his neck. "It's okay, Logos. He's very nice. He's our friend."

To Zeno I said, "Let go of my hand. Just let it drop. Then stand there."

I roughhoused with Logos on the floor for a few minutes. In the interval Zeno returned to his chair, shaking a little and silent. I led Logos back to his corner, restored to his earlier insouciance. Over fresh coffee, Zeno and I resumed our talk about our separate research and about the philosophers we knew.

Beyond all that, sometimes when I looked up from my writing or reading to see Logos lying fast asleep a few feet away, sprawled at perfect ease on the mat I had made for him, his sides heaving slowly, rhythmically, certain that that place, that very place, was where he belonged, the unalloyed pleasure of the moment would hold me motionless.

Yet, for all my understanding of loving, Ousia entered our household not for her own sake but to serve a purpose of mine: she was to produce one of Logos' puppies. Logos would exist in that puppy, then in a puppy through that puppy, and so on to the end of my life. It was my way of acknowledging that his life-term would differ from mine.

Still, it wouldn't be fair to the pup to bring her to live with us but to relegate her to the scullery, so to speak, until she was the proper age to undertake the business for which she was present. I'd have to keep an eye on her health up to and certainly including the mating, not only to ensure the health of the litter but to keep the threat of disease away from Logos. And in order to do that, I'd have to keep her groomed and free of ticks and fleas; I'd have to keep sharp and breakable objects out of her way, as I did for Logos; I'd have to train her, at least to some minimum level, to prevent her being a nuisance. How was I to give her all that time and attention without liking her? And how was I to like her when Logos absorbed the whole of my affection?

On a certain day I suddenly saw Logos as lonely for his own

kind, and there was the solution to my problem. I didn't have to worry about dividing my affection between Logos and a new puppy because he could like her *for* me! Far better for him to like another dog than for me to love two dogs: our loyalty to one another would be untouched by this way of allocating things.

Within two weeks I found the litter that contained Ousia. The breeder separated the females from the males, then, knowing Logos was current in all vaccinations, he humored me by letting Logos have some say in the matter.

Logos tumbled out of the car, straining against my leash in his haste to explore the new domain all at once. Zigzagging in front of me, behind me, to each side, he rushed into the midst of three surprised female puppies. Two of them backed away to watch him from a distance, but the third stood firm, shaking with excitement. When Logos swept past her, nose down to smell every inch of the ground, she took a step forward. Her tiny tongue touched his muzzle briefly, and then she stood happily back, proud to have been braver than her sisters in confronting the big intruder. With that kiss, Ousia chose Logos.

"I'll take that one," I told the breeder.

He lifted her into my arms, and I looked her full in the face for just a moment. She was fat and black and her ears still hung down. The intensity of her alertness almost stung my hands, but she was only an object I was buying for Logos. She was then just under eight weeks old.

I had it wrong, of course. Ousia may have chosen Logos, but he did not choose her. When I brought her home a few days later, he inspected her thoroughly, nosing her to stand still. She gave up trying to reach me, lay down, and rolled over onto her back. Her round pink unprotected belly was her admission to Logos that she knew he was king. But to him she stopped existing.

The first afternoon, although Logos did not let his eyes come to rest on Ousia after the early minutes of their acquaintance, he somehow seemed always to be backing into her or stepping near enough to a paw or her tail to make her withdraw it in time to prevent its being crushed. Ousia would then pad over to me. My automatic reaction was to quiet her apprehensiveness. My second reaction, which always intervened in time, was to stand up from where I sprawled on the grass and walk away into the house or to another part of the yard. If Logos were to see me even once as a refuge for Ousia, my whole plan for having them be friends would collapse. There would be time later, I told myself, after he has accepted her, to be quite natural in responding to her. So long as she doesn't hurt herself or eat anything dangerous, there's no need now for my even touching her. And each hour that goes by without adding fuel to whatever is smoldering in Logos' eyes might by that fact alone serve to bank it.

For the next few days the three of us circled one another in what would have appeared to any passing aerial observer as a strange and intricate country dance. Ousia would approach me, I would half-start toward her, then walk in another direction, perhaps toward Logos, who would stand next to me rubbing closely against my leg while I scratched his ears or stroked his back to let him know that he was still first, and then he would wander elsewhere, not even under these circumstances permitting me to touch him longer than a few seconds at a time. None of us was really satisfied by all this tact, and yet by the end of two days I had made certain facts very clear: Ousia was here to stay; she required certain attentions that Logos, being adult, did not; but Logos was indisputably Chief Dog. Each of us knew all of that.

Thereafter, morning after morning when all of us scurried out the back door into the yard, Ousia would walk straight up to Logos and kiss him unashamedly on the nose, then stand back, her long thin tail wagging violently in the soaring hope that this would be the day he'd see her. But Logos stared grimly off into the woods, never once even blinking, which was the minimal attention he would have paid a fly that had temporarily alighted on him. The fourth or fifth day when she stepped backward to watch the effect of her gift, he moved, but only to sit so that he could better scratch some unexpected irritation in his ear.

After three days, Ousia was house-trained and therefore free to go anywhere in the house. When we weren't outdoors, she could most often be found on the bed of cotton rugs I had arranged for her in the kitchen closet. I kept adding piles of old clothes to it, planning one day soon to buy a piece of foam rubber cut to the size of the closet floor, as I had done for Logos, to complete her comfort.

Logos found reasons to pass that inviting bed often, but if she lay there he refused to look inside. When she was elsewhere he spent some time sniffing it all around, incredulous that although he had deemed her not to exist she somehow still did. One of the days it was empty he walked in, turned around once, and lay down, stretching himself so that his entire back was flush with the rear wall, his nose against one of its sides, his bottom against the other. You will correctly imagine that no room was left for anything at all, even for the one small confused female shepherd who stood examining him for a long minute before she came over to tell me that something was definitely wrong.

I went to the closet and looked down. Logos had fallen so deeply asleep that he did not hear me call his name. "Sweet Puppy," I said softly, "that's Ousia's bed."

But it's my house, the unmoving body replied.

It didn't escape me that something new was on the verge of happening, but that day, for some reason I can't now recall, I wasn't up to whatever my suddenly deaf friend had in store for me. I took Ousia for a short walk by ourselves to divert her.

Over the next few days Logos found his way to that bed with a great deal of regularity. It soon ceased to matter to him that Ousia was lying there too. He still didn't look at her, and anyway, she took up only one small part of it. She surely didn't need that whole other wall that he could curl up against, his paws tucked up under him as though to show me that he too could still be a puppy, if he chose. From then on I couldn't pass the closet without giggling. Either Ousia lay there, not quite edged out by Logos, or else Logos sprawled there alone.

Toward the end of the second week of all this, Logos stepped onto the rusty edge of a can that had somehow missed my policing of the woods. I knew exactly what to do for the foot and I was very proud of the bandage I wrapped around it. Logos limped a little for a day or two, favoring the sore foot, and then he began to find the bandage a handicap. With his teeth he sought out the end of the tape and slowly started to peel it off. I happened along in time to repair my work, taping the end so that Logos would find it difficult to tear away. Nevertheless, in the comparative concealment of Ousia's closet he managed to get a good start on removing it by the time I made my way to the kitchen sink to clean the pans that didn't fit into the dishwasher.

"You stop that now, Logos," I said, irritated as much by having to wash the greasy cookware as by the prospect of having to redo the intricate bandage. Logos sighed, recognizing my tone of voice, and left off. He settled himself into a sleeping position that paid due care to his aching foot, so that most of his body lay on the rugs in the closet while the wounded paw spilled over onto the floor, the lifted corner of the bandage visible to any passerby. Which happened to be Ousia.

I was standing at the sink waiting for the flowing hot water to form a good head of suds in the dishpan. I glanced at her only long enough to watch her realize that she had been outmaneuvered one more time, and then I leaned into my work. I continued scrubbing the pots until the sink was clear of them, and then I rested them, draining and gleaming, on the counter. Some fifteen minutes had elapsed, therefore, during which I did not know that

Ousia had volunteered her friendly assistance to Logos and he, in full knowledge of the consequences, had accepted.

For Ousia was pulling the tape off Logos' bandage while his paw lay extended on the floor: the tape was already several inches long by the time I looked. Ousia was gently tugging at the end with her teeth while Logos exerted sufficient resistance to allow her smaller weight to rip the tape off just a little more each time. She'd let go briefly to catch her breath or to gather strength, and in that minute Logos would shift his body just enough to give her the exact purchase her baby teeth required. He lay quite perfectly still as she worked, although from time to time he opened his eyes to observe her progress. By the way he closed them I understood that he was luxuriating in the knowledge that he had nullified the threat by making her an ally.

And so began the friendship of Logos and Ousia.

I find it difficult now to remember my lack of real interest in Ousia herself during those early months. Then on a February day I brought her home after seeing the vet's X rays: she had hip dysplasia, a malformation of the fit between the hip socket and leg joint to which shepherds are liable because of the very standards American breeders have selected for their ideal dog. The disease would cripple her at age two or three, she'd be in great pain, and she'd die young; she'd transmit the heritage to half her young, and pregnancy itself would hasten the onset. She would have to be spayed.

I knelt next to her, the influence of the anesthesia needed for taking the X rays still cloaking her as she lay on the bed in the closet I had prepared for her not six months earlier. My three-year-old plan to have Logos always with me through his get and then his get's get had dissolved on an X ray plate that afternoon. From Ousia's ugly face, as I then saw it, my look traveled across the furry black sides heaving deeply in drugged sleep, to the skinny tail that was only then beginning to thicken out into its proper fullness. Her long legs twitched briefly: the day before she had made me laugh at the clumsiness with which she trotted toward me. Suddenly I saw in imagination the day her rear legs would collapse under a burden not of her choosing.

"She's only eight months old," I muttered. My hands clutched the air as though I could reach the inaccessible enemy, and then all at once I yelled to my empty kitchen: "She had nothing to do with it!" I burst into tears and fell in love with Ousia without reservation.

I set an appointment for the spaying the following Monday. At eight months, Ousia's first estrous could occur any day now, and then the ovariohysterectomy, which is as much major surgery in dogs as in human beings, would have to await its passing. But ten minutes after I hung up the phone, unable to believe there were no other choices, I called the man into whose hands I had placed money in exchange for Ousia. He urged me to have some shepherd breeders whose judgment he respected take a look at her.

I spent the weekend driving the back roads of Connecticut to place Ousia under the long-practiced eye of four different men and women. The one who seemed most sensible advised me to wait, to let Ousia have her first estrous. The hormonal changes sometimes straightened out a puppy. Her bones were still maturing and she might heal herself if the dysplasia were minor. Another X ray could be taken before her next estrous. If the dysplasia still appeared, the spaying could be done then.

Next morning I canceled the appointment. And in March when the signs preceding ovulation appeared, I absented Ousia to the vet. At the end of the critical days the vet phoned me.

"Come and get her. She'll still smell good to Logos, but that will be over by about Friday. Anyway, she won't let him near her."

My little white convertible sang all the way to the vet's, and

then I had Ousia with me again. I swear she had grown. At home
Logos took one whiff and let out a small cry. Ousia whipped her
rear around and faced him nose to nose. She drew back her lips
just enough to stop Logos in his tracks. For the next twenty minutes
the two of them did a little dance that constantly entangled me.
Ousia would come to me for protection, Logos would follow along
behind her, she'd turn on him and warn him off, but he'd just
stand there, ears sidewise and a silly patient grin on his face, until
she simply sat down. The sitting would happen in the broad open
space beneath my writing table, and then Logos would be there
too, and in a moment the tussle would begin again.

At the end of August that same year I scheduled Ousia for new
X rays with the Bridgeport vet used by the shepherd breeders I
had earlier consulted. What matters isn't simply skill and extensive
experience in reading X rays, they told me: the very way a veterinarian positions a dog for the X ray is crucial to what is finally
seen on the film. I waited for the vet to develop the films while
Ousia lay tranquilized on the examining table. There was no question in his mind: Ousia had dysplasia.

One year to the day on which Ousia came to us as the future
dam of Logos' puppies, I phoned to arrange her spaying for the
following Friday. Labor Day weekend the year before had been
thick with all the new beginnings Ousia brought with her into our
household. Too swiftly this year it brought me closer to the surgery
I'd have given anything not to confront. Friday morning, with
Logos and Ousia in the backseat and not hurrying at all, I drove
Ousia to the vet in Bridgeport. Without me, without Logos,
through a stranger's intervention, her whole life was to be changed.

On the way home, traffic was sparse after the morning rush. I
wondered what Logos and I would do with the long day we had
to ourselves. I caught his image in my rearview mirror. Had I
forgotten already the three years Logos and I had been together
before the black and silver puppy opened both of us out to her?

Why, we'd do those things we did by ourselves: walk along the beach, wander through the woods, swim in the pond down the road, take that lazy hike around the campground near Redding and keep Logos racing for sticks down its long meadow.

Late that afternoon I phoned the vet.

"She came through it very well. No complications. We'll keep her here tonight, of course. You can have her tomorrow around two o'clock."

When I hung up I rested my head against the phone for long minutes. Then I poured a drink, picked up the nearest book, and went outdoors to sit in the sun, reading idly, Logos on the grass beside me, sleeping off our holiday.

They gave Ousia back to me thinner than I remembered her thirty hours earlier. Her midsection was bound in a broad white wrapping secured around her back.

"Keep the bandage dry and clean. And keep her quiet. The sutures must stay in for a week. Come back Monday and let me check to be sure nothing goes wrong."

I settled her into the backseat and we started home. The journey that had taken fifteen minutes from Weston lasted an hour and a half on the return. I drove with one hand on the wheel, the other touching Ousia. We had made a similar trip, she and I, just one year ago. She was no longer that new puppy, but she needed my reassurance even more.

Ousia took a deep drink at the water bowl as soon as we entered the house, went straight to her familiar bed in the kitchen closet, and fell asleep under my stroking hand.

Ousia did not have dysplasia, it turned out. Two years after she was spayed, Whit, my new vet who had been taking care of her for a year, suggested that annual X rays would provide a useful check on the progress of the disease. No smallest malformation appeared on the films I asked him to take. A second set taken ten days later confirmed his negative findings. Perhaps Ousia had had a bad fall when she was very young, and a spur of cartilage had formed around the hip socket. Two vets had misread that temporary anomaly as dysplasia. For months Whit tried to get the earlier X rays from the vet who spayed Ousia, curious to compare them with his own, but his colleague did not reply to his requests.

So for years Ousia raced around the yard in pursuit of the rubber balls I threw for her, leaped over stone fences or whatever else stood in the way of her retrieving a stick, and swam whole afternoons away. If from time to time she limped, it was only because she pulled a muscle or exerted herself beyond good sense.

True: she could not have Logos' offspring. But I had her.

Although Ousia is fiercer than Logos when other people enter our ambience, I see her as an extraordinarily fragile creature. The merest sharpness in my voice, whether directed toward her or elsewhere, will bring her straight to me. She will sit in front of me, her ears will fall back, shaping themselves so closely to the sides of her head that you wonder whether indeed she has ears at all, her whole body will droop downward, and her marvelous soft eyes will plead with me to reconsider my rebuke. I continue my sternness for half a minute, fooling myself that I thereby show her I am consistent when I correct her, but then I cannot bear to have her beg me for a love she already has in all its fullness. I stoop next to her to stroke her earless head, which then seeks comfort in the darkness of the hollow under my shoulder. I rub her neck and give her some solid thwacks on her strong shoulders. She rises to her feet. Her ears come up; her tongue arches high; her tail swings sideways back and forth. She is ready to play, for we are friends again.

Logos refuses ever to admit that something he has done is wrong. The most he will acknowledge is that I'm big enough to be able to enforce a command, if I happen to be close enough to do so. When his ears go back, it is only a formality; deep down he does not recognize anyone as having rightful power over him. Unlike Ousia in similar circumstances, his heart is not breaking, nor does he construe my displeasure as the withdrawal of my love. Perhaps the reason is that long ago he learned that he can always change the subject: he can find some way to make me laugh. Faced with the actuality of a loud lecture, Logos wags the last four inches of the tip of his tail. He does it tentatively: out and back, then stop. If I have not noticed, he tries again. Of course I have seen it the first time: I have simply been trying to sustain my authority. No use. The experiment in apology always works, and he knows it: the large body standing contrite and immobile except for the last few inches of tail sending out its tiny plea strikes me as comical. I giggle or grin or in some way betray that I am easily had. Instantly Logos seizes the initiative. He wheels to look for a ball with which to lure me into a game, putting me in the position of trying to make up to him.

Ousia knows how to bring her body together with mine in a dozen ways. She has inventoried all the hollows on me and will place her head to fit snugly between my breasts, in my armpit, against my side. She will rest her chin on my belly as I lie reading, her head going up and down with my breathing, until finally I am laughing at the grave look with which she examines my face at that close range. Then nothing for it but we must play some game. Sometimes when she awakens very early, earlier even than the hour that sends me out of bed, she will place one paw on my covers to let me know she'd like some company; without speaking or opening my eyes I pat the place next to me and in an instant she has climbed up and fitted the length of her body to mine, and the two of us will fall asleep again, warming each other from our very insides.

Logos does not lie against me and parallel with me as Ousia does: he places his body at right angles to mine. He thus commandeers three-quarters of the bed, and as he makes small changes in his position, seeking his lounging comfort, I am slowly shoved to the far side. Maybe Logos lies that way in order to be able to get off the bed fast if necessary, or maybe, unlike Ousia, he simply has no sense of my body as a solace for his. But no matter how glad I am to have him near me, it is with a certain resignation that I watch him take up his position, his tail and rear against the side of my leg, his face at a 90-degree angle to the perpendicular of me, for in no time I shall be relegated to one edge of the bed while he reigns augustly over most of the rest of it.

Where Ousia is delicate and tender and loving, Logos is wily and original and always seeking some new way to outwit me. If Logos had been a human being he would have been awarded graduate fellowships in his junior year at college, taken his doctorate in no time flat, and then sat back to have his choice of academic appointments. He would have published four papers revolutionizing whatever field he was studying; in three years he would have been chairman of his department; in five, president of the university. Throughout his career new ways of doing things would have come out of his head as though he were a self-contained source of energy.

Ousia would have been a long-haired girl wearing organdy dresses that flowed to the floor. She would have sat in calm silence while young boys broke their hearts for her, and she would have chosen one of them for some reason that only she would know, and she would have remained faithful to him for all the days of her life.

Logos has a repertoire of sounds so extensive that it can very nearly be called a language. But Ousia makes sounds on only a few kinds of occasions. When she is in my car and someone, including other dogs, approaches within what she considers too near a range, or when a car drives into the road leading to our house, she barks with such menace that I have seen people draw back instinctively, even though they are separated from her by closed windows. She is of course protecting me, the house, and the car with this declaration. She uses some of the same sounds, including snarling, to warn Logos away from her food, interrupting her own eating and sometimes even startling me into dropping a spoon or a pan while I'm cooking. The growling at Logos stems from a summer stay at the vet's, where I had to leave her and Logos for two months, when she apparently felt so insecure for not knowing when she'd see me again that she began to search for things that clearly belonged to her, and ended by needing to protect her food from her own dear companion.

When I roughhouse with Logos, Ousia becomes so excited to join in that she utters a high-pitched puppy bark she uses under no other circumstances. Her tongue arches, she prances back and forth, her tail wags in deep curves, and she moves in fast to nip at Logos' body: she is teasing him into a game of tag. If she cannot for those moments have my attention, she will aim for getting the attention of him who has it. When I scratch or knead almost any place on her body, sounds of deep pleasure issue from her. Low groans reverberate in her big chest, something approaching a whisper slips through her teeth, and within this range her voice modulates through such a variety of sounds that she makes me laugh to recognize some of my own. If she could say: "Don't stop: more," she would be saying it in that tone of voice. When she is having a bad dream she makes an extraordinary sequence of sounds. It begins with a cry that would fall out of her throat if her mouth were open, bespeaking a sorrow that interrupts whatever I'm doing. I go to her at once and stroke her gently to blend in with what is running through her thoughts. My touch will stop the crying within a few moments, but the sequence is not complete until a moan begins, sweeping from the toenails of her rear legs through her entire body until it is exhaled at her mask. That final segment of sound takes a full minute to run its course, and I shake my head in wonder at the mental agony she carries within her that I know nothing about and that belies her daytime waking gladness.

Having written all this, I realize that Ousia, too, like Logos, uses sound to connect herself with other creatures in the world. The difference between her and Logos, however, is that she almost never directs sounds to me. Instead, she will come to sit in front of me, staring earnestly at me. That she intensely wants me to do something cannot be mistaken. We run through some possibilities. Out? A game? Hungry? Water? It may turn out that Logos is asleep on her bed at the very time she wants to lie there herself. My task is then to adjudicate the matter.

Logos directs so much deliberate sound to me that one day when he had been silent for twelve whole hours I took him to the vet to discover what was wrong. I had noticed the gradual loss of his hearing since the winter before, and I was afraid that it had abruptly turned into full deafness, that the reason he wasn't vocalizing was that he couldn't hear his own sounds. The vet found only tonsillitis and gave him an antibiotic injection. By evening Logos was back to commenting on all the events that ordinarily aroused his notice. Logos has such abundant vitality that I think the sheer overflow of it bursts out of him as sound. Logos silent is almost as though he is Logos absent, and, indeed, on the rare occasions when he has had to stay at the vet's overnight for some reason, every action of mine echoes in the quietness, and I find myself touching Ousia at regular intervals to reassure myself that all is well.

When Logos was a puppy we played a game in which I'd get on my knees, sit back on my haunches, then place one of his rubber toys on top of my head while I had him sit-stay behind me. Even though he was quivering to get on with it, he'd wait for me to say, "Logos, take it." I'd pat my shoulders with both hands to invite him to rest his front paws on them while he reached for the toy with his mouth. As he grew larger I'd rest on my knees to make him reach fourteen or fifteen inches higher for the trophy. We developed the game to the point where I'd stand, stooping only slightly to let him retrieve the toy by stepping back a few paces to

give himself a running jump. I never ceased to be astonished at
his extreme gentleness in these close dealings with my body. Even
though he was balancing himself only on his rear legs as he rested
his paws on my shoulders, he didn't simply grab for the toy so he
could get back on all fours more quickly. He'd bring his big teeth
slowly and cautiously onto the top of the object, never once touching
my hair, let alone my head itself. Because I wasn't facing him I
couldn't anticipate awkward moves on his part, but after the first
time or two my apprehensiveness vanished, for his coordination
and balance were almost perfect. When I'd say, "Take it," I'd feel
the lightest of touches on my shoulders, a warm breath being exhaled
at the back of my neck, and then the temporary weight would be
gone from the top of my head, as though a breeze wafting by had
blown it away. He seemed to think of the game as a test for his
concentration and control, and he it was who supplied the rule that
above all he must be careful of me.

When I taught Ousia the same game, it was the toy alone that
caught her attention, and I was merely an obstacle between her and
it. She'd watch me place the rubber ring on my head, and although
I asked her to sit-stay while I arranged myself, her excitement
would bring her to her feet and around to the front of me. I'd keep
turning on my knees in order to have her at my back, and often
we'd complete a full circle before the game could even begin. Ousia
had no slightest concern for my hair or my head or my clothes.
When I'd say, "Take it," I'd immediately have to shout, "Easy!"
in a vain attempt to remind her that in climbing onto my shoulders
she was not reaching toward a block of wood. Over the years I
finally managed to instill in Ousia a little regard for me when we
play that game, although her understanding of my entreaties has
turned it into a game of another sort. In her version she no longer
places her paws on my shoulders while standing on her rear legs.
She doesn't actually reach for the ring at all: she worries it to the
floor. She walks around and around me, occasionally touching me

with a paw as though to reassure herself that I am indeed flesh and hence forbidden. All the while her eye is on the ring, my eye is on her, and I am ready to leap aside in case she decides to take it by storm. But of course that's how she gets the ring: I keep rotating my head to watch her, giggling at the expression of rapturous concentration on her face; then, as she seems ready to spring upward, I duck to get out of her way, and *voilà!* one blue rubber ring protrudes from her grinning jaws.

From the very first time Logos heard thunder in my presence he pasted himself to whatever part of me was nearest him. He'd climb into my lap if I were sitting, slither between my ankles if I were walking, or sit on my instep if I were standing still. His terror was original with him, not communicated to him by me. I'd stroke him gently and talk calmly to him all the while. I sometimes thought wryly that if there were some way to bottle up the sound of thunder so that I could call on it when I needed it, I could make Logos come to me even from the midst of a dogfight, for he was never so docile as when the heavens were breaking apart.

Ousia paid no more attention to her early hearing of thunder than if a book had unexpectedly fallen flat from its customary upright position: it caught her attention only as a sudden sound intruding into our usual quiet. She'd go back to sleep or to whatever else had occupied her, except that I'd see her watching Logos hastily becoming one more appendage on my body. What she was seeing, of course, was Logos getting a powerful lot of caressing and sweet talk, and yet she was more than three years old before she decided that she wanted to get in on some of that too. The first time she came to me during a thunderstorm she made such a tentative request that I was almost brusque with her, not wanting her to pick up any more of Logos' bad habits than she already had. But in time she either persuaded herself that she was frightened or else some change in her way of perceiving the sound arose in the very heart of her, because now there's no question that she is equally as terrified of thunder as he. When I'm not on my bed, Ousia has the habit of lying there on the side where I usually sleep or read, as though when I'm absent it gives her some special contact with me. To that spot she now flees when thunder bursts into our lives. Logos, too, leaps onto my bed as though his arthritis did not exist. In fact, arthritis loses out to thunder every time. For two whole months after we moved into our house in Virginia, Logos would not join me in my second-floor study because he refused to climb the stairs, even though they were carpeted. One day I happened to go upstairs just as a thunderstorm began. I looked up from my desk to see Logos rounding the corner of the stairway, trotting swiftly toward me at the end of the hall. He ran the last part of the way as though he had never heard of problems with bone joints. Which is only to say that Logos will come to me in a thunderstorm wherever I happen to be, and when that place is my bed, where Ousia is already almost on top of me, my bed is a very crowded place indeed.

You are perhaps wondering at their names.

'Logos' and 'Ousia' are Greek words, philosophical terms. They are shorthand for certain aspects of the circumstances in which I found myself at the time each dog came to me, aspects I wanted to perpetuate, wanted never to forget. I like a name to do several things at once. It should say exactly what the named entity is or does or is supposed to be, and it should have a certain gracefulness in its sound.

The rainy night before I embarked on my longest journey, the poor shivering puppy I had just brought into my life was closed into the pantry, alone, in a house where I myself was not so welcome a guest. Upstairs I lay alone, trying to wrap around the puppy a name that would become him. On the island that awaited me, he would be my only contact with a living creature. He'd be my hedge against the silence I knew I'd encounter, the only being I'd be talking to.

Words.

Logos.

I remember opening my eyes and staring into the dark. I said the word over and over.

Logos.

Ho Logos: the word. In philosophy: reasoned discourse. As in the '-logy' suffix in the names of the sciences: biology, psychology, physiology. In ancient philosophy, the *Logos* was the rational principle of the universe, that which made the universe comprehensible to human beings, that which made it *be* the universe. That's what Logos would be for me: he would help me render things comprehensible.

It was the right name.

With Logos my whole world was uprooted, and he and I were the only two parts of it that had any prospect of remaining together longer than a few months. By the time Ousia came to us I had more stability than I had ever known. When I first laid eyes on Logos, I had had six addresses during the preceding year, and the very next day after getting him I ran for my life to Nantucket. The day I brought Ousia home, I had lived in the same house for two and a half years. With Logos I was in debt and I had no home. With Ousia I had long since paid off all my financial obligations; I had accumulated a houseful of furniture and a wardrobe of clothes that twenty-five years later still sustains my contacts with the human world. With Logos I knew neither who I was nor what I wanted to do, and I was even trying to decide whether it was worth continuing to stay alive. With Ousia I had already set myself free; I was saving money against the day when I'd be able to spend all my time writing; I knew precisely what person I was and exactly how I wanted to live, having long since decided that it was worth doing.

Ousia's name reflects all that.

'Ousia,' a term more common in classical than in contemporary philosophy, can be translated as 'substance' or 'essence' or 'the truly

real.' But is the truly real something palpable to the senses, something that can be punched, sniffed, tasted, heard, and seen, like
the rubber ball I now hold? Or is the truly real rubber ball a
statement of the essential features of any rubber ball whatever,
features that make this object on the rug *be* a rubber ball (and
nothing else)? The debate is as ancient as the word itself. For me,
'Ousia' meant all the reality that was at last within my purview.
And she herself, truly real, would make real for me the beginning
of the line of Logos' progeny. Then too, the '-ia' ending is feminine.
And finally, all the vowels made the word a perfect one for calling
her: oo-SEE-ah.

Should I have been surprised, therefore, that throughout his
life Logos understood so much of what I said, whether I spoke
directly to him or merely talked about him to others in his presence?
Should I have been astonished that on a hot summer day Ousia
would dig herself a bed in the cool earth for curling into? Or that
she loved to have me rub and knead and nuzzle and stroke her
body, while Logos barely endured two seconds' touch of my hands?
Because Logos in his own way and Ousia in hers came to embody
their names, which encapsulated the hopes I had for each of them
when they entered my life.

Kairos came to me at the worst possible time, even though his
very name defies my saying so. Yet it was I who chose both his
name and the time. They are, indeed, inextricable, for 'Kairos,'
also Greek, means 'the appropriateness of the time.'

In the fall of 1976 Logos had been dead eighteen months. I
had spent the first two of those months trying to learn from the
Maryland veterinarians in whose hospital he died the cause of his
death, the time of his death, and the circumstances surrounding his
death. Their conflicting answers and the inadequacy of their medical
records, which, at Whit's suggestion, I had almost at once re-

quested, convinced me that the only way I'd ever learn the truth was to sue them for malpractice.

Between May 1975, when I reached that conclusion, and September 1976, when the lawsuit was finally filed, I moved from northern Virginia to Maine, then back to Virginia, but to a different house that I soon could not afford, and so we moved again, the third time in that same eighteen months.

Only Ousia's presence checked my mourning for Logos. I fed her, walked with her, made some poor attempts to entertain her each day by tossing a ball for her to bring back to me, but in the seconds from the time the ball left my hand and Ousia flew after it until she was once again standing in front of me holding it I had stopped thinking about her and was once again immersed in my grief. Trying to spare her, sometimes I'd leave her at home and drive for miles, an hour, around the Washington beltway, crying out my rage and sorrow within the privacy of the rolled-up windows of my car. But just as, when Ousia came to us as a puppy, she had taken up into her being our happiness and security, Logos' and mine, so now she was being permeated by my despair. She herself was grieving for her companion of ten years, her lifetime. Day by day I watched her wilt, until I knew that unless I did something the life would run out of her too.

The something I did was to get Kairos for her. It was the appropriate time.

And so for the third time, as though I had learned nothing about loving through Logos and Ousia, a living creature entered my household not for his own sake but to serve a purpose of mine.

I have a couple of thousand photographs and slides of Logos and Ousia, together and alone. I have photos and slides of Ousia and Kairos, although fewer, together and alone. In Ousia's puppy photos, Logos is unmistakably glaring at her, his tail curled upward, his stance lock-kneed, a certain hard look in his eye. He is barely controlling his dislike of the intruder, and he is doing so for my sake alone. In the puppy photos of Kairos, the same unconcealed dislike is apparent on Ousia's face and in the stiffness with which she holds herself away from Kairos' floppy attempts at friendliness. First Logos, and then, eleven years later, Ousia, were telling me the same story: "We (you and I) don't need this puppy."

In bringing Kairos into our household for Ousia, I did not forget that Logos had promptly rejected the fat round black female. But neither did I forget that in time Logos and she played together and fell asleep together and studied me together. Ousia too would come to see the new puppy as a friend. I'd have to wait until then, hoping hourly that I was not overburdening her palpable unhappiness but rather lightening it. Mostly, selfishly, I was hoping that by giving her Kairos I could concentrate more thoroughly on trying to grasp the fact of Logos' death, on trying to slash away the new obstacles to the truth about his death that sprang up as I uncovered each new piece of information, on trying to hustle jobs that would support all of us and the lawsuit too.

But there were differences between Kairos' entry into our household and Ousia's, and my own overloaded judgment had not taken them into account.

Logos was halfway toward four years old when Ousia came to us. Even though six months passed before he sanctioned her entry into our group, both dogs were still young. For the next eight years, each could run as fast and swim as far as the other. It was only during the final year of so of Logos' life that I needed exceedingly fine attention to his pain on arising, to his inability to walk more than a few steps to retrieve the ball that he still longed to have me throw for him, to his wish simply to lie quietly for long hours.

When Kairos came to us, Ousia was seven months short of twelve. Except for a touch of arthritis in her left rear leg, she was almost as vigorous as she had always been. But she had spent the first ten years of her life with Logos. How was she to make room for a lumpish puppy? Yet she soon saw the advantages of her new position as Chief Dog.

Poor Kai. Between Ousia and me, he didn't have a chance. Even so, by the time we moved back to McLean, to another house whose two acres of lawn I mowed irregularly, Kairos was lying on the floor next to Ousia's mat whenever she rested there to wait out the muscle soreness that lasted longer each day. During her fifteenth year, her arthritis was compounded by a growing paralysis of her rear quarters. Through it all, Kairos kept her company in ways that must have assuaged some deep need in her that I, a mere human being, could not reach.

Yet Kairos, already three years old, had to be outdoors, had to chase the Frisbees I taught him to catch, had to have the long walk first thing in the morning that I myself needed. When he and I would return from the woods a mile away, I'd start calling Ousia the moment my key unlocked the door, singing out all her names, knowing she could hear me even though she could not rise to her feet to greet me. Kai and I would race down the long hallway, turn the corner, cross the living room, and rush to where she lay in my bedroom, I holding her, talking to her, reassuring her that we were all back where we belonged.

The day came when Kairos and I walked through that doorway and there was no Ousia to sing out to. I closed the door behind us and stood in the silence, and he watched me begin to grieve for a second time. I was aware of him, but I could not attend to him.

And thus did late winter slip into summer.

Washington in July is a place to be avoided. The air is wet, the sun beats down, the temperature does not drop during the night, and no breeze blows from the Potomac to relieve the dreadful humidity of its 95-degree days. Nevertheless, one hot July Saturday I, who lived in a country suburb of Washington, drove into the city so that Kairos could swim.

Off Constitution Avenue a pool the size of a small lake had newly been constructed a grove of trees away from the Reflecting Pool as part of the setting for the Vietnam Memorial. I snapped the leash onto Kai's collar, and we ran across the broad lawn toward the water. When I set Kairos free, he scrambled along the bank to scout the best wading-in place. And then he was swimming, leaning into the rhythm of his stroke, pacing steadily, turning idly from time to time to check on me whenever some new person approached the base of the tree where I had set up my watch. Then he'd sight and head for some distant marker on his next tour of the pool. Around the periphery, clusters of people stopped whatever else they were doing to watch him, none of them believing his casual endurance, the strokes of his forelegs seeming so effortless and yet having to be so powerful to keep him in motion so long.

A man standing near me watched him for a quarter of an hour and then said to me: "You have a happy dog."

I heard his words as though they were a foreign tongue that I had somehow to translate into a language I understood. The puppy I had given to Ousia as her companion was now in fact a full-grown German shepherd. During his three years with me, he had taken second place to Ousia, who in turn had taken second place to my search for the truth about Logos' death. The search was at an end, still without my knowing the truth, and Ousia was no longer with me. Yet somehow Kairos was. There, in the water. Happy, the man said. And I had done nothing to bring that about, except to take pity on him on a hot summer day. Who was he, that puppy grown into an adult, now happily swimming? By himself, he could be happy. But with me?

After a while I drove him home. He did not know how exhausted he was until he fell asleep before we even arrived. He did not know that from that afternoon forward I would begin to be his friend. The days I would give him might never be as golden as those Logos and Ousia had, might never be as joyful, might never, even for the two brief years they and I had it, be as stable. But the days from then on would be ours, Kairos' and mine.

I opened my eyes to see him for his own sake for the first time.

Kairos catches your eye first by his color.

"How strange," you'll say. "Isn't he an unusual color for a German shepherd?"

Breeders call it 'red.' If you're trying to imagine it, don't think of a fire engine or a male cardinal. Think instead of a redheaded boy or girl. Imagine the range of these reds: carroty, sandy, auburn, titian. Somewhere between sandy and auburn, with silver lights when the sun plays on his coat: that's the red Kairos is. Across his back and down both sides his coat is black, the familiar shepherd "saddle," but the rest of his coat is red, replacing the tan of the more common black-and-tan marking. 'Red sable' names this whole mix of coloring.

The next thing you'll notice about Kairos is that he knows you've been talking about him, wondering about him. Your gaze has bent out a hook toward him, and he connects to you almost at once. Even though you've never visited us before, he sees your attention to him as inviting him to make the first gesture of friendship: he will bring you his Frisbee, perhaps his ball. He will place it at your feet, and then he'll take a few steps backward, his look raking your face, his eyebrows furrowed.

"Play with me," he is saying.

People who have never thrown a Frisbee in their lives stand happily and toss it for him. It goes straight up, then thuds to the ground, or it wobbles off to the side a little way before it falls flat, or it does one of the many things Frisbees do when they know they're in inept hands. But the visitor is charmed by Kai's immediate race to retrieve the bumbled throw, his swift return with it in his mouth, all but prancing. He lays it at the feet of the new person, steps back, and waits again. To Kairos the game never ends: it is merely interrupted for longer or shorter intervals, no matter that an entire night may intervene. Once awake each morning, he seeks that person, usually me, who will throw whatever object he currently treasures, so that he may run for it, dazzlingly fast, and bring it back.

Ethologists who study wolves describe one of their vocal sounds as a squeak. I know the sound well through Kairos, but the word is wrong. Yes, the sound is small, even minuscule, and yes, it's high-pitched. But the mouth remains closed. Try humming your highest note, then drop down a few tones. But instead of sustaining the hum, cut it off, not abruptly but casually. 'Squeak' is clearly not the name for that sound. A squeak has a certain harshness about it, a tenseness that's the consequence of its being forced, prompted by some untoward pressure or event. But Kairos' high soft brief hum is deliberate: through it he keeps me informed of a wide variety of fluctuating interests and moods.

Say I have been sitting at my desk for some time, one hand on the sheet of paper I should be covering with words, the other holding my pen but instead supporting my chin as I stare out the south window at the daffodils. If I remain in that odd posture, unmoving because focused on some matter I may not yet be able to articulate, and most especially unaware that Kairos has been closely observing me, lounging nearby on one of the four mats I fabricated for Logos and Ousia, now his, placed for him at particularly desirable corners throughout the house, he will decide that I have been inattentive to him too long.

"Um," I will hear. Or perhaps "Ee" is a closer transcription for the page. There may be a slight rising or falling cadence but the sound will be so modest in extent that you could not time it with the sweep-second hand of your watch. Kairos has reminded me of his presence and that I am of this world, his, where Frisbees and balls await being thrown, where strolls along the country road on the other side of our stone fence deserve to be taken, where, best of all, the car stands ready to bear us to the sands of Long Island Sound minutes away or to some park or forest that he and I, together yet independently of one another, can explore afresh, changing as it does no matter how daily our reconnaissance.

When you consider it, that sound is courteous. An intrusion, of course, but sometimes welcome. Other times I say to Kai, "Not yet," and he'll curl up again into his bed to wait for other minutes, soon to come, when I'll roll back my chair and turn my full attention to him. 'Not yet' doesn't always get me off the hook. Some days Kairos comes straight up to my chair and sits very near me. Nothing for it but I must interrupt my thought, put down my pen, use both hands to stroke his head, scratch his throat, touch lightly the extraordinarily soft edges of the tips of his ears, and finally lay my face against one side of his long muzzle. We have made contact. With no further protest he'll return to his mat, and thus will I have bought an additional hour of concentration to whatever project litters my desk.

Kairos' nose is the part of his body he uses in some of the ways I use my hands, and to my hands he directs the subtle variations of its use. He will head straight toward me and, in the very motion of passing me or of curving toward the direction where he wants to lead me, his nose will graze the back of my hand so fleetingly that, if I were a stranger, I might believe the touch to be accidental. Like the tiny high sound it is polite, but it also displays a clear firmness of purpose: he wants my hand to do something for him. Most of the time I know his wish at once: I am to open the outside door for him; his water bowl is empty; his ball has rolled beneath the bureau too far for him to fish it out with the noisy clacking of his nails that shows me how serious are his attempts; I have let the time for his evening meal pass; there is some treat on my plate that he knows I would want him to have if I were my usual thoughtful self.

The nose can be insistent too. In this mood his gesture does not touch my hand directly but only indirectly through my elbow. It can instantaneously disorganize some occurrence so ordinary that you would not be alert to the possibility of its disruption. The pattern of it did not penetrate my obtuseness for a few years. One invariable factor was my holding a cup of hot tea or coffee, preferably that I be in process of raising it to my lips to drink. Comes the nose abruptly in a swift upward movement aimed at the visibly crooked elbow from underneath. Hot liquid that is suddenly no longer constrained within the boundaries of a vessel has a tendency to spread out, then drop where it listeth.

But consider the matter from where Kairos stands. My hand is occupied with the cup instead of lying in my lap or hanging at my side. The elbow, however, is being all but deliberately provocative, suspended in the air where it never otherwise is. It is easily the most accessible point at which to connect to me. A gentle touch, as on the smooth skin of my hand, would seem ineffective against that knob of bone that protrudes into the air.

In time I warned my guests before I poured their drinks, hot or cold.

"If Kairos approaches you, hold on to your cup (or glass)," I'd say.

They'd laugh as I mimed the likely consequence, but then we'd become absorbed in our talk and they'd forget. I'd forget. Until the split second before the nose thrust beneath, then upward on, the bent elbow. Too late I'd shout. Rarely could I intercept the gesture: any dog can move faster than any human being most of the time in any circumstance you can name.

One sunny morning a Very Famous Person was leaning comfortably into one corner of the couch in my living room while I sat curled into the other. He had stopped by to pick up the galleys of my first book, perhaps afterward to write some comment that would find its way to the back cover, there to entice readers to buy the book. He had only a few minutes to spend with me, and you may well imagine that I hoped to make the best use of the time. Focused on the VFP, I did not notice that Kairos was moving in for the thrust until the man's cup flew into the air, spilling hot coffee over his clothes, the couch, and the rug. Fortunately, he was wearing jeans, there was neither cream nor sugar in the coffee, and the couch was upholstered in black wool. I raced for towels, one for the man to dry his clothes, the other to sop up the surroundings. He was not burned, no; a little surprised, perhaps. With grace he continued our talk a few moments longer, and then he left with the large envelope containing my not-yet book. (He did not write the praising lines for the back cover, but not, I think, because of Kairos.)

Intermediate between the graze and the upward thrust is the nudge. Here the nose signals its owner's excited anticipation: "Hurry. Why are you fussing so?" On dark winter mornings I often explain to Kairos that I need more time than he to be ready to go out into the snow. Nevertheless the nose pushes two or three times at the pile of sweaters I'm ringtossing over my head and slithering down my body, at the jeans, at the boots. I talk him over to the chair near the door where coat, stocking cap, gloves await. Two more nudges at my leg while I zip or button, and then he can leap out the finally opened door. It is the fastest I move at any point during the day. I do it because I consider the demand legitimate: he has, after all, restrained his bladder and intestines through the entire night in deference to me. Without the nose, I'd still get him outside first thing; with the nose, he goes express.

Shoved at the purse I'm filling for the day's excursion to library or grocery or meeting, the nose almost always swings the balance in his favor in case I haven't fully resolved whether to take him along. He's telling me how helpful he can be when I must hurry —"Could you do it so fast without me?"—and I laugh or curse depending upon whether I'm on the right or the wrong side of the world's schedule.

Is that entire hunk of cheese on my plate for me? And all the crackers as well? The nose gets as close to the food without touching it as though Kairos had plotted the asymptote. He doesn't "beg," in that appalling posture or sound some people have taught their dogs. He simply nudges, then sits quietly, politely, waiting. Unlike the trick-trained dog, Kairos will leave my side if I send him away. He'll even go off to another room. I try to be wise, lengthening the interval so that he will not think his near-swipe at the Cheddar has resulted in his actually receiving some. But there is no such interval. At however many minutes later, two or twenty, that I go to him, there he lies on his mat, head up, paws straight in front, eyes searching mine, he is ready to accept the portion I carry to him for his delight.

Think of his gift to me: he lets me please him. How many human beings do you know whom you can please? Simply, plainly, please. Two boys I knew raged through their adolescence in different ways, one on drugs, the other on sheer willful perverseness, because nothing they ever did pleased their omnicompetent father. The near-addict was retrieved through a generous judge, who ordered him to live in one of the state's better rehabilitation houses, where he learned to articulate his fury. He emerged new, calm, but devoid of ambition. Still, he is happy now and married to an easygoing and creative woman who saw him through the last of his battle. The other could have won college scholarships but deliberately provoked suspension from a series of schools before joining the Marines, who sometimes make a man of a boy. This time they failed. He now finds work as a security guard, a frightening job for a man whose wrath still smolders. Two lives blunted, and all because their father refused to be pleased. What else, dear heaven, can we give one another?

I do not always please Kairos, although when I displease him it is less because I have set out to do so than that I have been so intent on my own purposes that I fail to take his into account. We are at odds on two scores: the length of time I work at my desk, and the length of time I'm behind the wheel of my car.

I learned early that I can't take a break from my work often enough to suit him, but I've taught myself to drop my pen, mid-sentence or no, so that I may amuse him more often than my unprompted inclination would otherwise. We go out into the clear New England air in every weather except rain (and even then sometimes we must); I toss a ball or Frisbee to let him run; we wander through the yard, I observing the growth and decline of the perennials, Kai wanting only to play; and then we come in. Five minutes, ten at most, have passed. I have cleared my head, although occasionally I have also lost my path through a clutch of ideas that I had wanted very much to chart, and Kai is content to nap for another hour or two until the next time. Sometimes, however, this agreeable compromise must be jettisoned: I have only a day to complete a project that deserves three; or deadlines not of my making glare back at me; or a piece of writing so thoroughly absorbs me that I cannot leave it until some natural pause lifts my pen from the page. Some part of my awareness registers my friend's unhappiness for being so long unoccupied, but I do nothing about it until I can avoid it no longer: six or seven hours have often thus streamed by without intermission for either of us. When I finally stop, my first words aloud are: "I'm sorry, Kai." He knows them well: he hears them regularly. Then ensues joyful barking, laughter, movement, games, outdoors.

I leave off my work for Kai in these ways because I am his sole source of diversion, now that we no longer have Ousia. He cannot read, go off to art museums, watch television, phone a friend, do some desultory sewing, play the lute, or seek out music. Since Ousia died, he has no companion to chase and tumble with, let alone to lie up against or to tease. He'd find amusement enough, I know, if I were to leave him outside without me, but he'd also find other things. Cars frequently hurtle down our road as on a racecourse. Other dogs with temperaments less even than his may consider him an intruder into their territory and, although few dogs, even other males, will pitch into a German shepherd, some are foolish and a few are bigger. There is also swale nearby, the muck of which leaves a lingering stink on fur and skin even after the most strenuous bath. Ponds, a river, small enclaves of standing water: all invite a lone dog to swim. The problem arises for the same reason human beings are warned against swimming in most of the open waters of the land: they are polluted. Every dip Kai takes more swiftly than I move to prevent it ends up with a skin infection of months-long duration. He hates the medicinal bathings and daily anointings with smelly salves; I swear at the time I lose for nursing him.

In a word, I have opted for his safety and health over his unconstrained freedom. And because I have taken that from him when I must and want to work, I am committed to giving him something else in its stead. No matter that my gift does not equal what I have deprived him of. It is one of the prices, perhaps the highest, that each of us pays, I with regret, he with unfeigned sadness, for being one another's friend.

It's more difficult to accede to his wishes when we're in the car. A few years ago I briefly turned my attention from the road to check on Kairos and was startled to see him sitting huddled in the corner formed by the backseat and the back door on the passenger side, making himself into the smallest possible package a full-grown male German shepherd can become. My impression was that he was about to be sick. But we were traveling at highway speed and it was impossible for me to pull off the road in that instant. I snapped my eyes forward again and instituted an unbroken series of soothing, cajoling comments, all the while scouring the route ahead so that I'd be prepared to take immediate advantage of whatever shoulder safely offered itself. But as the miles rolled along and my words kept flowing and I kept glancing back at Kai, I realized that he was perfectly well and that in fact his look was one of reproach rather than appeal. I sighed in relief and continued to talk to him, but now along different lines. I reminded him that he knew we were going for a long ride, that he wouldn't have wanted me to leave him at home, that we probably wouldn't stop for at least another thirty miles, and would he please lie down instead of leaning against the door? But he continued to sit, almost puppylike in the diminution he had managed to achieve. After a time I became silent, turning to check on him only at my usual intervals of half an hour or so.

Since that day my swift backward glance has caught him in the identical position on any trip lasting more than ten minutes. He ducks his head so low that he all but tucks the tip of his nose into the notch of his collar bone. The final touch, and it is masterful, is that he seems to be casting his eyes upward at me, an illusion he emphasizes by keeping his brows raised at the same time. But the seeming derives from his head's being so deeply lowered, chin to chest, because in fact his eyes are looking straight ahead, which is to say: at me. It is a position of unmistakable dejection. And he is always in his chosen corner which, mind you, is just outside the scope of my rearview mirror. To see him, I have to turn my head.

I sympathize: "Poor Kai!" I explain: "I have to do these errands." I promise: "And *then* we'll go for a walk." Words cannot draw him out of his mood. The large brown eyes reply: "Why are you doing this to me?"

One day, on impulse, I changed my approach. I didn't sympathize: I laughed. I didn't explain: I created a high level of excitement. I didn't promise for the future: I offered him something desirable then and there.

"Hey, Kai! Come on up in front with me!"

The forbidden front passenger seat was what he had been playing for all along: to annihilate the barrier between us.

From one instant to the next, the downward-oriented, curving-shouldered, miniature-appearing dog leaped to all fours, thrust his now big head into the space between the two bucket seats in front, and nuzzled my hair and neck while I transferred the full guidance of the car to my left hand, my right hand sweeping to the car floor whatever lay on the seat beside me. The tail was thumping against the backseat now. Sounds close to rapture were audible. One fast glance assured me that the lock-button on the passenger door was down, and I patted the seat in invitation.

The newly large and lively shepherd slipped through the opening between the front seats, settled into his side of the car, and stared intently through the windshield, helping me drive. In a moment or two he turned his head to look at me, and I reached over to stroke the strong neck. Say what you will, but he smiled.

"All of this you've been writing about loving has concerned only dogs."

Yes. Logos, Ousia, Kairos are dogs.

"Are there no human beings?"

Of course. It holds as well for human beings.

"Is there no man?"

There was a man.

"Well?"

Nothing.

"Is that all you're going to say?"

It came to nothing.

8

MONEYING

IT CAN TAKE years, half a lifetime, to split apart the two ideas of work and a job. Once you know what your work is, you probably won't immediately be paid for doing it. To get the money that will buy time to let you do your work, you have to give up some of the rest of your time: you need a job. But you need it only to pay bills: rent, heat, electricity, water, phone, food, medical, car repairs, gas. People who work are constantly aware that time they spend at jobs is letting them buy time to work.

People who don't know what their work is need a job not just to pay bills but to have something to do, some way to fill their time. People who have jobs use their money to buy objects. But for each object that you buy, you're exchanging the amount of time you spent earning that money for the amount of time others spent making and selling that object. Money is the medium in which the exchange occurs, but that which is being exchanged is time: your time for the time of those who made and sold the object.

With a job, you're letting someone else place a value on your time. With work, you set the value for your time. And although you hope that enough other people (sometimes it takes only one) will value your time as you do, so that you need no longer find jobs but can then only work, you continue to do your work anyway, because that is what you have chosen to do with your time. It is this perspective on time that separates those who work from those who hold jobs.

Until you know what your work is, you look for a job that will use your interests, your education, your talents, give you room to develop, let you meet exciting people. Some job may come close to meeting those requirements but may not pay the minimum level of money you also seek. You take the job anyway because it comes with an implicit promise that there will be more money later. In the meantime, the job gives you a certain prestige and uses the parts of yourself that you consider important.

But once you know what your work is, a job has to meet only two requirements. It has to give you enough money to pay your bills, and although it takes your time it must not use the creative energy you need for your work. Thereafter, the operative rule is: do anything for money that doesn't require you to break too many important laws.

The only other rule worth knowing about money is: take it any time anyone wants to put it into your hands. If the giver claims to expect nothing in return, squirrel away the statement, and haul it out shamelessly when he later asks you to square accounts. It's a mistake of judgment to let any other principle stand in the way of accepting money from someone who wants to give it to you. I have stupidly refused it too often.

The implication of all this is that, if you know what your work is and are not yet being paid for it, getting money involves at its very core lying to the people who give it to you.

Everyone who has to earn a living knows how to perform the trick of telling oneself the truth while putting a gloss on it for someone else, although few people seem able to remember that it's only a way to keep the bills paid. Under the pressure of surviving, I finally turned to it myself. By then it required me not merely to remain silent when I would have wished to speak plainly but to lie outright. Never once have I fooled myself into believing that I was doing anything other than gathering income necessary to live. Whether I fooled all the people from whom I took money in exchange for my time is another question. I did the job for which I was being paid, and I did it well, at least as well as many others who might have been given the job instead. The only matter I lied about was that doing it mattered to me. Knowing that winning an assignment would eventually come down to that, I cut short the waiting by starting with it: "This project is something I've been thinking about for a long time. It would be a special pleasure to do it."

Consider the moneygivers' side. They always believe, must by the nature of the circumstance believe, that the person doing the job wants something more than money from the job. Pride of accomplishment, they'll say, if you press them. They've mixed things up, of course: you take pride in doing your work, not theirs. But they have the money, and what they're buying is having the job done well. So you do it well, and in passing you give them the words they want to hear. Telling the truth isn't one of the requirements for getting money that will give you time to do your work.

Not yet understanding the distinction between work and a job while I was in graduate school, I assumed that the differences were only between jobs: between the hundred jobs I had held up till then, each of them simply enabling me to stay in school, and the job that would reward my education and my talents. The job for which my doctorate would qualify me was teaching in an American university, but while I was writing my dissertation I did little to find one. I wanted only to have done with the thesis, to pass the orals, then to get away from Harvard so that I could untie myself from the demands I had allowed it to place on me. So that I could find out what I wanted to do. It is a question one ought to ask at the beginning, not at the end, of eight years in graduate school, eight years that included time away in order to earn money that would let me return. Even so, even in spite of my not knowing during my final year at Harvard whether I wanted to spend my life teaching philosophy, I would have accepted an appointment if one had been offered to me. There would have been time enough to raise my question and try to answer it while I was earning money in the higher learning.

A few weeks before the sweet June morning in Sanders Theatre when the ancient and honorable community of scholars welcomed me into its midst by slipping the doctoral hood over my shoulders, I asked one of my professors how I should go about getting a job.

"Too late in the year," he replied. Too late forever, had I only known.

I spent that summer in the steamy Boston offices of Houghton Mifflin as a first reader. It was the lowest rung of the editorial ladder, a job I could have held at any time since I received my bachelor's degree. Had I endured eight years of graduate school merely to be reading unsolicited manuscripts? What did knowing the transcendental deduction of the categories have to do with culling the slush pile for a novel that might be worth a senior editor's attention? The editor-in-chief tried to keep me by holding out the bait of a small raise "a little later," but I scurried to New York where there were no promises at all.

I imposed on friends for the use of their couch, and I tramped around the city. At Columbia I discovered that the University Press, preparing the third edition of its fat *Encyclopedia*, needed someone to add, delete, revise the philosophy articles. The pay was $1.50 per hour. During my junior year in high school, my very first job had paid me 37 cents an hour. Three degrees and twenty years later, I was still earning the minimum wage for unskilled labor.

But Columbia had a bit of education lying in wait for me. Wandering along Broadway near 116th Street one autumn afternoon I saw Ernest Nagel, and on impulse I introduced myself. Nagel, whose work in philosophy of science is known throughout the world, turned the talk toward me.

"What are you doing in New York, and why haven't you visited the department yet?"

I described my freelance job at the Press.

"But, my dear, you shouldn't have to fend for yourself like this. Your department should have helped you get a teaching job."

My jaw must have fallen.

He stared at me. "You didn't know? Those people at Harvard!" He shook his head. "Now listen to me."

I was to go at once to the chairman of the Columbia philosophy department and ask to be placed on the mailing list for departmental colloquia and guest lectures. By that invitation alone, Nagel was welcoming me to the gatherings of my peers. But more: I was to ask the chairman to try to find me a teaching job.

"You understand that we have to assist our own graduate students first, Dr. Koller, but there's bound to be a job for you. In fact . . ." His forehead wrinkled while he searched his memory.

I waited, unable to believe what I was hearing.

Then: "Yes, I'm positive of it: there's an opening at Barnard next semester. Or is it next year? You must forgive me for not knowing the details. I'm not on committees this year, so I don't keep current with all that. But the chairman knows. Ask him about Barnard specifically. And of course tell him I sent you."

There was an opening at Barnard for the spring. I was interviewed. Admiring remarks about my candidacy were later relayed to me. But something made the committee decide not to fill the position in the spring, to wait until fall instead. The details elude my memory; perhaps the incumbent changed her mind about leaving.

I turned to the Harvard philosophy department. Since they had an obligation to me, my not having pressed them to fulfill it had in effect relieved them of it. I arranged to meet then-chairman Roderick Firth at the annual philosophical convention the following month. To reach the meetings I took a train to New

Haven, then walked to the convention hotel. I picked my way through the crowd and the noise and the smoke to find Firth. He looked at me as though we were meeting by chance and said, "There are no jobs for you." While I sat in stunned silence he turned to a male graduate student and said, "Let's go. Professor Blank is waiting to talk with you about the job in his department." He did not care that I heard him.

Midsummer of that year I crossed the country to Berkeley. In a little hotel I sat whole days at my typewriter, tapping out two hundred nearly identical letters to West Coast colleges announcing my availability to teach: philosophy, humanities, general education, even freshman composition. In between mailing out batches of envelopes, I was revising a section of my dissertation to submit as an article to one of the philosophical journals.

On my way out for fresh air one morning I stopped one of the maids in the hallway to ask for clean towels.

"I have them right here," she said. "I just didn't want to interrupt you. Every time I pass your door I hear you typing away. You writing a book?"

How to smile? "No," I answered, "just something that has to be done fast. And I don't mind your coming in when I'm there."

"I'll fix the room while you're gone. And you stay outside for a while. You shouldn't work so hard."

I looked at her buckets and mops and linen wagon and vacuum cleaner, and I said, "You too."

She took care of me very well for the rest of that month, and when in early September the philosophy department at the university of California at Santa Barbara offered me a last-minute opening, I managed to find a five-dollar bill to fold into her hand the day she knocked on my door and found me packing.

At Santa Barbara I held the rank of acting instructor (someone who only acts as though she were an instructor?), a status beneath the university's lowest rank, thereby enabling UC/SB to pay me a salary lower than its published scale and to ignore the custom of paying moving expenses for new faculty. As though to compensate for the niggardliness, the department chairman gave me the use of his family's spare VW. Without it, I would have been tethered to the city bus that scuttled between my apartment in town and the campus twelve miles away on the ocean shore.

Of the three courses assigned to me, one was a section in a colleague's lectures. A second course, in ethics, filled me with dread each time I entered the classroom. Not me alone: one student always seated himself directly within my line of vision and, whenever I caught his eye, lifted his gaze to the clock on the wall behind me and stared at it fixedly.

My third course was a smash hit, not to be predicted from its plain title, "Philosophy 1." Students rolled up their beach blankets and came out of the water to attend it. Some brought their friends. Auditors showed up and never left. I knew why: students were discovering how to explore their own thinking.

My way of teaching philosophy is not to lecture about schools of philosophy, history of philosophy, problems of philosophy. Not to lecture at all. I place students in the way of *doing* philosophy. Like standing them on a railroad track in the way of the train that will come rushing along: they can't avoid being struck. My students don't simply memorize Hume's statement, "All the perceptions of the human mind resolve themselves into . . . impressions and ideas." They catch the troubling quality of the problem that so profoundly perplexed him. I send them in search of understanding how that opening sentence of his *Treatise of Human Nature* was the beginning of his proposed solution. I use 'catch' here as in 'catching measles.' The intoxicated Alcibiades, bursting into the drinking party Plato celebrates in the *Symposium*, accused Socrates of having seduced him by philosophy. That's what I had in mind: to get my students seduced by philosophy. Unless that happened, they'd repeat lifelong, "Aristotle said . . ." or "According to Kant . . ." without ever understanding why philosophy is the inquiry that Western civilization knows to be its crown.

The day before Christmas recess, I walked into a classroom draped with red and green streamers, those students having turned the final class into a surprise party. My present was a lavender plush dog half my height and around whose neck they tied a ribbon holding a stainless steel dog tag inscribed 'Plata,' the feminine, they informed me, of 'Plato.' I drove home with Plata sitting next to me on the front seat of the VW, her head tall enough to seem to be looking through the windshield. Waiting at a traffic light, I happened to glance at the car next to me and found the driver staring at my enormous companion. For the rest of the way home, I looked straight ahead when other cars pulled alongside, not giggling until I left them behind.

From Santa Barbara, the MITRE Corporation whisked me back to Boston, doubling my puny teaching income because of my degree and also, I quickly understood, because of my big blue eyes. By then I knew I was doing no more with my education than peddling its trappings to whoever would pay me.

In a few months, in rage, in fear, I was walking the sands of Nantucket. When I left the island in February 1963 I knew for the first time how to say what I meant, and I could then look to see whether what I said was true. One part of what was true was that I could use my degree to support myself while I tried to find out what my work was.

The job at the contract research firm in Stamford was simply the first one to present itself. During the year and a half I took its money and gave it my time, I also tried to locate an academic home. The Radcliffe Appointment Office had merged with the Harvard Appointment Office, ostensibly to give women access to the job information that poured into Harvard, but in fact men continued to be plucked out of the larger pot first. And the Harvard Appointment Office was not the place from which philosophy departments hired philosophers.

I was beginning to piece together what had been happening on my periphery during graduate school. The late fifties were a time when professors could arrange teaching jobs for their male students as deliberately as they chose their dinner guests. Prestigious universities sent one another their graduate students, well knowing that the first job would lead to the other jewels that perpetuated the system: chairmanships of influential committees; high offices in professional associations; editorships of important journals; juicy research fellowships; visiting professorships here and abroad. Lesser colleges and universities had their own versions of the identical game.

The system didn't lie idle, waiting for the student to receive his degree. Long before they submitted their dissertations, sometimes five or seven years before, most of my male classmates were already teaching at Princeton, Berkeley, Michigan, Johns Hopkins. They had been taken in hand toward that end early in their Harvard careers; were introduced to the right colleagues; were seen attending the right meetings for which it was arranged that they contribute papers; were urged to write articles for the right professional journals whose editors would cast a friendly eye on their efforts.

Of these things, Harvard did none for me. I was left on my own to seek the elusive plum that was to be had (how could I have known it at the time?) only by the friendly phone call: "John, I have a fellow here who will be a real help in your department." These days, in the lip service paid to affirmative action policies, the phone calls are still made, but they're a little more discreet and it takes just a little longer for them to be put into action. But in those days, without the phone call: nothing. Yet I, almost alone among these men, had completed my dissertation, had received my degree, ignorant that the dissertation, the degree, were the last things that counted. I had crossed the finish line but, not having been coached in the rules of the game, I didn't know that at some point near the first turn the track had been shifted elsewhere.

When I harvested the research grants that affiliated me with Connecticut College, I entered upon a life of working alone in my study and in libraries, walking through the woods, playing with Logos and Ousia, all at times of my own choosing. Meanwhile, I was learning that I could, wanted to, had to, write and think. Both. Like a formless mass of dough that, under proper conditions of warmth and shaped by one's hands as well as by the pan, rises before and during baking into a recognizable loaf of bread, I had expanded into the fullest shape of my own freedom, filling all the little corners and gulleys and chasms. Nothing could ever take it from me. It was my doing, yet the grants were its necessary condition: I knew month after month for two years that a definite and comfortable sum of money was available to me.

To find out what work I wanted to do, I let my thinking play only on what it would be like to be doing the work. Whether I'd become famous doing it, whether I'd earn a lot of money, wouldn't be considerations. The only matter that would count would be whether I was totally absorbed by it while I was doing it, not noticing the passing of time. Doing it only for its own sake.

Did the doing of it use and nurture the best of the talents I cherished? When I wasn't doing it, did I continue to think about it, still trying to solve some technical or substantive problem it had set for me? Did I know when I had done it well, done it just as I wanted to do it, just as I wanted it done, regardless of what anyone else said of it? Did I know myself to be a master in it? Did the doing of it feel totally familiar, like an old sweater, and yet always fresh, like early morning? Could I imagine being prevented from doing it for the rest of my life? Could I imagine doing almost nothing else but that work, if almost everything else were taken away from me?

Finding what work I'd do wasn't simply a problem to be re-solved, one among many: it was the problem on which all other problems balanced and were ordered.

Initially, mistakenly, I assumed that money would be given to me for my work. Later, when I had to spend a good deal of time, most of my time, looking for jobs, having jobs, I understood that I could count myself successful only when the money I earned came only from my work. People would then be paying me so that I'd spend my time doing my work, doing the thing I'd do whether I were paid or not. Having my time restored to me, not having to spend it looking for jobs, letting me use it to do my work: this is the essence of being successful.

The lessons I was then learning about money are so elementary that I blush to set them down. Read them in the context of my having money for the first time, of having been a student all my life up till then, even though alternate years saw me out of school—Goodman Theatre, University of Chicago, Harvard—so that I could earn enough money to return, where 'enough' meant only paying tuition and buying food, shelter, books, and an oc-casional movie when movies cost fifty cents.

I was probably twenty years behind most people my age in discovering that some things are costly because you're also paying for the shop where you buy them or because their national adver-tising must be recouped, but that other things are costly because they fulfill important purposes, are well made of excellent materials, and will therefore endure, so that their ultimate cost is lower than something initially cheaper that I'd have to replace frequently. I learned to ask, not just: "Will it serve?" but: "Do I need it only now, or will it continue to be useful for a long time?" By choosing certain objects carefully the first time, I never had to think about them again: from then on they were there when I needed them. But exactly because almost nothing that fulfilled only a present need entered my newly enlarging household, I came to think of my belongings as perduring. I'd take the time, or find the person who knew how, to extend the use of the thing by some patch or new part. Persons of another bent find this habit penurious, even old-fashioned. I retain it because I've been without money often enough, before and since, that no amount of it for no matter how long a time can make me forget that it may still pass through my hands again without being replenished.

I soon learned the sophisticated way of thinking of money as solidified chunks of time. For my time I received money: with money I could buy time. I began to pay someone else to clean my house when it would have been costlier for me to do it at my hourly rate than to pay Mrs. Johnson to do it at her hourly rate. You can weigh the value of your time against someone else's, of course, only when you have money coming in. Only when someone else values your time as you do.

The offer to teach philosophy at Connecticut College arrived one snowy December noon when the Air Force grants still had five months to run. The college was looking to replace someone going on sabbatical the following September, but the one-semester position might stretch over a couple of years because of consecutive sab-baticals other members of the department would be taking.

The invitation caught my undivided attention by walking up to me and quietly tapping me on the shoulder, a breathtaking contrast to my fruitless thrashing about before the grants began.

Yes. Well. Before the grants had given me my head to explore my thinking, to let me discover that my work was writing my think-ing, I had thought I wanted to teach. Did I want to teach now?

I could teach: I knew how. I could write: I knew how. The question was only: could I do both at the same time? To prepare for fall classes, I'd have to start a month or six weeks in advance: August. I'd finish the *Hornbook* in April, and so I'd have only three or four months to work on the Nantucket book. I'd have barely immersed myself in it when I'd have to put it aside to start thinking about the courses I'd be teaching. And when the semester began, there'd be only evenings and weekends to write.

Ah, but there are no evenings and weekends free when you're teaching three new courses. Not the way I teach. I ignore as much as possible that it's a *class* I'm teaching. A class is a convenience for administrators but an inconvenience to students, antithetical to their purposes as individuals. I blunt the fact of it by concentrating on the purposes and competences of the separate persons who compose it. In my hands a class of twenty becomes twenty nearly distinct tutorials. I connect with each student one at a time, two or three during every class meeting, and whatever that person and I are doing manages somehow to interest everyone else. The midwifery Socrates showed me how to perform on the thoughts of others is as deeply engaging to those who observe it as to those who undergo it. My encounter with one student on a given day may only distantly concern some of the others, but they know that their own turn will come, and more than once. And they seem to find that worth waiting for. I've merely been down the road ahead of them; I merely know where the ruts are and how to avoid them, where the rocks protrude and how to get around them.

That kind of teaching is almost never lecturing. It's always and only trying to find the hook within the student to which I can tie my words and ideas, to draw him or her out so that, after a little hand-holding, the person will pursue his or her own path. Will not need me, or any teacher, ever again, except as someone to touch base with from time to time when the territory looks more than ordinarily terrifying.

Teaching that way can be a sixty- or seventy-hour week. Excluding faculty meetings and conferences with students. Excluding reading the professional journals to keep current. Excluding driving to New London, an hour and a half each way three or four days a week. Because I had no intention of moving to New London solely on the strength of a one-semester teaching appointment.

But why should I give up all those hours, even for a semester, when I'd have enough money saved to write full time for a year? Once I knew I wanted to write the book about Nantucket I had cut my living expenses sharply, saving nearly half of each month's salary. By the time the grants would end in April, I'd have a bank account of more than eight thousand dollars. Today the sum couldn't support even a frugal year of writing, but my close figuring made it suffice for then. More than suffice: I had even tucked away enough for another two or three months beyond the year of writing in case I had to wait that long before signing a publishing contract. (My estimate was off by thirteen years.) And once the "Journey" was published, I'd never have to think about money again. From then on, I'd be paid to do my work. (I was wrong about that, too.)

Why, then, did I even consider the offer to teach? The answer lies among a cluster of ideas whose nucleus is the fact of my doctorate. The cardinal feature of that degree is that it entitles me, announces me as qualified, to teach at a college or university.

Six years stretched between receiving my degree and lifting the Connecticut College envelope out of my mailbox. Of the twelve semesters that had elapsed, I had taught during exactly one: at the University of California at Santa Barbara. Six other semesters had seen me affiliated with Connecticut College, but only to do the Air Force research. The remaining five semesters had been living catch-as-catch-can.

After the year of writing, might I not want to be at a university? The easiest way to assure that was to nail down the tentative offer I held in my hand. Write during the summer, teach next fall, then pick up the writing again summers, holidays until it was done. Meantime, I'd have an academic connection whose long-term advantages might balance off the long-term cost of losing time from my writing.

I phoned the chairman. "Tell me more."

His second letter followed swiftly, full of details. Then two months of puzzling silence. In February he wrote complaining that my phone seemed to be out of order. But I had sent him my new phone number weeks before. Worse: we had misunderstood one another. I was waiting for him to decide whether to make me an official offer; he was waiting to hear that I was definitely interested.

The tedious correspondence resumed, still without an invitation to talk face-to-face. More of my time was being requested: it began to appear that I'd be expected in New London daily. The matter of texts arose. And with it, my way of doing philosophy lurked in the wings as a potential source of conflict with that of the other members of the department and of their long-range plans for their students. And that disagreement, if it persisted, would nullify my reason for considering the offer at all: that the appointment might last beyond one semester, an inducement the chairman had mentioned in not one letter but two.

Rank and salary weren't at issue: neither was even mentioned. The chairman knew, or could easily have found out, that the college considered my rank under the Air Force grants to be equivalent to an associate professorship. My salary figure under the grants was also in the college files. I assumed, mistakenly, that the college would match both. When the official offer from the college's president reached me, crossing in the mail with my letter to the chairman declining, I discovered that I was correct about the rank but that the salary was nearly 20 percent lower.

Afterward, the chairman acknowledged his tactical error: he should simply have invited me to his office where we could have discussed and arranged all the details at one time. I agreed. In fact, his administrative incompetence was one of the reasons I decided against the job. Low on the list, to be sure, but I believed then, and I still believe, that any man in a position of authority over me—even that unique academic authority of being first among equals—ought to be able to dispatch the duties of his position at least as efficiently as I. If he and I were to be colleagues for half a year, I'd have to hold my tongue when knowing what I felt and saying what I meant had become one and inseparable to me.

I hadn't yet learned that my freedom was so securely mine that it could let me separate them. I need not have feared that, by sitting quietly or nodding agreeably each week for the hour or two that I'd be encountering this man, I might have reverted to my former crimes against myself. I thought that, unless I said what I meant, which in turn was the spontaneous outcome of how I felt, I might go back to my old way of lying to myself. And the one thing I understood before I left Nantucket was that my life depended on never doing that again.

I turned down the Connecticut College offer because there was something I wanted to do more than teaching philosophy at a college; more than having a stable income for the months of a single semester, to be followed, perhaps, by four others in a row; more than being part of the academic world again, talking with peers about philosophy, writing letters on stationery to which recipients felt obliged to reply.

And that thing was: to write the book about Nantucket. To pick up where I had left off the inward journey, a journey backward, that would disclose to me the journey I had undertaken from before Nantucket to here. Nothing I had ever contemplated doing matched the plain wanting to write that book. Not writing it on the side, nights and weekends, but writing it to the exclusion of everything else.

In the years since the offer from Connecticut College, I've come to see it as one of the most important decisions I've ever made. A decade later during a sequence of ever-deepening darknesses—in heavy debt, on welfare and food stamps, having no phone while living sixty miles away from all potential sources of income—I thought of that decision as a major mistake. Even in lighter hours I've called it a grave error.

Now I know what the mistake in it was: I was without the power to foretell the future. I couldn't know that nearly twenty years would pass before I'd ever again have the reserves of time and income that the Air Force grants lavished on me. I had held the grants only two years before receiving the Connecticut College offer, but their great gift empowered me to discover how I wanted to live my life, what would be my works and days. That I actually continued to want that life when it came to my hands made me one of fortune's darlings. From that pinnacle, how to imagine that it would only once and briefly be repeated? It had come so soon after I had started the new course of my life that I was lulled into believing that from now on, finally, things would go well.

Just as I acknowledged that the disordered life I had lived before Nantucket was mainly my own doing, even though I had been led by the child's heart in me, so did I now affirm that the life since I had thrown off that crippling love was, and would forever be, of my own fashioning. Whatever portion was luck in the old and the new, the difference was that then I was incapable of recognizing it, whereas now I was not only setting a course for it but was able to sail with the wind quartering when I came upon it.

So the grants were luck, but luck that I had sought. I knew the art of it, I thought: I just had to keep looking in the right place.

As a child, Henry Adams believed that everyone's grandfather was, like his, president of the United States. I didn't have the excuse of being a child when I believed that my talent and hard work, my willingness to seek out my own good fortune, would perpetuate the circumstances that had let me find the seed within me, sustain it, and nourish its growth.

□   □   □

The following spring I completed the *Hornbook*, and the year after that, "Map of an Inward Journey." Two books in two years: it is the paradigm for the use I make of my time when I have a full purse.

Response to the *Hornbook* began arriving when I was halfway into the "Journey." Winfred Lehmann at the University of Texas/ Austin, reading the book while waiting at an airport, nearly missed his plane. Rulon Wells, a philosopher at Yale, was using it in a linguistics course he also taught there. Requests for copies came from Czechoslovakia, France, Italy. A graduate student sent me a book of haiku: I had inspired him, he wrote. Invitations arrived to enter into scholarly correspondence, to submit articles for state-of-the-art collections, to review books for linguistics journals.

On this unanticipated attention to me as a philosopher and writer I cast a grateful but distant eye, so caught up was I in the "Journey." I was wrong, of course, about having to wait only two or three months before someone would want to publish it. For more than thirteen years I lifted the returned manuscript out of my mailboxes around New England and suburban Washington, spent a bad night, then packed it up again next morning to send it off one more time. But all that was in the future.

Watching six months slide by as publishers kept rejecting the "Journey," I rethought my plan. In addition to my degree, I now had the asset of the *Hornbook*. The research community, academic and other, had sought me out at Connecticut College, on the assumption that I was a full-time member of the philosophy department there: the *Hornbook*'s cover announced it as my affiliation. If I were now to hint to any of those persons that I was available for hire, would I not receive offers to teach? And teaching, I was finally beginning to understand, was the way people who wanted to write and do research supported themselves. More: it gave their work continuity by providing a source of income that could be relied on, that they could augment with research grants, invitations to lecture, perhaps books.

I phoned Rulon Wells. We met for lunch, talked about Yale, about Harvard, about philosophy, about linguistics. At the appropriate time, over tea, I asked about openings in his department.

"We may have something next year."

It was then October. In the academic calendar that has guided my life since I was five, years begin in September, not January. 'Next year' meant the September upcoming, eleven months hence. But in fact applicants make themselves known a year in advance. Appointments are offered and accepted by February. For once, I was on the right side of time.

"And the field?"

"Oh, almost any field would do."

I was puzzled. Usually you bring your specialty to your department. One of the marks of a good appointment is that you're permitted to teach in your special field, preferably at the graduate level and most desirably a seminar. One of the marks of a run-of-the-mill appointment is that you teach whatever course the department needs to round out its offerings. Only after you've been there for a few years, and only maybe, will the department schedule you to teach the field of philosophy that you know best.

"Except philosophy of language?" It was the field the *Hornbook* plowed, the field I had been exploring for the nearly three years of my grants. It was also his field.

He smiled. "Not necessarily."

I let the ambiguity pass. "And the rank?"

"Instructor."

"Instructor!?" I should have kept the startle to myself. "But you're using the *Hornbook* in your course."

"Yes." For a moment he had the grace to be uncomfortable. He knew, and I knew, that having published a book, even a book distributed by the federal government, but particularly a book that was being talked about and used as a text by linguists in the important universities in the country, qualifies its author to advance at least one rung on the ladder of rank. But instructor is the rank for brand-new Ph.D.'s.

Wells looked me full in the face. "What teaching have you done?"

He had me there. One semester in California.

I asked a few more questions about the mechanics of applying, about salary. I forget what silly topic we discussed walking along the New Haven streets to the corner where we parted. I drove home, twisting my body in the driver's seat every few minutes until I realized that I was trying to rid myself of a sense of oppression that was foreign to me. And yet, familiar. Why familiar? Noticing it, even naming it, did not make it slip away.

The moments of greeting Logos and Ousia briefly displaced it, but all the while we walked in the woods I kept replaying my talk with Wells.

No matter that in the writing of two books I now understood my relation to philosophy, was productive in it. What mattered only was: had I held a teaching job immediately after receiving my degree, and had I been teaching in that place or elsewhere all this time? And the answer was "No."

Next morning over coffee I tracked down the familiarity of the feeling that still clung to me. It was like being at Harvard: being on a playing field without knowing it, without anyone's having taken me in hand to tell me the rules, and then the game was over by the time I figured them out. On Nantucket I cast off their rules and I began making my own. Now they won't let me into the game, even though what I'm doing is the whole point of philosophy.

Preparing the morning meal for Logos and Ousia I decided not to apply to Yale. In the same moment the heavy hand weighing me down disappeared.

Not that there were other alternatives.

I wonder today how I managed to get us through the next eight months. Savings designed to cover three months until someone would want to publish the "Journey" were somehow stretched to span twelve.

And then Jan Narveson arranged a job for me at the University of Waterloo in Ontario. After the moving van departed Weston for Canada with my belongings, I piled Logos and Ousia into my car and we left behind that house of stability, six years' worth, to begin the odyssey that has not yet ended.

The job was not in the philosophy department, where Jan had tenure, but in a new program called Integrated Studies, and I was one of four persons hired expressly to establish it. We were to select students by the seriousness of their intent to learn, rather than on the basis of their previous grades. We were to experiment with unusual ways of teaching. We were to assist students in using the resources of the entire university, and they were to design their own programs without having to meet any of the standard prerequisites.

The place seemed right up my alley. The time, however, was preposterous.

Anyone who had anything to do with a campus during the academic year that began in September 1969 knows that insanity exploded everywhere. The hot undertaking wasn't to experiment with studying and learning but to run the university. Hours-long, days-long, meetings were held in the common room the university set aside for our group. And since ten minutes' discussion of administrative matters has always seemed to me eight minutes too long, I disappeared politely and quickly into my office, there to be available for what I considered to be my job: teaching philosophy to anyone who wanted to learn, guiding into the higher learning anyone who requested my judgment.

About 60 percent of the students quietly devised and undertook the independent study that Integrated Studies was supposed to sustain. But the "management committee" wanted governance as well: from hiring the faculty to evaluating their own academic performance, all to be achieved by votes taken at meetings. Some of these students gained access, by unknown means, to the files of the academic vice-president and uncovered (it was their word) my Air Force grants. You will recall that at the time the United States Air Force was devastating Vietnam. The student newspaper promptly trumpeted me as the enemy, and I became the target for daily and ugly hostility. No matter that the facts were distorted. No matter that I had been withholding certain taxes from the United States government to protest my country's involvement in Vietnam. No matter that in point of academic freedom my political beliefs were to be separate from my qualifications to teach. No matter that Canada was hiring American scholars because Canada did not then have enough Ph.D.'s.

Only one student came to me to ask about the Air Force grants. And when she understood that their purpose had been to explore the foundations of linguistic theory, she went to other students to try to stop the hate-campaign. But the lie was easy to tell, and so the truth became irrelevant. That the whole matter was irrelevant was also lost on all my colleagues except Keith Rowe. He and I spent weeks seeking clarification of the university's policy for Integrated Studies from the liaison vice-president. We sought as well administrative support for ourselves as faculty. The university administration remained silent. It was a signal the students made good use of.

Keith, a Canadian, held tenure in the mathematics department: no matter what happened with Integrated Studies, he had a safe haven. I had a two-year contract: my haven would vanish in another year. But I stopped caring. I began crossing off the days until I could leave. In May I returned to the United States. In September I resigned. No other job was in sight.

You see the mistake, don't you? I was treating a job as though it were my work. The university vice-presidents who were silent understood that they held jobs. Why didn't I? The vice-presidents weren't going to antagonize two dozen vocal young people, whose grade averages hovered near C-minus, by defending my academic freedom. But I let them deprive me of my source of income.

Couldn't I simply have gritted my teeth for the three or four hours every other day that I had to meet with students in our small tutorials, then gathered up my books and file folders and driven home? People who go down into mines longer than that every day grit their teeth. Men or women who are the sole support of children they have brought into the world grit their teeth each day they walk into their offices or shops or factory floors. Who was I not to be part of that great multitude?

Well, you see, I still hadn't learned to take money when it was put into my hands. No one at the University of Waterloo asked me to murder or rob or forge checks. Forget my beliefs about what constitutes an education, my understanding of how to teach, my sense of the interpenetrating connection between writing and thinking. I should have relegated all that to the privacy of my study. For the job, I should have done what needed doing. And that, as the vice-presidents clearly showed me, was to remain silent. To sit and smile and wait for it all to pass. Meanwhile to pick up my paycheck.

Stupid Alice.

It was my last teaching appointment.

I accepted one other appointment, then resigned it a few months before the academic year even began. It was in the South, which would have turned every smallest action of my day into a political one. And much as that department said they wanted me, the best they could do for salary was exactly what I had earned under my research grants nine years earlier.

Why did I accept the position in the first place? Well, I have this funny idea about belonging at a university. I had held it for so long, thirteen years beyond my degree by then, that I temporarily ignored the actuality before me. When I abruptly understood that I would not simply Be At A University but be at this university at this time in this place under these conditions, a black hole opened up beneath me and I stumbled into it, falling, falling.

After my second swift visit to my projected new home I returned to Washington, still the congressman's speechwriter. Exactly ten days later, on the last day of May, the congressman fired me. He called me to his office at four, indicted me, and ordered me to leave at once. Persons on the staffs of members of Congress have none of the protections civil servants have. No law prevented the congressman from firing me. Nothing required him to give me notice or severance pay. From the decisions of princelings there is no appeal. He, however, saw himself as generous by arranging for the Treasury of the United States to provide me with two weeks' salary. I had planned to resign by August in order to move south, so I was not mightily troubled. I merely had to trot around Washington to unearth some job that would carry me through the summer.

With my days free, apart from hustling money, I began preparing my courses for the fall quarter. Philosophy 1: early and middle Plato. Philosophy 2: Descartes through Berkeley. Ancient philosophy: pre-Socratics and Aristotle.

Plato first. It was like coming home, hefting the collected dialogues in the Bollingen edition, leafing through the thin beautifully printed pages with the now-rare bookmark: a ribbon sewn into the binding. I started by outlining the *Protagoras*.

Rereading the dialogue, I found myself arguing with Socrates, noticing complexities I had not sufficiently attended to in graduate school, trying to sort them out, clarifying the line of reasoning. But more: the fresh standpoint on the world I shaped for myself after Nantucket gave me new eyes in philosophy as well. With those eyes I had written the *Hornbook*, working my way through traditional problems by hacking out new paths. Almost as though I were starting philosophy all over again, coming upon my own views by shaking off those of others that I had ingested as a graduate student. So that now, picking up Plato again, not just casually, to confirm some small point as I frequently did, but seriously, to lead unsophisticated students into his thought, I was rethinking my understanding of him.

The *Gorgias* was next. My notes stop halfway.

I can't conceive teaching any of this until I've thought it through again. As I did in the *Hornbook*. I can do it. I *have* to do it: it would be intellectually dishonest not to do it. But there are only weeks before classes begin. Ten weeks to cover these and three others of the major dialogues? Rethink each and every one of the dozen dialogues I am to begin teaching in three months? Impossible. And that's only Plato. What of Descartes? And Spinoza and Locke and Berkeley? And Aristotle? Aristotle!

From one moment to the next, fear flowed into my fingertips from the marks my pen was making on the page. I rolled back my chair, awakening Logos lying beneath my desk and Ousia in her far corner of the room. We scrambled down the stairs and outside, I leading the way for the long walk I knew was in me.

During the next several days I repeated that sequence often: studying, taking notes, flinging down my pen in panic, rushing outdoors with the dogs to try to gain perspective.

What was petrifying me?

I had not been doing technical philosophy for a long time: four years since Waterloo (if you consider that to have been teaching), six if you harked back to the *Hornbook*. Oh, I had the philosophical skills: I used them in my writing. But I had not been doing philosophy *quâ* philosophy, as philosophers say, for the hours and hours you must do it every day, reading and writing and thinking it, to make it into the perduring equipment of your mind, as you do when you teach it. Instead, I had been huckstering it to bring in money, to stay alive.

I can't do it. Not so soon.

I must do it: I've signed a contract.

For two weeks I went round and round the circle, burrowed beneath it and looked up, hovered above it and looked down. In the middle of June I wrote to the chairman of that philosophy department asking to be released from the contract.

In the deep place within me from which my clear hard eye looks out onto the world, I knew that my backing and filling about philosophy was merely a bad case of stage fright. I had not done philosophy for a while: that's what it had all been about. Sitting down to my desk every day for the hours that would have been necessary until classes began, doing it rather than thinking about doing it, would have made that part of the terror wither away. The image that would not go away was living in that small town in inimical circumstances: the wet heat penning me into an air-conditioned house for endless months each year; not living alone in the country, as colleagues and realtors urged, because sooner or later there would be some violent intrusion into whatever country solitude I might inhabit. For the rest of my life. That was the real source of the terror: that once installed in the deep South I'd never be able to leave. What philosophy department in the North or West would come looking for me there when none of them had seen fit to hire me during the seven years that had passed since I declined the Connecticut College offer? The best I could hope for from that southern college was that by working hard I'd be invited to remain there.

It was the fatefulness of it, the intractable sense that I could never undo the move south, that kept me wakeful during the night, trembling at my desk during the day, in the weeks following my signing of the contract. I could bring that feeling of dread to an end only by asking to be released from my legal commitment. And when I no longer faced my own annihilation in a foreign land, I took deep breaths of fresh air, even though it was Washington air, and Washington air in June.

Fired from one job. Resigned from another. Both within two weeks. You'd think that the first would have been sufficient to prevent the second. Particularly when no income was in prospect from any other source.

The problem of course was that I had somehow held on to the idea of justice too long. Somewhere deep within me, ineradicably, is the belief that the privilege I had earned of being centered at a university as a philosopher and writer has been denied me. I belong there but I have almost never been there. If several teaching jobs had been offered me, I would not have accepted the southern one. But in seven years there were no offers (I exclude Waterloo). Aware by then that declining Connecticut College had been a mistake, even though I could not have known that nothing else appropriate would come along in the interval, I seized on the next thing that came along, appropriate or no. It ought not to have been the only thing to come along. I ought not to have felt compelled to take it on pain of having nothing else ever come along. And 'oughts,' as any philosopher will tell you, are connected to the concept of justice.

Six months later a little coda played itself out. A woman I knew, one of the early and now well-known feminists in philosophy, told me about a job in her department. Her advocacy took me as far as the short list. My qualifications for the job and its rank as associate professor were not in question. Then one of her colleagues, a man, protested that the salary I'd be paid would exceed his. She backed off. She understood, as I then did not, the irrelevance of justice in such matters.

I remember deciding never again to apply for a job in philosophy, but my memory plays me tricks. A file folder I've just reread shows me that for another whole year I wrote to departments of philosophy asking to be considered for the openings they advertised. The letters became longer as the year progressed: I was explaining to prospective colleagues that while my route since graduate school had been unconventional, so was the knowledge I had gained thereby. The replies were uniform: "No." Compared with the other letters in the folder, the final letter I wrote is very spare. It is dated ten days after Logos' death. The futility of the whole endeavor had at last become very clear.

Since publication of *An Unknown Woman*, I am often invited to read from it publicly and to answer questions afterward.

"What have you been doing since you left Nantucket?"

At the first few readings, I stood for long moments before answering, not knowing how to compress all this into a brief reply. It was easier to compress the life of moneying, and so I said, still say, "I've been a freelance writer and editor."

Because after Waterloo, and it was, my attempts to be at a university were happening on the side while I tried to find money.

Not long after the firing, the resignation, an acquaintance came to my house for coffee. We traded assessments of Washington, my six months against his several years.

"A friend of mine left his government job to become a freelance writer, and now he's earning a hundred and fifty dollars a day," he said.

"That's three times what I earned as a speechwriter! But how often does he work?"

"Every day."

I stared at him. The possibility planted itself before me, and tendrils began winding around me. "Would he talk with me?"

"I'll ask him and let you know."

We probably talked, that friend and I. The life is wicked enough that you never forget what you had to do in the beginning, and so you hold out a hand to someone who wants to enter. Not much of a hand, because you can't open the door to your own competition.

But you can suggest a few steps to take, the overall scheme of the thing.

First, you get on the phone.

The thing everyone at the other end of a phone in Washington has is information. And they're willing to give it to you. Free. In fact, they're waiting for you to call so that they *can* give it to you, directly by phone or in person, or indirectly through the people who represent you. That's their job: to acquire information that will be useful to you. (This is the theory, anyway.)

Some people have more information than others. The formula is: the more information you have, the more power you can wield. Even: the more power you have, the more information you (probably) have.

So if you're looking for money, you need to know who has it. To find the person, you look for the places where information accumulates. To find the information, you have to ask questions. And one thing philosophers know how to do better than anyone else is to ask questions. The beauty of Washington is that you don't even have to know the right person to ask. All you have to do is get on the phone and ask whoever answers. The odds are extremely high against finding the right person with your first call. But the answer you receive will include another phone number that will get you closer to him or her. By the eighth call, the same odds say, you will be talking to the person you're looking for.

Money in Washington isn't only in the federal government, although that's what draws all the rest of it there. The private national organizations, lobbying for their causes, winning research funds. The companies who contract with the government to do work it has announced needs doing. The subcontractors to whom work is farmed out: freelance editors and writers and illustrators and lettershops and drivers and, and, and. But all these people need restaurants and taxis and garages and refrigerators. They build buildings, attend the theatre, visit museums, read newspapers and magazines and newsletters. Some of the federal government's money finds its way to these places, and so you look there as well.

Thus did I place my pen and my expensive education in the service of living by my wits.

"Hello. I'm a writer and editor. Does anyone in your shop have a project for an extra pair of hands?"

"Full up right now, but try me in November. I expect to be starting something that you might be right for."

"I'll do it. But do you happen to know someone who has something now?"

Pause. "Try John Bee over at Agriculture. Here's his number."

"I appreciate it. Thanks, Harry. I'll call you in November."

You dial Agriculture. "John Bee, hello. I was just talking with Harry Cue at Labor. He tells me you might have a piece of work for a freelance writer."

"Well, how's old Harry? I haven't talked with him since we worked together on the migrant labor bill. I do need a writer but I haven't any money for you."

"I also edit. Do research. Policy analysis."

Pause. "I can't really hold out any promises, but why don't you come by and talk? How about Wednesday at two?"

You go. You talk. Nothing comes of it right then and there, but he learns how you handle yourself, whether he can work with you. So that when you call again he may have something. Or know someone who has something.

You return home and get on the phone again. "Hello. I'm a writer and editor."

After a while you join organizations that have job banks: organizations for writers, for women. More names to add to your list of people to call. You refine the approach by dropping names, listing credits. But getting on the phone is something you don't stop doing until someone says: "How soon can you start?"

Sometimes I found the money. I'd hang up the phone and shout and clap my hands. Immediately I'd take Logos and Ousia swimming or for a long walk in the woods or keep them chasing balls until even they were ready to stop, repaying them for all the days, the long days, on which I had done nothing but sit at the phone or drive into Washington to meet potential clients, days on which I had barely gone through the motions of being their good friend while they waited, sleeping, hoping, their time slipping by. The next thing I'd do would be to buy myself a gift: a pound of fresh fruit whose cost had heretofore excluded me, or a cheese I had been longing to try. If the new assignment came on the heels of the old, so that I still had some cash on backlog, I'd buy something substantial: a pair of shoes, say. Most of the time the interval between jobs was lengthy, and always the money would not come to hand for a month or more, so that my gift would only be that I could then buy a week's food at a time without having to allocate my pennies into exactly what we needed each day, no more.

Next morning I'd be at my desk before dawn, free to do my own writing again, picking it up from where it had been dangling since the last assignment ended, since the money ran out. When I have no money, I can concentrate only so long on my own work, and then, in the middle of a sentence I'm trying to shape, my thoughts will of their own accord begin circling around ways to start income incoming again. I pick up the phone, make the calls, hear the "No," or "Try me next month," or "Our budget for writers has been cut," until the business day ends. Dreiser knew what five o'clock means to people who are looking for jobs: it frees you to do anything else for the whole evening; it absolves you from looking until the next day. Having no money and not knowing when I'll have it again marshal all my thinking into the search for it, divert my whole mind away from my work. But when I know money will be reliably in my pocket, even for weeks, even for a few months, I can then throw off the burden of the looking and begin writing again. Try to begin writing again. Because I shall have lost the thread, lost the momentum of each new word inscribing itself on paper, lost the sweet discovery.

All the while I looked for freelance jobs, I still went to my desk at four in the morning, claiming for myself the hours until offices were open, until the dialing had to begin. But I was not working. Finally I did not even go to my desk, although I could not do other than awaken at my time. The dogs and I walked. I read. I waited for nine o'clock. And every day I carried the question around with me: "Can I not write anymore?"

It took three months to land my first assignment. Doing the actual writing had the peculiar effect of reassuring me. But hiring out my pen was one thing. Could I write for myself too?

If the job were long enough, I could. I'd give my benefactor the workday that began at nine, but during the very early hours of the morning I'd sit in my chair with my fingertips on the typewriter keys or holding a pen, the paper in place, and wait for the words to appear.

Those hours became lessons in understanding the most intimate rhythms of my way of working. It was enough to be sitting in my perfect chair in the dark silence of four in the morning. Perhaps nothing got itself written that day or the next. But by simply being there, alert to whatever fragment might float along, ready to seize it, let it play itself out on the page, I'd have something on paper, even a sentence or two, to read the next day. Sometimes, picking it up from where I had had to lay it aside the day before, I'd wonder where I had thought it might lead. Other times I'd see, and half a page might get itself written. And the following day more paragraphs would somehow become two pages. After a time of doing this, of patiently watching for the thing in me that is the why of me, of letting it know that it can come out now, that it no longer need huddle frozen, inert, at least not for a while, the words would come. And even though I can't let them tumble about through my thoughts during all the hours of my day because I have to do the job that's giving me the money that lets me free them up each time I sit down to them, they know that they're being held back only until the next early morning and only by the thinnest of silken threads.

I was not intent on a career as a writer for hire. The jobs were only to let me pay the bills so I could write my thinking. The moment the phone calls netted me an assignment, I'd stop looking for money. And I wouldn't get back to the phone again until the money needed replenishing. Foolish Alice. Not the way to proceed. The thing to have done was to make fresh phone calls immediately after getting a job. To line up the next job and the next, so that the flow of money never stops. The successful writers in Washington spent as much time looking for new business as doing the jobs they won. Their reputations grew and, unlike me, who had to scrounge on the phone, they were sought out: people called them. But that was how they spent their time: the jobs were their work.

For two years I kept us fed, the rent paid, the phone connected, fuel in the tank, vets and doctors current. No cushion at all, of course, in the event of emergency. And then Logos died. For three days I did not eat. Coffee sufficed for the morning and vodka for late in the afternoon. You could not say I slept. On one of those mornings that was not distinct from the night I carried a cup of coffee to my desk at my customary hour and took up again the article on women and power that had engrossed me during the same hours before Logos' last weeks. I wrote until daylight, and then I pushed back my chair. But Logos was not lying against the wall beneath my desk, ready for me to take him and Ousia for our morning walk. Logos *was* not. Ousia and I walked out alone. The day crawled past me: I could not work, I could not look for jobs, I could not think. And yet each morning at four I'd end the sleepless night and go to my desk, writing until the light filled the room and showed me how empty it was. And then the empty day cycled around to night. For two weeks the sentences of that article poured out of my fingertips as though it were writing itself and I were only the medium by which it could get itself transferred to the page. But I could write only from the time I heaved myself out of bed until the darkness lightened to dawn. And when I finished the article, when it finished getting itself written, I did not write anything else of my own for eight years.

But I wrote. I edited. I analyzed policy. Whatever the subject and whatever needed being done to it, I did.

Construction of the Baltimore subway.

At street level the engineer led me, hard-hatted, toward the excavation. "We'll walk down," he said as we approached the landing of a steel staircase. He walked to the railing and called me over to look. "There it is."

I cannot, but I had to, look down into a hole three hundred feet deep. My stomach disappeared and my head flew away. We began the descent. I had my choice of walking next to the pit with one hand on the railing or next to the wall but without support. Oh, the wall, I thought, keeping my eyes on each stair with each footstep. But after only two landings I was hanging onto the rail and counting. You'd think my stomach would know when we reached bottom. But how to acknowledge that you're on solid ground when you can look up and see solid ground three hundred feet above you?

For minutes at a time I could attend to the engineer's descriptions of his company's earthmoving equipment, of the cut-and-cover operation, of how the tons of soil were disposed of. I heard myself asking questions. I saw myself taking notes. But all along, my stomach played counterpart: "You have to go up again."

My editor was so pleased with my article about the Baltimore subway that she assigned me to report on the Washington subway.

And then to write about ornamental wall railings, friezes, spandrels, and grillwork crafted of bronze, aluminum, or stainless steel by an architectural metalworking firm. About digging and grading equipment used in street construction and along highways and banks. Flashing safety barricades. Cranes for erecting steeples. The design and construction of the rational city of Columbia, Maryland, and of the festival that is Faneuil Hall Marketplace in Boston.

The Baltimore assignment took four and a half days: travel to and from the site, digesting the written material from the engineers, making sense of my own scribbled notes, phone calls for clarification of some technical point that made no sense as I tried to put together sentences about it, choosing the story line and organizing the material around it, writing the piece, rewriting it, editing it, delivering it to the editor's office among the seductive shops of Georgetown. For all this, one hundred and fifty dollars: about four dollars an hour.

For the second assignment I lopped off a day. For the third assignment I wrote out a set of questions in advance, and they became my formula. By then, I was delivering the article in one and a half days and my fee was up by twenty-five dollars. Once a month for nearly two years, that reliable little assignment took care of our food and kept the car going. The rent was another matter. And the phone. And heat. And electricity.

I learned the trick of referring casually to the technical information I was acquiring. So that when another construction magazine wanted someone to do an article about hot-dip galvanizing, I was the person they hired. In galvanizing, a zinc coating is electro-chemically bonded to iron or carbon steel, thereby forming an impermeable barrier against corrosion, whether in fresh or salt water, in the atmosphere, or in the soil. Hot dipping is done to finished and to semifabricated articles. Its advantage over continuous galvanizing is that it completely seals all edges, rivets, and welds, leaving no joining exposed to the oxygen that is metal's enemy.

Six hundred dollars, publication in a glossy magazine, and a by-line. The article took me a month. But the magazine would not pay until the article was published. A wait of six months or seven or eight: a writer has no say in the scheduling of an article.

I instituted a battle with the editor. "You walk into a store in December to buy a lawn mower. Try telling the salesperson that you're not going to pay for it until April because you won't be mowing your lawn until then."

"Alice, this is how we pay. This is how we've always paid. As soon as the piece appears, we make out a check request, it goes to the treasurer, and you get your check."

"Another month added on!"

"I can't change the procedure, Alice."

"You mean that someone else can?"

"No."

I wrote a strong letter to the publisher. He did not reply. After a couple of weeks I wrote again. The editor called to say that I could pick up my check by the end of the week.

He gave me other assignments. I fought for my money the same way each time. They liked my work but they hated me.

A chemistry professor at American University teaching science to physically and emotionally handicapped children needed someone to help her write a book that would enable elementary school teachers to use her methods. I wrote the procedures for the laboratory experiments. How did I qualify? I know how to ask questions.

I imagine doing the specific experiment. There is a gap in the explanation.

"How does such-and-such happen?"

I listen. "Oh, you mean that-and-that?"

Not exactly.

"Then what happens to that-and-that?"

I listen. "I get it. You mean this-and-this."

Yes.

I am silent. "But then so-and-so."

Or for nearly half a year. Among all the things needing to be written at the Academy, Phil found the person who had a project for me. The person found one thing, and, when I finished that, another. The first thing concerned the health effects of radiation accidents. What did I know about radiation? Only how to use a library. Only how to ask questions. The second thing concerned the social and political consequences of solar, nuclear, and other alternative energy systems. A set of chapters, each written by a different specialist, needed to be rewritten into a book as though by a single author and having a beginning, middle, and end. A book that people would read. It mattered not at all that my name would not be on it.

When there was not one small thing else for me at the Academy, not even a full-time job, I got on the phone again.

Nine years and more of writing for hire, mere moneying. I specialized in editing jobs: reorganizing, cutting, clarifying, tightening someone else's writing. Editing used only the left side of my brain, and that was the only part that was functioning after Logos' death. They did not support me, these jobs. Friends loaned me money that I often could not repay for months, a year. A certain piece of federal legislation helped me with a hospital bill. Another paid my midwinter fuel bill so that the oil company would deliver its sustenance to my house again. Food stamps twice. Welfare once.

You will not believe that I did not understand until two years ago when it all happened again that I had been living in poverty. I did not call it that because I continued to assume that one day I would be paid for my work. That conviction rested on rock. It kept me shipping my "Journey" to the next publisher each time it was returned to me.

"Why did you wait fourteen years to publish *An Unknown Woman?*"

I always laugh.

□   □   □

For a long time I thought that the circle connecting work and money was small and tight: money to let me work; work that would bring me money. It was the idea of deserving that so closely linked these arcs but that was absent from the large and loose circle of money and jobs. For your work you deserve to be paid; for a job you take as much money as someone will pay you.

What is it: to deserve? When something I am or do or have is rewarded commensurately with the value I place on the thing. And since my writing jobs had only money value for me, no deserving was involved. With jobs what mattered was only: how could I get as much money as possible for the time the job was usurping from my work?

The jobs I hustled in Washington weren't any part of my work, yet they kept me at work among words. Never mind that it was · with one hand tied behind me. Because when I returned to New England after my long exile and began my own writing again, my pen was more finely honed than before, my eye made harsher demands on the connection of my sentences, one to the other, my ear more swiftly eliminated extraneous syllables.

Perhaps, then, there aren't two circles, one connecting money with work, the other connecting money with jobs. Perhaps there's only one circle of money and work that contains an indeterminately long arc for moneying. Perhaps the shadings between moneying and work, still not clear to me, turn on the plain fact of doing your work every day in whatever guise it makes its appearance to you. It is unexpected, that arc of moneying. But then, in the circle of loving, taking-care-of unexpectedly shades into caring-for, being-concerned-about.

For too long I let deserving connect money and work but not money and jobs.

During the two years following publication of *An Unknown*

Woman, I lived off its royalties and advances without having to hustle jobs. Came the October day when my publisher's semiannual royalty statement contained a check totaling exactly one hundred dollars. I had not counted on the feast's ending so soon. I did some calculating. My bank account would support me for six months. Long before then, I'd somehow have to begin my own writing again, leaping over eight years' absence from it.

On my desk was the first of my half dozen "Hers" columns for *The New York Times*. The topics were to be of my choosing, and the only limitations were the twelve-hundred-word length and the weekly deadline. The crafting of an essay thus long, to be in an editor's hands by thus day, became the impetus that sat me down to my own work. Because one of those columns was in condensed form an entire book that I had projected a year earlier, and I began writing it.

The writing went well enough for me to submit the manuscript to a publisher for an advance against royalties. I received an offer. It was larger than any sum I had ever had in hand at one time in my whole life, the equivalent of two or three years' worth of free-lancing income. There was a catch: I was to write a letter (it would be part of the contract) saying that I would not write about my lawsuit against the veterinarians in whose hospital Logos died. I thought hard about that condition. The attorney I consulted said: "If you take the money and write those chapters anyway, they'll demand their advance back from you, and you will have already spent it."

If I had considered the money to be only payment for a job, I'd have written the letter and signed the contract. The book I wrote would have contained the unwanted chapters, but the publisher would be seeing them written rather than imagining them in the abstract, and she would have liked them, would have seen them as integral to the whole manuscript.

But I considered the money as payment for my work. And for my work, only I decide what is and is not to be included, or that it is to be done one way rather than another. I declined the offer.

I was not totally mad. My hole card was writing a newspaper column that an editor and I had discussed. She was on vacation when I had to decide what to do about the book contract, and when she returned I told her I'd write the column for her. But I had misconstrued the firmness of the offer. In the intervening weeks, the newspaper had instituted a policy of cutting back on columnists.

The life of freelancing began again. This time I was living near the wrong city. Disaster overtook me faster. I put aside the book I had continued writing anyway in the early morning hours, packed my belongings, moved them into storage and, with Kairos rather than with Logos and Ousia, drove back into the past of inhabiting friends' spare rooms.

Almost immediately I received an invitation for an interview from a company whose blind advertisement I had answered before becoming homeless. They had described themselves as "an energy-related company" without naming themselves; their letterhead now identified them as one of the major utilities in the country. I went to the interview: my Washington background in energy would win me the day. They liked me, they liked my writing, the salary was more than acceptable, the benefits would have made you rub your eyes.

And then the editor leaned back in his chair. "How do you feel about nuclear energy?"

Good-bye, job. "I oppose its use."

"And your reasons?"

I started to speak but he anticipated my words. "Disposal of radioactive waste and no viable plan for evacuating populations in the event of an accident." He had heard the answer many times: it was the reason he had not named his company in his advertisement.

I nodded. "But there are so many aspects to energy. Surely I can write about everything else." Lame.

And he knew it. "We're committed to nuclear power. A large percentage of the energy we deliver derives from nuclear reactors. It would touch every article, every speech, every brochure you'd have to write."

In minutes I was walking back to my car.

It was only a job. Why couldn't I have seen it as only a job?

For eleven months I barely kept us whole. People I had known for years turned away from me. Others sent me money without asking when it would be repaid. In the spring I applied for a job teaching in a college's new writing center, a program I'd help design. After two or three very long phone conversations, my candidacy collapsed. By phone I tracked the woman who had been so eager to meet me. A colleague, with apparent prompting, spoke in her stead: "The committee decided that you've been away from teaching too long."

"But I never pretended to have been teaching during these years. The *vitae* I sent her makes that obvious."

"I'm sorry."

"Once you know how to teach, you never forget it. It's like driving a car."

"I'm sorry."

Late that afternoon, while Kairos and I climbed a hilly path in the woods a few miles away, what the committee meant emerged from what the committee said. Next morning I rewrote my résumé in such a way that twenty years fell away from my age. Within two weeks I received two job offers, and I took the one that paid the most money. Pity I didn't think to lie sooner.

The summer before last I met a man who gave me enough money to write a book. This book. I am being paid to do my work.

□ □ □

Whenever a moneyer is talking with me about hiring my pen, there's a proper point in the discussion for asking what I'll be paid and when. I'm never reluctant to raise the topic or to pursue it when it seems to go into hiding. Driving to meet a potential Washington client, I'd arbitrarily decide to raise my fee by fifty or a hundred dollars, pushing it ever closer toward the highest fees that I knew were being paid for comparable projects. I'd name the figure casually during our talk, not justifying it. If some faint dismay appeared on the client's face, I'd point out that of course the moneyer could hire another writer for less money but the project would take longer and might not be done as well, might even have to be redone later. If that ploy failed, I'd accept what I was offered but, once at my desk, I'd cut back on the time I gave to the project. Because I *was* doing it faster, and I always did it well.

As much money as possible and as soon as possible. A singer I know told me that her union requires theatre managements to deliver checks to all singers thirty minutes before a performance, and if there are no checks there is no performance. The only writers' organization in the United States that could make comparable demands for writers refuses to use its clout, and so each writer stands alone to face the moneyer's whim. I want to be paid the moment I hand someone my pages of writing, whether a job or my work. When I lecture or read publicly, I take my cue from the singers, although I'm willing to wait until after the performance.

I do not find it peculiar that I want my money immediately after earning it, but the persons who hire me give me to understand that I am not well-bred to press the matter. An author should wait graciously, which for them is silently, during the weeks or months until their procedures wheel around to doling their money out to me. But I must deal with two separate groups of people: the editors or deans or faculty who hire me, whose concern is the quality of the work and that it will be delivered or read on time; and the accountants and clerks in the business offices who actually sign and mail the checks to me. The editors, the deans, declare themselves to be at the mercy of the business people, and they, the ones who hand out the money, aren't going to be hurried: that's their work, that's all they do. Backed against the wall (and I have done it), both groups insist that they are merely carrying out the policies of their institution: "This is how we always do things." But they know, and I know, that the larger the institution the easier it is to bypass rules. Yet there is no compelling reason for them to try to imagine my need. All of them receive their salary checks, week after week and on time. It does not, it cannot, occur to them that the well-dressed woman standing in front of them lives by hanging on to dimes, almost never has savings to buffer illness or periods without income. The money I earn goes out as soon as, sooner than, it comes in. I'm pushy about having it at once because I have none, because there is no prospect (now, today) of getting more. Until I lift the phone again: "Hello. I'm a writer. Do you have any . . ."

Last winter a young woman contacted me to address a seminar whose members had been reading, among other books, mine. My fee would be paid from two sources: one check would be given me that evening, and within a few weeks the other would be mailed. I met with the group, and afterward the woman and I had a long talk. She told me that the night before she finally reached me, she had lain awake for hours trying to think of some good reason that would persuade me to come to talk. I spent the whole first check the morning after the seminar: it kept the phone connected and the heat on and half-filled the tank of my car. I planned to allocate twenty-five dollars of the second check for buying Kai's food and mine, but when it arrived it was twenty-five dollars short. No other money was on the horizon. I phoned the young woman. I had, it seems, misunderstood the amount of the fee. No doubt something difficult seeped into my voice. When we hung up, I figured ways to use the staples in my cupboard until I had grocery money again.

dollars. I wrote to thank her, suggesting that we stay in touch. She did not reply.

Thus do I have a reputation for being greedy, for always grasping after money.

People tell me that I'm hard to find. They have only to look for me at the moneying station. It is the station of solitude that seems to have my name on it, so lengthy are my interludes there. In twenty-five years I've left it only twice: once for nearly four years, and once for nearly two. A total of five years, say, out of twenty-five. Only five years of having enough money to live on without constantly having to try to earn it so I could do my work. Since I consider people to be successful when their money comes only from their work, I can't at all count myself among them: I have had to give up 80 percent of my days merely to survive.

And then I think: I searched for a work I'd love doing, a work I'd do independently of whether I'd earn money doing it. And I've had my wish: I found my work, and money has rarely been part of it.

9

SINGLING

IT IS A single life I live, in many senses. Single in being without other human beings, not a member of a group, unaffiliated. Single in being individual, of my own design, unalike. Single is being unmarried. But also single is being integrated into an unbroken whole, unified.

Like the web spiders weave out of their own substance, each of these aspects of singleness is something I've made, whether from reshaping to my own purposes circumstances over which I otherwise had no control, or by making an initial choice that thereby excluded other related choices, or by drifting into a situation that I in time acknowledged and then turned to my own account.

The threads of my life correlate with these meanings.

Living in the country I am without other human beings. My work is my singularity. These two threads are primary.

Being unmarried is only a special case of being unaffiliated, but it is also a consequence of my individuality. Unifying my life into an integrated whole, I wind together into a single cord the two strands of my work and my life in the country. These two threads derive from the first two.

Single: unaffiliated.

On Nantucket with Logos, I found myself in a landscape of

open space and silence that I almost at once recognized as my natural habitat. Logos and the sea and the moors and the isolation were inextricably first, chronologically as well as in priority. I never returned to Nantucket again, but those of its elements that spoke to me I imported into all the places I've lived since. Each day I awaken, fall asleep, do as many other things as possible for as many hours as possible as near as possible to the natural world. This thread, living in the country, arose from and included at its very core my commitment to Logos.

In the beginning, in my first country house in Weston, I still carried my ignorance of wildness born of living in cities. Certain creatures were acceptable and could wander at will through my yard, in my woods, across Logos' and my paths in our own meanderings: deer, raccoons, rabbits, squirrels, opossums, skunks, foxes, porcupines, any bird. Other creatures were banned: snakes, to start.

"You want to watch out for copperheads," said Tommy, not one to pass up a chance to intensify someone's apprehensiveness. "They're the only poisonous snakes around here, though."

"What do they look like?"

"Well, they've got a diamond pattern on their back. Just be careful when you cross stone fences. That's where they like to live."

I thought of the stone fences marking the boundaries of former meadows in the woods where I walked every day.

Tommy watched me. "But you don't have to worry about the other snakes around here."

"What other snakes?"

"Milk snakes. Of course, the pattern on a milk snake's back looks a lot like a copperhead's." Tommy was having a good time.

"Then how do I tell the difference?"

"You use your eyes. What have you got eyes for? Look over there. See that black snake on the wall?"

"No. Where?"

He cupped the back of my head in both his hands and turned me toward the stone wall at the eastern border of his meadow. Twenty feet away a thick black stick gleamed against the rocks. "That snake has lived in that stone wall for I don't know how many years. Now be quiet and watch him."

Minutes passed.

"He's just taking the sun. He'd want to get out of your way as much as you'd want to get out of his. Unless you surprised him, maybe stepped too near him in the woods, he wouldn't bite you."

"Bite me?"

"But the copperhead: well, you're just going to have to learn what he looks like. He can be trouble." He marched over to his yellow pickup truck, switched on the ignition, and was gone.

Three days later I saw a copperhead. I phoned Tommy. No answer. I drove to his house. No one at home. I ran down the lane to the house he rented to two men.

"Please come over to my house! There's a copperhead on my lawn!"

One of the men stopped to make a forked stick from a fallen dogwood branch. They followed me back to my house in their car.

They looked first where I had seen the snake, near the steps leading to my back door. Then they poked along the length of the stone wall that separated my yard from the swale to the east. But in the fifteen minutes that had elapsed, probably within the first seconds of seeing me, the snake had moved off to quieter places. The men returned home.

The following week I found a diamond-patterned snakeskin near the back stairway to my house. I took it to Tommy.

"My gosh!" he said, "you had a copperhead." He was grinning.

Olive shook her head. "It's an ordinary garden snake, Alice." As a young man Tommy had rented a room in her mother's house, the very house where we now stood talking, and within a few years she and Tommy married. For more than forty years, therefore, she had observed Tommy and his games, and she took it as one of her tasks to warn the unwary. "Copperheads moved toward the hilly land up here when excavations began in Norwalk and Westport for the Turnpike. But that was years ago, and most of them have gone farther north by now. Tommy's the one you have to watch out for."

Early in September, Tommy again:

"You don't want to let your dog swim in the millpond. Snapping turtles lie on the bottom there, and they just reach up and grab hold when something juicy shows up in the water. Their jaws are like a vise. A snapper could drag any dog under."

For weeks I kept Logos out of the water. Then, on a path through the meadow that was slowly being reclaimed by staghorn sumac, a snapping turtle stood face-to-face with me. I grabbed Logos' collar and ran the whole length of the winding route to my house. Tommy and Olive were out of town. I phoned my nearest neighbor.

"Rocky, there's a snapping turtle in my woods."

"So?"

"He could kill Logos. Please. Do something."

"The football game just started, and I'm all set for the afternoon."

"Please, Rocky." I heard him sigh.

I met him at the road, then led him to the place where the turtle surprised me. The turtle had moved only a few feet farther along. I walked quickly back to my house, but the dull thudding of heavy blows followed me into my yard. After too many minutes the sounds stopped. I returned on the path to find Rocky standing quietly, a large stone in his right hand. He stared at me, then heaved the stone at the rock wall from which he had taken it.

"I feel like a murderer," he said, then turned and walked away.

Rocky, so do I.

In Virginia years later, I crossed my kitchen on my way outside and reached for the knob on the screen door. A long black rope curled around and hung down from the outer handle.

Did I leave the leash outdoors? And then the tip of the leash slowly twisted, becoming the king snake who had wrapped himself around the knob, there to hang in the sun.

It did not occur to me to utter a sound while I stood unmoving, studying him. Then very slowly I closed the kitchen door so that Logos and Ousia, now sniffing out the strange scent, would not frighten him away.

He made himself visible afterward in enough other places to teach me that he lived nearby. The only action I took was to let the wildflowers grow nearly waist-high in the front lawn, refusing to mow it, then avoiding crossing it, because it might conceal him. I did not want my dogs to come upon him unexpectedly as he took the sun, idling in that green disorder, but neither did I want to have to watch for him perpetually wherever I walked, barelegged and almost barefooted, in the murderous Washington heat. For the wildness I was letting surround my house was wildness unqualified. I had waived the privilege of issuing invitations: "You come, but not *you*."

If I had kept the grass trimmed, the wild raspberries would not have prospered. But I had no machinery for mowing and no money for hiring mowers. I would not give up half a morning each week to the task, nor pour pollution into the air, nor contribute to the ambient noise. By sparing energy, my own and that of the fuel I did not use, the creatures of the woods that bordered my house could count on the refuge of my lengthening grass as they reestablished paths denied them by all the groundskeepers who preceded me in that house. The land rewarded me with a thicket of raspberries densening in tandem with the sweetbrier roses that are their cousins.

With no assistance from me, the raspberries continued to grow day after day. Their accessible presence gave me a sense of abundance that I suppose permeates the rich always and farmers in summer. Every human being should have at least one such thing, at least for a brief time.

Nothing hostile competed with me for the raspberries, neither bees nor wasps nor any stinging thing. Snakes did not rest beneath the brambles' crown, nor did I notice the predations of raccoons. Creatures with fur or with unprotected skin must have taken warning enough from the prickles and thorns that studded the whole length of the canes. Not creatures with feathers, however: I was in contest with the birds for the fruits, and unfairly. One cardinal in particular, whose territory I invaded merely by living in that house, regularly scolded me as I stood filling my little bowl. I reminded him that for a year and a half he had done very well on my sunflower seed, and didn't he remember past favors? He tried a little unfairness of his own. Hadn't I noticed his pair of juveniles as they stood next to him, almost his size but still yelling to be fed? I pointed out to him that he was hourly at my feeder, where I continued to place enough sunflower seed even during the summer, so that those very young out of whose mouths he was accusing me of taking food would have substantial protein. You are talking about the past and the future, said the cardinal in reply; what matters is now, now, only now.

But there was enough for the birds and me both. The berries having only four or five drupelets were so small that my fingers would have crushed them had I picked them. I left them on their stems. So it was nature's variety, not my generosity, that assured the cardinal a raspberry from my bushes every now and then.

And when there was less than a week left of wild raspberries, I knew a place deep in the woods where a massed stand of blackberries was slowly ripening. I kept my eye on them, and in about two weeks I was able to fill a bucket with them each time I went that way.

In Connecticut one autumn near midnight a low deep call sound-

ing only a few feet from my bed awakened me. I lay alert and
listening, but now Logos and Ousia were awake too. The call came
again, three times, four times, catapulting the dogs into wild excitement. I, who always keep a flashlight with a powerful beam
next to my bed, carried it to the doorway opening onto our broad
balcony, held it flat against the screen, and flicked it on, the dogs
roaring next to me, battling about who would rush through the
doorway first. But the great horned owl slipped away without my
seeing him. I played my light into the trees, searching, hoping,
but the beam reflected only stillness. The call began again, more
distant now, but the dogs were unconvinced that the creature from
whom it issued could not be chased and done away with. I flicked
off the lantern and stood in the darkness, leaning against the open
door for a long time. First Logos gave up, then Ousia. The hoots
in their distinctive series fitted in with the night, progressing toward
distant perches, moving slowly out of earshot. Not too many weeks
afterward, walking in the dry woods of early winter, I raised my
head in time to see the great horned owl lift himself from the bare
branch of a maple fifty feet away. I caught my breath at the span
of his wings, even at that distance seeming as wide as I am tall.
Silently the owl wove a line of flight through the branches as though
a highway were open to him. The dogs were close at hand, and I
grabbed each of their collars to keep them near me. I had no fear
of the owl for my sake, but if he were considering Logos or Ousia
as prey, I wanted him to understand that they were too large for
him and, most particularly, that they were with me. Had I been
alone, I would have stood motionless to fill my eyes with the sweep
and silence of the owl's movement. From time to time during the
winter we heard him again, sometimes as near as on that first
midnight, but I simply lay listening to him, and the awakened
dogs, watching me do nothing, quickly fell asleep again.

Deep in the Virginia countryside, evening after evening I listened to a whippoorwill sing until dusk faded into darkness. You

can go to a great deal of trouble trying to transcribe that rush of air and sound into a sequence of syllables readable from the page, but you will not succeed. The first syllable isn't sounded so much as it is a forceful exhalation you can approach imitating by whispering "who-ee," and cutting off the "ee" into short "i." The second syllable barely exists, a brief puff of air: "puh." It's the third syllable, eliding into the fourth, that rivets your attention: WHEE-el. Over and over, countless times a minute: who-i (split-second pause)-puh-WHEE-el. I identified the song and called its maker by that centuries-old name the first time I heard it. Once, before evening came on, I left Ousia and Kairos in the house and, lantern in hand, stood waiting next to an unused shed near the house. The sun had barely set when the first "who-i-(pause)-puh-WHEE-el" sounded from the ground two feet away. I did not move during long minutes of repetition. Then, sure of the bird's location, I edged quietly toward her, shining my light on her for a split second. If she were not pouring beauty into the air you would not have been able to distinguish her from the dry leaves and grass on which she rested. The flash of my lantern did not startle her into silence. A moment's break, perhaps, and then she picked up where she had left off. Slowly I moved away from her, not wanting to frighten her into flight, and then I stood listening until the night began. When I went into the house to bed, my ears and all of me reverberated to her sound. Somewhere somewhen later, a woman I met left me speechless by complaining about a whippoorwill outside her window who kept her from sleeping until long after midnight.

What made the difference? By what route did I proceed from fearing snakes to making room for them within a few steps of my very dwelling, from demanding the slaughter of a snapping turtle to listening rapt in the night to a great predator's call? Was it by reasoning? By mere habituation?

Some of both. More by loving: by watching, listening, discovering patterns of growth, of activity, waiting to see whatever there would be to see.

With Ousia and Kairos I drive to the woods a mile from our northern Virginia house. Every morning before sunrise, sometimes just afterward, our walk begins at a certain path's beginning. Every morning: summer, spring, fall, winter. In winter when the leaves are gone you can see far into a forest. Paths appear that you didn't realize existed when greenness cut off your line of vision. But as the months of winter wear on, and your eye has taken in the shades of brown and grey and black of bark, grateful for the stands of white pines and the scatterings of firs, late in January you start looking for the first green tips to emerge above the snow. In these woods it will be bloodroot, the plant low, its petals waxy white, eight of them, cupping fine short yellow stamens. The distinctive leaf teaches you how to count all over again: one leaf with lobes curving into one another, or three leaves (or five)? The answer lies in whether the leaf attaches to the stalk in one place or many. And where did I see bloodroot last year? Ah, here, near the base of this yellow poplar. There, behind the jutting rock. Not yet. Another morning: not yet. And then one morning, half a leaf, still a narrow cylinder, rises above the duff, finding the vertical tunnel of air in the frozen soil that lets it claim its life in our air another year. Each succeeding morning more of the leaf shoves upward, another tip appears, both cylinders uncurl, and then there is the flower still closed: I am too early. I make a second trip the same day and am rewarded: the bloodroot is open. Every morning thereafter, stopping to look at the flower, now joined by its fellows, begins and ends my walk. Not alone to know where the first spring bloom will appear, but also, and mainly, to have the moment of looking at it, to know a mile away at my desk that it thrives in its own home, to know that I can, for a few weeks anyway, stop what I'm doing at any time and go to that place because it will be there, white and green and beautiful, to know that next year it will push its way upward into the winter silence, uncurling in just that way in that same place. That is my continuity.

But next year will I be here to see it? Not just because between now and then I may die, but because my own search for sustenance may disinter the shallow roots I myself put down, may move me elsewhere. And yet, wherever "there" is, I'll seek out some woods to tramp every day, my eye peeled for the growing tip of bloodroot as January ends, or February farther north. If I cannot have continuity by being able to return year after year to the same wooded place, I can have it year after year by finding wooded spaces wherever I am. In whatever terrain of land or water or admixture of each.

With Logos, Ousia, Kairos. But also with red squirrels and blue jays, with starlings and bats, with field mice and foxes, with cardinals and mockingbirds.

Among these living beings I first understood loving, first came to hold precious a living being for no reason other than his being what he is, her being what she is, the bloodroot's being what it is.

Among these living beings, apart from human beings, I spend the hours of my day that are not taken up by my work or by the too frequent busyness surrounding it. That I live apart from human beings is now my preference, although I did not institute it. How could one institute it? Persons loving God in one or another of the names given to that Being have dedicated their lives to Him/Her in solitude, but they make it clear that they are absenting themselves from the warmth of human connections for the greater warmth of their connection to the divine. Persons hating human beings for one reason or another have taken up solitary lives, but they make it clear that it is precisely because there is no warmth of human connection that they live in the wild or locked away in apartments in the center of large cities.

Neither of these is my reason. I had no reason. It was not I who instituted my being unaffiliated.

Three years after I received my Ph.D. from Radcliffe, Radcliffe became a college of Harvard University, and an official letter informed me that my doctorate would henceforth be considered a Harvard degree. By the time that letter reached me I had already begun an education beyond that rank. It might as well have swept me to the far reaches of the galaxy for the distance it separated me from other human beings. That had not been my intention. I had not even conceived it as a possibility. In fact, I thought I was on my way back in from the outside.

I did not begin living in the country until after I left Nantucket, but living in the country did not stand in the way of a university affiliation. I could have driven however many miles were necessary into (wherever) for the customary two or three classroom hours a day three days a week, for faculty meetings, conferences with students, the library. Never mind that an academic teaching schedule is a sixty- or seventy-hour week. To me it would have been work, not a job. It would have been a seamless life.

"Are you bitter?" a man asked me over lunch. He is a philosopher, the holder of an endowed chair in the department that abdicated its responsibility to me. He alone, too late, made some feeble gestures toward opening academic doors for me.

"Enraged is closer," I replied.

He was prepared to have me say that the public response to *An Unknown Woman* wiped the slate clean. But I am not a saint: I am only a philosopher.

Yet what's philosophy to me or me to philosophy that I should have raged for 't?

It became, it was, it is, myself.

Single: unmarried.

I am a woman. I have never thought of myself, felt myself,

wanted to be, a man. My life without other human beings has not changed my sexuality: I want only a man's body next to mine.

"Why have you never married?"

I answer the question automatically now: "Just lucky, I guess."

Not being married, not having a man connected to me in any of the ways women now connect with men, has nothing to do with my age. I am not old but neither am I young.

I have never married because the solitude I created has room at its center only for matters I cherish for their own sake: loving my work, loving Logos and Ousia and Kairos, loving the country. Loving a man and his loving me would have to be of the same sort: having no purpose beyond our loving one another. I would not be his mother, his teacher, his audience, his child, most especially not his housekeeper, his concubine, his punching bag. He would not be my father, my teacher, my audience, my child, my provider. I would not need him, nor he me. We would only want one another: want to be part of one another's lives, want one another's good, want to be one another's best friend, want one another sexually as the supervening benison on our being one another's best friend.

Wanting is an arena separate from needing, beyond needing. If a man needs me to be his mother, he will in time see me as failing him because I cannot be his mother. If he needs me to assure him about his work, he will in time see me as failing him because only he is the proper judge of his work. If he needs me to have someone to guide or to dominate, I'll always fail him because I am my own guide and I do not take kindly to domination. Needs such as these, or others too idiosyncratic to imagine, exist in persons who have not even set foot toward the first station of solitude. Not loving themselves, they do not know how to love someone else. A man who sees a woman only as someone who will serve his purposes has no conception of loving her for her own sake, loving her only because she is the person she is.

I have never married because the men I've met are still at the level of needs. I have needs, but they're not carry-overs from my childhood. I call on friends for the loan of money that I continue to owe, on neighbors for a hand with a carton too heavy, a piece of furniture too bulky, for me to lift myself, on acquaintances for an introduction to persons who might open doors for my work or become moneyers for me. I repay these gifts by actions that often sport garments unlike those of the original, but that is matter for another essay. In the main, my life without other human beings has taught me to rely on no one other than myself for solutions to matters great and minor, foreseen and emergency, as they arise. With that habit of mind, I have no need for a man. I'd only want him. A man, loving me, would only have to be himself. There is no empty space at the center of me waiting to be occupied: the center of me is now full but I can always make room for things valuable for their own sake. That is the intimacy I reserve for a man, only for a man.

But my life is not absent of intimacy, now with Kairos, and before with Logos, with Ousia. My interconnections with the natural world abound in intimacy. Years ago I wrote some chapters whose calculated focus was Logos and Ousia and the wild creatures we encountered in the course of our country days. One editor returned my essays with a comment that nearly shuddered off the page: ". . . too personal, almost an intimacy." What 'almost'?

Being unmarried comes closely along on the heels of being unaffiliated.

I've lived so long at the very edge of poverty, even for a time in its depths, that all erotic longing has vanished from me. I find myself not simply neutral but faintly repelled at the thought of physical contact. Other urgencies appropriate my attention: will I have money for food tomorrow, can I keep electricity and phone connected, pay the rent, repair the car, buy gas? My daily existence is far too insecure for me to have room in my thinking, my feeling, for a man, even to notice him more than fleetingly if he stood before me. This too was new for me, integral to my individuality: not looking for a man to rescue me. I'd have to be stably located somewhere, assured of an uninterrupted income adequate for my work, before my attention could rest on a man. But only twice in these twenty-five years have I been thus assured. And even though the few years that those two occasions separately encompassed seemed long to me, long enough to let me write two books during the first, to begin a third during the second, both had time-bound endings.

Being unmarried is what most people mean when they talk of being single. Before Nantucket, I thought of it as a failure I might never surmount. Now it is the least consequential part of my life.

Single: individual, one only, unlike.

Long ago I understood that it wasn't merely my being a woman that was preventing my being welcomed into the world of what I long thought of as my peers. It was that I had succeeded in an undertaking few men have even attempted: I have become myself. Worse, I compounded my sin of overreaching male achievement by taking my education seriously: I used the philosophy that is my profession to free and then to shape my own life. "Know thyself," said Socrates. "Physician, heal thyself," said another great teacher. I have done so. It has brought brick walls tumbling down over my head.

Because once you know who you are, it is impossible ever after not to know that you know. Like climbing Everest, you cannot not know that you have reached the peak. Unlike Everest, however, from which you must in time descend, knowing who you are is a permanent locus you occupy, one you cannot even temporarily abandon. It is not a fact about you that you forget most of the time, like having dark brown hair, thinking of it only when you're buying clothes or filling out an application for your driver's license. It is not a fact at all but rather the cast of mind through which you view everything you observe or in which you participate: the way you enter a room of strangers, drive a car, confer with a doctor. It is something that happens to you through your having brought it about, and it continues happening to you because it is you and you are it.

During the early years after I left Nantucket, the education I began there by discarding every need, desire, purpose, habit that was not mine but that I had somehow allowed to be imposed on me opened me wide toward a world every aspect of which appeared and felt new. I was becoming free, and at such a pace that I didn't yet understand that that's what I was doing, that that's what was happening to me. Like a tapestry whose warp and woof you distinguish exactly when you stand close up but whose pattern does not emerge until you step back a certain distance, the life I was fashioning seemed to me then to be filled primarily with practicalities.

What to feed Logos. Where to buy it. Where to buy my own food. The most comfortable bed for Logos. How to keep my bedroom dark. The doctor who would accommodate his time to my health needs. The veterinarian who would do the same for Logos. Logos' safety outdoors within the fence I helped build. My safety indoors and out. The care of my car. The best desk at which to work. The best chair.

V. Sackville-West's white garden at Sissinghurst Castle in Kent is one of the most famous gardens in the world. Before she planted it she had in mind only that, from a certain rough wooden seat at the end of a short path of grey flagstones, she'd look out over a sea of low grey foliage through which tall white flowers would rise here and there. Once planted, the garden so thoroughly achieved the white, light grey, blue-green grey, bright silver effect of coolness she had aimed at that she found herself unable to convey an impression of it in words and could only list the plants she had used: silver mound, southernwood, cotton lavender, a creeping silver-leaved yarrow, velvety rabbit's ears, white delphiniums,

white foxtail lilies, white foxgloves, white hydrangea, white roses
climbing up white-flowering almond trees. The list continues and
is long. Each plant separately is familiar, not exotic. But having
to describe the architecture of their conjoint line and color moved
her to silence.

Just so, I can't set forth the formula whereby each of the
hundreds of details that made up my days flowed as a tiny rivulet
into, was tributary to, the rushing stream that became my personal
freedom. Consider only that each day turns within a circle of practicalities, and that, once my Air Force grants began, my day was
totally within my power to shape. Then the practicalities I have
listed, partially and at random, are for your mind's eye to bring
together, make of them what you will.

At that best desk, a long and wide teak table with four drawers
across the front, each reaching the full depth to the back, and in
that best chair that tilts backward, raises and lowers, has no arms
to get in my way, rolls on casters, holds my body as in an upright
sling, the chair fitting together with the table, both of them lean
and beautiful, I learned what my work is and how I want to do it.
The furniture was there, is here still, because it pleased my eye,
served my purposes. The words that appeared on paper were not
at first the ones I wanted, but they opened doors into hallways into
caverns where I found the ones I wanted. They were not lying
there, waiting for me to carry away. But where I dug and pressed,
they came to hand. Some would at once take a polish. Some stayed
dull until I lined them up with others like them, and then they
would set one another to gleaming.

Is this what I mean to say? Does it belong here, right here, no
other place? Suppose I move it to the last chapter instead. But then
those final lines are redundant. Throw them away. Those good
lines? Nowhere else for them? Not here, anyway. Perhaps back in
the early pages? No? Well, keep them for something, sometime.
And this word: how could I have read it a dozen times and not

noticed that it doesn't at all say what I want it to say? It needs unpacking, that space I thought so small: this poor word covered over a chasm. I write the sentences that fill it out. Now the words lie quietly, one to another, and my eye runs from beginning to end without stopping, unstartled by some misshapen idea, some ill-fitting sequence of words, some rhythm that breaks where it should flow, some awkward element in the pattern of sound.

I it was who chose the furniture. I chose it in accordance with a criterion deep within me of suiting me, belonging with me. At the same time it met contributory criteria of line and color and function. I it is who choose the words. In their final form they are on the paper exactly as I wish them to be. That I write, rather than paint or compose or sculpt or design jewelry or houses or clothes, is some elemental component of my being. I did not try all these other things or medicine or botany or physics to learn whether, after all, one of them is what I wanted to do. I did not deliberately look for my work at all. What I did deliberately was to sweep away the habits and purposes and needs that were not intimately mine. "Can I write?" "Do I want to write?" "Am I good?" "Will my writing ever be published?" These questions were the barriers that had kept me from writing. When they fell away, I left myself open to see what would occupy the newly cleared field. At the appropriate time, the time that was right for me, I simply started to write. To write my way. To write my thinking. About the matter I wanted most to understand. The two faces of freedom again: I freed myself from not writing; I became free to write.

Because I simply wanted to understand the steps that led me to Nantucket and away from it, I wasn't at first thinking in terms of publication. Understanding was powerful enough by itself to keep me at my desk, piling up pages, for the year that writing the "Journey" eventually took. I was writing because I wanted to write: I had come to understand that I like building sentences, choosing and rearranging the words that compose them, designing them into a line of reasoning or a tale, that I know how to make sentences say what I wish to say, and that I need have no reasons for writing other than those. I was writing, not to instruct anyone, nor to win anyone's approval, but to please myself first of all.

One other reason made publishing the "Journey" irrelevant to the writing of it. I believed that what I knew was true for myself alone: I felt no necessity to extend to anyone else the highly specific conclusions I had reached about myself. I cared least of all whether anyone else agreed with what I had come to understand. But finally, I saw no reason why anyone else would consider what I had done important, or even interesting. I was absolutely certain of what I had done on Nantucket, but my achievement was a gift for myself alone.

Ninety-three pages into the "Journey," I stopped writing to let the work salt for a time and to return to the *Hornbook* to finish off my obligation to the Air Force. But the Nantucket folder was only out of sight. Its contents intruded into my thinking while I played with Logos and Ousia, walked with them, drove to the grocery store, prepared our meals, fell asleep at night. After a while, I understood that the pages then written, and whatever else I could get onto paper, could be for other persons as well. I was free, and by my own hand. I was therefore able to lay open to other eyes exactly what such a journey was like. Not as a pattern to be imitated: certainly no one else needed to go to an island, let alone my island; or to go there in winter; or to spend three months, no more nor less; or to take along a dog, or anyone or anything else whatever. By rendering visible the everydayness of what it was like to free myself, I could make it less mysterious even though I couldn't make it less frightening. I could place the map of my journey into a reader's hands, intending it, not as a map for his or her journey, but only as a sample map that would best serve its purpose when the reader could lay it aside to draw his or her own. When I was a graduate student, a swimming instructor helped me overcome my fear of water by persuading me to keep my eyes open under water, against my every inclination to close them. She told me that, although the water would blur when I submerged and first opened my eyes, if I could force myself to hold them open for just a few seconds, the water would clear and I'd be able to see. Just so, my Nantucket book is my way of holding a reader's eyes open during the time it takes to learn that you can see.

My central purposes changed very little once I let that unknown reader in. I was still writing to please myself first of all. I was still writing to reconstruct as though it were the present the brief period that continues to astonish me. I still used the present tense to render the immediacy of my Nantucket time. I still believed that what I knew was true for myself alone. The beginning and the ending remained the same. I merely had to say a bit more for the extra pair of eyes than if only I were to see the page.

I accept the compliment wryly when someone speaks about reading my "journal": he, she, has seen only half of what lies on the page. The rest is the process I rendered transparent, and I extend unalloyed gratitude to those who see it and use it to think through their lives. Having made explicit my own understanding, I thereby laid open the path along which anyone else's understanding can travel. The philosophical skill I deliberately cultivated of being able to say exactly what I mean lets me articulate my own thinking in such a way that readers believe I am articulating theirs.

And along with writing my thinking, I write my seeing, my hearing, of the natural world that is the context in which I flourish, that, with Logos and Ousia and Kairos, is the centering point out of which arises my joy. I did not set myself tests ("Can I describe the call of the mourning dove?"). I simply turned my pen toward the creatures I looked at and listened to whenever I set foot outdoors, whenever the cardinal's song cut into the silence of my study, whenever I lay in bed next to my open windows tallying the summer night sounds. I did not want simply to copy these things (else why not photograph or tape-record them?). I wanted to have forever the whole of it: song, color, ambience. And an essential ingredient of the whole of it was my loving it. I do not write about my loving it: my writing it *is* my loving it.

From there, only one step remained, but I did not see to take it for a very long time.

Single: integrated into a unified whole.

When Logos was teething, at about age five months, I gave him a raw marrow bone to gnaw on to ease the ache in his gums. Within two days the bone became the center of a new game. I'd hang on at one end of it while Logos fastened his teeth firmly onto the other. I'd loosen my hold, and Logos would draw me forward; then I'd tighten my fingers and haul him back toward me. One evening I deliberately did not pit my weight against his: I merely held my end of the bone lightly and let him draw me wherever he wished to go. At first he was surprised to meet with no resistance, and then his gleeful eyes kept turning to gloat over me trailing behind him, as though his teeth themselves weren't telling him that I was still at the other end of the bone, being led by his whim. Suddenly I closed my hand hard around the bone and caught him off guard. For a moment I was able to drag him around the room, still clamped onto his end of the bone. But when it was his turn again, and ever after, he was alert to the instantaneous changes in tension his jaws felt whenever we played that game.

I was not intent on teaching him anything: I wanted only to let him win sometimes in a contest against a creature three times his size. But he did in fact take a lesson from the game: he learned that he could lead me wherever he wished by means of his teeth.

A week or so later I was switching off the downstairs lights for the night, and Logos was following along behind me. As we passed the corner cabinet in the living room he sniffed the floor, barked, looked at me impatiently, then barked again. I was at the other side of the room by then, and I turned to grin at his way of letting me know where his ball was. In the next moment, he came straight toward me. Very gently he placed his jaws around my wrist. My reflexes drew back my hand. But curiosity won over instinct, and I stood quietly to see what he would do. He tugged, just a little, and I relaxed into his pull. My wrist in his mouth, his teeth not even indenting my skin, he held his head high, prancing with the trophy across the room to the cabinet. He dropped my hand and stood looking at me expectantly. I caught my breath, then knelt, reached under the cabinet for the ball, and handed it to him. He took it gravely, lay down facing me and waited for me to start the game of try-to-get-the-ball-away-from-me. His seriousness made me laugh out loud. I reached over to hug him. He tolerated me, clenching the ball in his jaws all the while.

The extraordinary element is the reasoning Logos displayed. His problem was to get me to understand not only that his ball was under the cabinet but also that he wanted me to retrieve it. His solution made use of facts known to him:

1. When the teething bone connected us, he could lead me where he wanted to go.

2. But the teething bone was absent.

3. But my hand, the part of my body he most closely associated with our game, was present.

Therefore, he would now lead me to the ball by connecting directly to my hand.

I do not say that he actually followed these steps, marshalled the data in just this way, then drew his conclusion. I say that these premisses are logically required for his conclusion. But even when human beings reason, we rarely move stepwise from premisses to conclusion. All that is required is that the reasoning follows (logically, not temporally) an accepted pattern of inference.

Logos had abstracted a broadly applicable principle from his understanding of a specific situation, and he had applied it to an appropriate new situation. These are two widely accepted criteria for intelligence when the beings displaying it are human beings.

Thereafter Logos made use of all the means at his disposal to let me know what he wanted, to discover what I was going to do, and to make me do what he wanted done. He brought into play his teeth, his nose, his eyes, his head, his whole body, and, perhaps most of all, his voice: he cultivated a repertoire of sounds by means of which he intended me to understand him, and the seriousness of his intention could never be mistaken. Within the limits of his vocal range, Logos articulated most of the possibilities of sound, both in gradation and in volume. He did so, I think, primarily to multiply the ways in which he could communicate with me.

From our earliest hours together Logos became accustomed to the flow of sound I directed to him. All his life I talked to him quite naturally, and he listened to me carefully. Not only did he seem to be trying to understand what I said: he succeeded so often that chance withers away as an explanation.

Logos taught himself to understand an unbelievably extensive range of the straightforward English I spoke to him, just as he taught himself to understand what can be called 'the implications' of whatever I did. I mean only that I did not instruct him in any deliberate way, certainly not by conditioning him. I conclude that Logos learned what he knew by means similar to those human beings used: he observed me ("studied me," a friend once said); and he drew conclusions about what I generally did in certain recurring situations when they affected him. How, exactly, he understood so much of what I said, I do not yet try to explain. Yet Logos understood me by any tests anyone would wish to devise in deciding whether human beings understand one another, short of requiring him to speak English or French or . . . But then, as most philosophers will tell you, no one yet knows what it is for human beings to understand one another.

One day while Logos was still alive I tried to write out a list of all the phrases and sentences he understood. When I filled two pages, containing roughly a hundred requests, announcements, and questions, I shook my head and never went back to the task. It was not the number of sentences (certainly not the number of words) that could measure Logos' intelligence: it was the fact that his *intention* to understand whatever I said to him was almost palpable. People who watched Logos listen to me invariably caught their breaths, then laughed in nervous surprise. Because Logos listened to me as one person listens to another, and the way he went off to do the thing I asked him to do was not spit-and-polish obedience at all but a way that could only be described as attentive and appropriate. In a word: as intelligent. That intention to understand is currently the basis of much philosophical work on the nature of human language, but I have yet to read an unbiased reason for confining it to human understanding of language. In philosophical terms, attentiveness and appropriate response may be necessary conditions for understanding without also being sufficient conditions. But then, conditions that are both necessary and sufficient are very rare in any science, let alone in that art of psychology that passes for science. Logos kept on learning new things, and he did so not because I set aside a certain part of each day to teach him but because he could.

Logos did other things that are considered intelligent when human beings do them. He initiated actions of his own. He chose among alternatives presented to him. He invented games. He knew how to pretend. He grasped the way something was done after seeing it done only once. He figured out ways to alter an unfavorable situation so that it served his best interests. He successfully predicted many of my actions long before I actually entered upon them. That he was in as nearly constant a communication with me as a human being would be, that his pervasive intention was to be in (non-physical) contact with me, was merely one more aspect, although perhaps the driving one, of his being minded.

I will be pardoned if my description of Logos' intelligence does not conform to the prevailing views of what nonhuman animal intelligence consists in. Ethologists base their views about what nonhuman animals can or cannot understand on the views of linguists (and occasionally philosophers) whose theories are about human language and human intelligence. They gloss over the point that the concept of understanding a language remains opaque even for human beings, and they seem unaware that the views of linguists are cluttered with unsupportable assumptions.

Dictionaries will tell you that ethology is the science of animal behavior. The very definition exemplifies the problem that has occupied my philosophical interest for more than two decades. Because the proper definition is: the science of nonhuman animal behavior.

'Nonhuman' preceding 'animal' affirms that both human and nonhuman beings are members of the same biological kingdom: we are all animals. Ethologists impatiently grant the point when they consider their subject only in strictly biological terms: they know that a pig embryo at a certain stage of development is indistinguishable from a human embryo at a comparable stage. But ethologists don't study genetics or physiology or anatomy or embryology: they study behavior, what (nonhuman) animals do. (When you see the word 'nonhuman' in parentheses from now on, you'll know that it's my correction to what ethologists would be saying if they were to speak precisely.)

Now, it's certainly easy to pick out nonhuman animals from human ones: most of them look different from us. And those that swim and those that fly and those that customarily walk on all fours do many things differently from the way we do. None of this needs to be said.

But then ethologists smuggled in another belief so obvious, they implied, that it too did not need saying because everyone knows it to be true: human beings are superior to (nonhuman) animals. This assumption appears over and over in a hundred disguises in the writings of ethologists. Sometimes its bare skin shows. It was, it remains, so firmly held, so deeply buried in every aspect of every piece of research, every hypothesis, every conclusion, every chunk of theorizing, that most practicing ethologists would assent to it if confronted by it and would at the same time wonder why I bother to mention it.

According to them, human superiority is apparent merely by our possession of language. (Ignore for the moment what counts as language.) By virtue of being able to talk, write letters, read books, pass and obey laws, the stupidest human being is superior to (not just smarter than) any nonhuman animal of no matter what level of "intelligence." And they place double quotes around the word, these theorists do, to signal readers that they too know that the word doesn't really apply to the creatures being talked about.

But this assumption of human superiority is not innocuous. Nor is the belief, by now considerably pared back, on which it is based: that only human animals possess language.

I began reading what has now become a vast literature on (nonhuman) animal behavior when Logos was still with me, still young, still surprising me every day. I spent uncountable hours observing him, wondering what could explain the astonishing creativity of his intelligence. Was it the circumstances of his and my life together? Was it rather his own natural endowment? Perhaps the way I chose to deal with him? Or some combination of all these? I therefore had extensive hands-on experience in and reflection on a matter that absorbed my attention for its own sake. I turned to ethology with the expectation that persons who spent their lives studying nonhuman animals, as I spent mine thinking and writing, could illuminate it for me.

The first thing I learned was that Logos was not intelligent: he was merely conditioned to respond in order to avoid pain or to obtain whatever reward to which I had conditioned him: food, stroking, a dry bed. He was not intelligent because he was not capable of being conscious of himself, and also (or was it 'therefore'?) he was not capable of using language. It was the same old line: nothing had changed since Pavlov, and he himself had merely frozen into supposedly objective terms the orthodox view of Claude Bernard, who had accepted it from Descartes, and he from Aristotle.

I laughed out loud.

It did not take long for me to recognize that the animal behaviorists' assertions about (nonhuman) animal communication were taken straight from the pages of linguists who wrote about human communication. The number and kinds of philosophical problems that lay unnoticed on the pages of ethologists reporting research supposedly as objective as any conducted by, say, physicists, bore an astounding resemblance to those I had just finished collecting, analyzing, and writing about in my *Hornbook of Hazards for Linguists*. My purpose there had been to bring these very problems to light so that linguists (and engineers and psychologists and others involved in the research) would understand them to be philosophical.

But philosophical problems aren't resolved by merely opting for one solution over another, or by merely quoting one philosopher's view rather than another's, as many linguists then did, as many still do. Philosophical problems require clarification, not experimentation. More carefully still: they require clarification first, so that what can be experimented with or on is sorted out from that which does not permit experimentation or cannot yet support experimentation. Requiring clarification means that concepts, muddy and otherwise, irrelevant and otherwise, are all tangled up together. Who is to know which is which until someone whose work it is, who has the appropriate skills to untangle what does not belong together, subjects it all to hard thinking, sorts it all out? You can't know what's true until you know what you mean. One of the outcomes of a philosopher's clarification of scientific work is that it brings into the open the assumptions that underlie, and may thus bias, research that prides itself on not taking anything for granted unless it has previously been shown to be warranted by careful experiment. But no matter how painstakingly a scientist may conduct an experiment, if his or her hypotheses hide unexamined assumptions, contain concepts the clarification of which is in dispute, then the results obtained are as tainted as though the researcher had ignored contrary cases in publishing the outcome.

Human reasoning can go wrong in two major ways. It can be formally invalid, by breaking any of the well-known canons of formal inference. Or it can be materially fallacious, resting on various kinds of ambiguity or illusions of proof. Formal fallacies are gratifyingly rare in scientific books and articles. Material fallacies, however, are frequent, although they're almost never deliberate. Most often they occur because certain concepts crucial to the science have not been adequately clarified. The job is one for philosophers, who gladly appropriated it early in the twentieth century, thereby adding the new field of philosophy of science to their traditional work.

So I was simply doing one of the things philosophers do when I noticed that most of the befuddlements I had carefully pointed out to linguists were making their appearance in the work of ethologists. In much the same way that cloudy concepts rendered suspect the linguistic hypotheses or conclusions containing them, ethological hypotheses and conclusions were discredited for relying on the identical concepts.

I understood why it had been done. The task of studying the behavior of all animals except human ones is staggering. The biological kingdom *Animalia* includes about 8,700 species of birds; among land mammals there are, to start, some 3,000 species of rodents and 290 species of carnivores; marine mammals alone fall into 117 species. What a break, what a lessening of original labor, if ethologists could simply adopt whole-hog the most current views in linguistic theory, and then fit them somehow into the (nonhuman) animal behavior they were busily recording and analyzing and reporting on. After all, linguists too believed that (nonhuman) animals were incapable of devising and using language. The whole thing worked out very well.

But understanding why it had been done didn't mean I could condone it.

Lorenz and Tinbergen by their pioneering work established ethology as a field and named it. Lorenz discovered that, if their mother is not present, newly hatched greylag goslings will follow the first moving creature they see, no matter that it is tall hulking German smoking a pipe. Tinbergen discovered that it is the red dot under the mother's beak (and nothing else about her) that prompts herring gull chicks to peck at it, thereby motivating her to disgorge the food she holds in her craw, food she has in fact brought for them to eat. Men and women thereupon eagerly studied and reported on eating and nesting and mating behavior for as many (nonhuman) animal species as were accessible. All this was considered to be noncommunicative behavior. Communicative behavior was something else again. Here, too, a genius led the way. Human beings had been keeping bees and stealing their honey since recorded time, yet only in the middle of the twentieth century did von Frisch discover that the dances of honey bees, by their patterns and speeds, tell other members of the hive in what direction and how far away nectar is to be found, and the telling is so precise that the bees immediately go off and find the nectar while the dancer remains behind.

The limitations ethologists placed on what they would consider communicative behavior in (nonhuman) animals and what is thus communicated blur a distinction philosophers make between acts and actions. When I, not knowing a stove is hot, touch it, then reflexly draw my hand away, I have performed an act: I have done something primarily because of the neurological and physiological patterns of my body. If, however, I walk over hot coals barefoot, having trained myself to ignore or otherwise gain ascendancy over the pain, I have performed an action: I have done something primarily because I am able to consciously project a goal for myself and then work to achieve it.

According to ethologists, nonhuman animals are not consciously aware of what they do and so they cannot perform actions. Ethology therefore had no need to distinguish between acts and actions: animals could only act, could do things only in line with their built-in, hard-wired instincts, and they could learn only whatever was consonant with those instincts.

It is not logically impossible for a nonhuman animal to be conscious: nothing in the concept of a nonhuman animal forbids it. No experimental evidence provides a high degree of probability, let alone proves, that nonhuman animals are not conscious. Tests capable of proving with certainty whether a creature is alive or dead cannot distinguish among living creatures those that are conscious from those that are not, except by criteria heavily loaded in favor of human beings. To assert therefore that nonhuman animals are not conscious, cannot have purposes, cannot intend to fulfill them, cannot perform actions, is to do what logicians call 'stipulating.' A stipulation doesn't require being argued for: it's a mere declaration that something is the case. When you stipulate, you're announcing that you're stacking the cards. You do so in order to explore paths the stipulation may open up. Sometimes the fresh territory is glorious to look at, but its price is the stipulation you carry every inch of the way: you've obtained the view by fiat, not by fact. The honest thing to do is to go back to the starting place and try to find the evidence that will turn your stipulation into an hypothesis, then test it to see whether it lets you walk unencumbered on the same land where only the aid of a crutch let you enter before.

Ethologists were not aware they were stipulating. They certainly were unaware of the thicket of problems now polluting their work by their having imported current linguistic theories into their research without examining them. Not being philosophers, they weren't equipped to subject those theories from another field to hard analysis. Let alone closely examine any of the rest of the concepts they worked with every day. Only rarely did a Menzel, working with rhesus monkeys, or a Fentress, working with timber wolves, publish some doubts about the methods and the theoretical framework of the field. Only as late as 1972 did Donald Griffin raise the question of animal awareness, and then in 1984 title another book *Animal Thinking*.

But I am a philosopher and I saw the problems. I had laid bare whole segments of the conceptual foundations of linguistics, even though I was not a linguist. I now began to lay bare the conceptual foundations of ethology. Without university or foundation support, of course.

And then Logos died, and I fled with Ousia to Maine. Not to forget him: I do not even now forget him. And I was still, from that long distance, gathering the evidence that would let me file suit against the veterinarians whose conflicting and ambiguous and unsubstantiated statements were preventing me from discovering why and at what time of what day and how Logos died. I was in Maine for no good reason.

In Maine a man pointed out to me that I had two heads.

Because while I was busily uncovering vaguenesses and ambiguities and inconsistencies in the writings of ethologists, I was engaging in some inconsistencies of my own. I was killing non-human animals left and right.

Not that I severed a chicken's neck from its body. Not that I took a heavy mallet and brought it down on a cow's head as she turned her terrified eyes up at me, lying at the bottom of a chute she had been forced to slide down. Not that I took a three-week-old calf from its mother and placed it in a cage too small for it to turn around, left it in the dark, fed it a diet so lacking in minerals that it chewed the iron bars of its confining cage, all so that when I'd slaughter it four months later its flesh would be pale and would bring me the price of choice veal. Not that I placed eight or ten chickens in a cage too small for even one of them, the cage's bottom sloping downward from all four sides so that the eggs could be more easily gathered even though the chickens could never stand upright, and, in the ferocious crowding, would peck one another to death, the feathers at their necks worn through to the skin from having to slide their heads between the narrow bars of the cage to reach the corn in the trough attached to the outside. Not that I myself ulcerated the eyes of rabbits by pouring shampoo into them to test whether it might burn my own eyes, to render it tear-free for me. Not that I left Pacific spotted or spinner porpoises to die, fighting to regain the safety of the ocean, when they were caught in the nets of men who were fishing for tuna.

And yet I conspired in all this agony and death: I put money into the hands of persons who did the killing and torturing for me. I sautéed carefully chosen portions of chickens' bodies. I ate the eggs collected from the nadir of their cages. I stewed cubic sections of the backs and chests and thighs of cows; I used their cured and tanned skins to walk in and to carry my money in and to sit on and to wear over my shoulders and around my waist, and I admired and coveted books bound in them. For the care of my body and the enhancement of my beauty I used oils and creams and waxes extracted from the bodies of animals after death. Sometimes, as with the musk I used in scent, the animals were alive while the material was drawn from them.

Part of the reason I did not notice the inconsistency myself was that I thought I was doing everything possible to prevent harm to nonhuman animals. I did not wear furs, once shaming a friend for the mink coat her husband had just given her. I fought hunters wherever I could, singing noisily in the woods in late autumn to warn the deer, provoking arguments with hunters so that they'd see themselves as they were: only bullies, only relieving themselves of family burdens for long weekends of getting drunk with the boys outdoors. Their faces reddened as they turned away from me, cursing, or, more often, cursing me before they turned away. They would not answer why they were not content (if hunting is a sport) simply to sight a deer along the barrel of a gun, knowing thereby that they had matched wits with a wild creature, why they then had to pull the trigger, why they carried ammunition at all.

I railed against zoos where lions who in the wild prowled an easy thirty miles a day were confined to cages wide enough only for three paces in one direction and three in the other, deep enough only for them to sprawl at a diagonal while they slept. I detested rodeos, where steers and horses are made to buck only because their penises are held tightly against their abdomens by the flank strap: they stop bucking the instant the strap is loosened.

I had two heads, you see. One was for Logos and Ousia first of all. It included cats and horses and wild creatures. The other was for: but ah, I did not even know it was there.

The man who noticed it was my landlord in Maine. As a boy he had worked in his father's greenhouse, which he later inherited and was prospering in when I knew him. He had never, I think, taken a course in logic.

The house I rented from him lay a dozen yards above high tide on an inlet to Muscongus Bay. Only two other houses occupied the spit of land. One, barely visible behind white pines a few hundred feet off the rutted gravel path that was my driveway, was lived in year-round by a pleasant older couple whom I saw only occasionally. The other, considerably closer, was owned by my landlord who, although audible and visible when he and his family spent a few hours or overnight, was almost never there.

One Sunday afternoon I drove slowly along the unpaved road-way toward my house, Ousia with me in the car, Logos not: Logos buried on a hill three hundred miles away while I, every minute of every hour of the six months since he had died, since he had been left to die, tried to understand what had happened, could not let him die until I understood. My landlord's car came into sight as I maneuvered the final distance. I did not want to talk to him, to anyone. At that moment he happened to come around the back of his house, saw me, and came toward me. He spoke of some business connected with my house, then on impulse invited me to join him and his wife for dinner on their porch overlooking the water.

"Come by in about an hour," he said. "We're just grilling hamburgers."

I fed Ousia, left her in the house, and at six o'clock crossed around to his door, searching my mind for subjects to talk about. My mind held only one subject, and I would not talk about Logos with my landlord, who knew nothing about him, then or ever, not even that he used to walk the earth. Not-Logos, then, would be our subject. So flowers or Washington or the nearness of the Thomaston prison. I knocked on the door.

At the end of the meal I told my hosts about the hunter I had seen across the cove a little north of where we sat. "Yesterday morning. I yelled at him to go away: I walk near the water here every day with Ousia. I'm sure I surprised him. He started to lower his rifle, and then he shouted something at me. I couldn't make it out but I guessed what he said because he didn't move. I told him I was going to stand there until he left. And when he was gone, I went home and called the game warden."

My landlord's wife was silent, but he spoke. "I don't hunt anymore: I don't have time. But people have been hunting around here as long as I can remember."

"They're not going to be hunting in my backyard. Ousia is here. I'm here. We're outdoors half a dozen times a day."

My landlord opened with the first of the standard arguments for hunting, and I countered with the standard refutation. Back and forth we went in that contrapuntal discussion that parallels the arguments for and against the existence of God, where knowledgeable opponents argue to a draw, one of them declaring, "Nevertheless, I believe," and the other, "And I do not."

Even if the meal hadn't been at an end, it quickly became time to leave. My landlord walked me toward my driveway.

"Thanks for dinner," I said.

"We had hamburgers, so you eat animals. Why do you care when people hunt them?"

"Well, that's different," I said, and went home.

Ousia and I walked around the shore before high tide came in. You eat animals. But that's different. You eat animals. But that's.

The words came into my head and stayed there all the way home, all the time of preparing for bed, all the hours of trying to fall asleep. They were there when I opened my eyes in that darkness long before dawn that is my time for awakening, but now I heard myself saying, "It's not different at all."

By the time the sky was becoming pale grey, Ousia and I were already prowling the nearby deserted logging road to the north. Then we headed south, curving eastward to what passed for a hill in that flat landscape, except that, when you finally made your way through the blueberry bushes that covered its rise, you could look out over the bay, could watch the sun begin to light up the water and the world for another day.

At home I opened the refrigerator door. A cellophane-wrapped package of chicken breasts rested on the top shelf. Suddenly I saw the pinkish-white skin as devoid of feathers, the breast cavities as having held a heart and lungs, as mine still do, as having once been connected to other viscera, to a brain in a head, to legs. The chicken that had been was no less an animal than Logos had been, than Ousia was, than I myself was: all merely animals, they merely nonhuman, I merely nonphasianid, merely noncanid.

I did not become a vegetarian in that moment. I had become

one during the night at some point between my landlord's taunt and my awakening. But holding that package of the parts of what used to be a living creature let me understand in matchlessly concrete terms that during the hours since dinner the evening before I had made a decision that was forever irrevocable.

No living creature would ever again, because of me, suffer pain. No living creature would ever again die because I paid other people to kill him or her, then used words like 'beef,' 'pork,' 'leather,' 'veal' to clothe my conspiracy, words that gave me a second head with eyes that would not see, ears that would not hear.

I stopped thinking of the dismembered body in the package in my hands as food. It was the last death I bought. It was the first step along a route all the branchings and byways of which were yet to be disclosed to me.

What to eat was a problem for little less than a week. Three years earlier, Adelle Davis' writings had already revolutionized my way of eating. Millions of other people had changed their lives because of her well-substantiated but impossibly titled books on nutrition. I, however, had a digestive tract five or six feet shorter than normal. Twice my doctor had surgically removed diseased segments of my intestine, then anastomosed the divided ends, prescribing for me the only diet medicine then approved: white bread, crusts removed; white rice; no whole grains in any form; no nuts; no raw fruit or vegetables; some vegetables forbidden; all vegetables to be cooked to maximum softness, then mashed or puréed. I was also daily taking the highest sanctioned dose of a drug made from belladonna. This regimen would not cure my disease: it would only hold it more or less in check. And if the disease worsened, we'd cut out another piece of intestine, then take up the diet and the drug again. People didn't die of my disease, but it dictated the timing of almost every activity of my day and it would accompany me to my grave.

Adelle Davis argued for whole grains in bread and pasta and

cooked or raw as cereals. Vegetables and fruits were to be eaten in unlimited variety, raw whenever possible, their skins not peeled but merely scrubbed. When cooked, only brief steaming was needed, and the cooking water was to be saved and reused because it contained some of the nutrients formerly in the food. Now, fifteen years after my surgery, it's the diet doctors prescribe for the illness I used to have. At the time I would have had to defy my doctor to adopt it. Still, with his diet, I was totally at the mercy of my gut, which could never improve. With hers, others far more sickly than I had already become healthy.

I did not die the day I ate my first salad in ten years. I was not even in pain while the forbidden roughage made its way along the length of my shortened gut. After that, the rules about what I should or shouldn't eat were easier to break. Because up to the moment that my teeth came together on that first leaf of lettuce, that first chunk of fresh tomato, I had obeyed doctors my whole life long. Thereafter, I became the final judge of what to do with my body: I took back the authority over my health that I long ago gave to medicine by not having known that sound alternatives existed. Now I look first to nutrition. It was nutrition that let me cure the disease medicine had told me I'd have to tolerate to the end of my days. Nutrition's research is as scientific as medicine's; it is in fact part of medicine, even though medicine ignores it. From time to time I consult a doctor. I attend seriously to his or her analysis of test results, diagnosis of what I have not been able to assess myself, advice about what I in consequence ought to do. But then I pit my opinion against his or hers. It still feels a little like standing on a bridge while you're building it: at the unfinished edge you see only open water beneath you.

Considered solely in terms of food, therefore, my decision not to eat the dead bodies of the other animals required only a comparatively small modification to a way of eating already familiar to me. But the vow I had taken in Maine during a sleepless night wasn't simply about eating: it was about not contributing to the killing of other animals, not participating in any way in any action that might bring them pain.

I now have one head only.

If you see me wearing, holding, or sitting on a leather object, you know it's at least fourteen years old. I have in fact given away my leather clothes and gloves and purses. Three belts I bought twenty-five years ago still hang in my closet, but I almost never wear them. The perfect chair I bought for my perfect desk has a removable leather seat that I suppose could be replaced with canvas, if the store from which I bought it is still in business. But food and shelter have made more pressing demands on me, and anyway, arrangements are in place for that chair to go to the friend who will also inherit my desk, and so I almost don't think of either object as mine any longer.

Shoes and handbags become a problem when I need them. The triennial project of buying my pair of plain black pumps, my black purse, can last weeks, going in and out of stores in spare half-hours when other matters take me near some shopping center.

A clerk approaches me.

"I'm looking for black shoes, medium heels, not leather."

She examines me briefly before replying. I look and sound as though I could afford leather, and yet . . . "We sell only leather shoes," she says. A certain note has crept into her voice.

"Do you have a dog at home?" I ask. No. "A cat?" A cat; birds.

"Why don't you walk around in their skins?"

Occasional silence. Occasional glimmer from having heard me.

"Think about it," I say. I turn and walk out of the shop.

From time to time (and only after a silence) a clerk will ask: "Why not leather?"

"No animal has to be killed to keep my feet dry and clean," I answer. Or, ". . . to let me carry my money around."

The professional face momentarily becomes aware of having

two heads. I stay and talk a while, then. I doubt that people I encounter this way stop selling leather shoes because of me, yet I continue to prepare the ground, to drop the seed.

My new shoes and purses and belts and books and chairs are canvas or nylon or vinyl. And yes, sometimes they need replacing sooner, but they also dry faster.

My shampoo has not destroyed the corneas of rabbits, and anyway, I'm not so clumsy that I can't confine shampoo to my hair. No law, federal or state or local, requires manufacturers of shampoos, toothpastes, detergents, or cosmetics to test their products on nonhuman animals to prove them harmless before selling them to human beings: there are other ways to prove them harmless. Nonhuman animals are maimed, tormented, and destroyed because human beings do not know that it is being done, do not protest to the internationally known corporations that do it, continue to buy products that result from it.

Do you use skin cleansers, masks, fresheners, lotions, moisturizers? Perhaps bath oils, tanning lotions, body powders, nail polish? Surely makeup base, blusher, lipstick, powder, eye shadow, eyeliner? How about perfume, cologne, after-shave? No federal law requires manufacturers (who fight the proposal) to label cosmetics that contain segments and products of and were tested on nonhuman animals, but you can be sure they do if they carry no label to the contrary. Everything from lipsticks to lotions can be manufactured without killing other animals or using them or parts of them in any way. With minimal effort you can find out the names of the more than eighty companies whose products are cruelty-free and where you can buy them.

Nor do I acquiesce in the experimental use of primates, dogs, cats, mice, guinea pigs, so that new surgical techniques and drugs can benefit human beings. Acute toxicity tests using nonhuman animals, bound by chains, their vocal cords cut so the experimenters won't hear their cries, correlate poorly with human traumas and therefore are useless when extrapolated. In vitro methods and those using mathematical models are available and more accurate.

They also happen to be less costly. Not only to the creatures who pay with their pain and their lives. But to you who pay for the purchase of each creature, its cage, and its upkeep, which includes the salaries of technicians, custodians, and experimenters who would otherwise be productively employed.

I hold an uncommon belief about living creatures: they are not "things," and hence they are not ownable. No one therefore has a right to use them in any way, particularly if, when they cannot give their informed consent, they might suffer harm of any sort or die. The earliest records of human history show that victors with skin colors that ranged from pale pink through black made slaves of those they vanquished, whose skin colors ranged from black through pale pink. The spoils of war, they said. Little more than a century ago people in one part of the Unites States owned human beings. By virtue of our superiority, and of course by economic necessity, they said. People in other parts of the United States believed that human beings are not ownable, matched their belief against those who believed the contrary, and won. Now, except for South Africa, it is the common belief throughout the world. Uncommon beliefs of a certain sort have a way of becoming commoner over the course of time, but they are not less right before they become common. The price of the product to which the former slaves unwillingly contributed their labor goes up for a time, as cotton did, but then it levels off and soon declines again. By then, those who grow and sell the product have found some other way to do it. We call it human ingenuity.

For its own sake. It is how I love. It is how I work. Through the single thread of my commitment to nonhuman animals and the natural world, I weave together my work and my love, living with no demarcation between them, as much one as I can make them.

Persisting in unifying my life holds no religious significance for me. It is, rather, a moral and an intellectual pursuit. Moral, in being about the kind of person one is or can become. Intellectual, in being unceasingly concerned to clarify and to bring together into one consistent whole what would otherwise be the erratically joined parts of my mind and my actions, each within each, each to each. The philosopher I am is inextricably entwined with the person I am.

10

CONNECTING

YOU WILL FIND it all but impossible to depart from this most seductive of all the stations of solitude. I urge you not to head for it until after you have stopped at least at these others: begin the new constructing, know the intimate rhythms of your day and where you are at home, find your work, uncover your source of income. (I hesitate to promise you comparable gain from the station we just left: you may not be equivalently drawn to singling, may stop there only casually to look it over before moving on.) If you alight here first, your connectings to other human beings will heavily influence, may fully determine, your decisions about what work you do, where you live, when you start your day, why you love, and how you earn your money, and so the odds are very high that you will never leave.

But is it possible to choose the ways you will connect with other persons? Don't you simply like some, like others more, like still others not at all? Aren't you now connected to other human beings? And aren't those connectings unalterable? Yes, yes, yes, and no.

After you unbind at the first station and stand open at the second, you will no longer be the same person who set foot upon the line of travel. Some of the people you knew before may not like that outcome, may quietly walk away. You yourself may end connectings that will then seem spurious to you. Other persons you knew before may afterward mean more to you. Some may not understand until you explain, but they'll be willing to see whether the old connecting can be modified to adapt to the partner you now are.

Any and all of these eventualities are exceedingly likely to occur. I have given you fair warning. If that frightens you, you will, I think, abandon the prospect of coming to know who you are and who you can become, and I shall have lost you as a companion at the stations that remain. But if you decide to make your own circuit after all, bear in mind that there is a profusion of ways to connect to other people, that you may not yet have tried them, may not know they exist. It could be an adventure.

For perhaps a whole year after Nantucket, there were only two ways that other people could divert me from constructing the new life that was my preoccupying priority. They could be on my side, be with me. Or they could come crashing up against me, against my purposes, against Logos. Everyone else was simply other-than-I, not-I. In point of logic, it is the minimal way of marking the difference between two entities: it merely separates off one of them from everything else. Until I figured out all the other possible ways there are to be with other people and which of them were worth trying, until I got around to fitting other people into my scheme of how I would be in the world, I noticed people no more than to draw in my skirts a little so that I wouldn't brush too closely as we passed one another in the course of my going about earning my living, becoming at home in the country, finding and then doing my work, loving Logos, buying the goods and services that kept us fed and sheltered and healthy.

Almost from the day I rented his house, Tommy Phillips riveted my attention by being so completely himself. When you know how to do ten thousand things, as Tommy does, you tend to believe that everybody else should know at least a thousand of them. During the six years he was my landlord he was there for me to turn to when household emergencies arose, but there is of course a great deal of leeway in construing what counts as an emergency. Water not draining out of a tub was pretty low on Tommy's list of things that needed doing. Water leaking through a ceiling could get him to my house instantly.

Where he assessed the matter, touching, looking, listening, closing the master circuit breaker that he, with Olive's help, had installed, closing off the inflow of water at the main valve, then phoning one of his friends. His friends are the plumbers, the carpenters, the well diggers, the plasterers, the painters he's known for fifty years. All of them owned, still own, vast tracts of land in the town and, retiring from their occupations in the years since, have sold off parcels of their real estate at great profit. Some of them moved away; many remain, still driving their pickup trucks, wearing work clothes and old sweaters, the holes sometimes darned and sometimes not, plowing driveways for the newer residents who can afford the now exorbitant cost of living in Weston only by commuting daily to their New York offices, not realizing that each Jim or Tom or Anson or Rocky they hire as a workman has at least as much money in the bank as they.

Plumbers never answer their phones on Saturdays, but that Saturday the plumber arrived in fifteen minutes. He and Tommy sawed open the ceiling to look for the break in the line, the loose seal at a joint, the pinhole in the copper piping that was causing the leak. For several hours there was much coming and going of trucks and helpers. In between, Tommy went out into the backyard where Logos was waiting for me to play, dipped his ungloved hands into the snow and threw snowballs for Logos to chase. I watched, laughing, loving the gift for the spontaneity with which it was given.

It took me a while to figure out how to deal with Tommy. The trick was that first I had to try to fix the thing myself. That could require my figuring out how to dismantle the offending part so that

I could take it along to a hardware or building-supply store ("I need one of these"); learning the names of objects I never knew existed ("The circuit breaker?"); acquiring hammers, wrenches, screwdrivers, pliers, files, and learning what each of them can do. All this gained me a repertoire of skills not ordinarily part of a woman's education, let alone a woman who had spent most of her time in libraries and in apartments looked after by someone else.

Only when Tommy was convinced I had done everything I could possibly do myself could I persuade him to listen to my problem when I'd call. Even then, whether or when he'd fix whatever had gone wrong was completely his to decide. If he thought it could wait, waiting might melt into months. Then one morning I'd look out my study window to see his yellow truck pulling in and Tommy getting out, singing to himself as he rummaged in the side panels among the layers of boxes for the tools he'd need.

On the other hand, ask him not at all and he was there to do something I didn't even know could be done.

One bright summer afternoon I looked up from my book to hear a heavy piece of machinery slowly climbing the hill in front of my house. By the time I reached the window giving onto the scene, Tommy, sitting high on his tractor, was turning into the upper entry of my horseshoe driveway. Logos and I raced outside.

"Hello, bad dog," said Tommy, barely looking at us, intent on guiding his equipment around the boulder jutting out of the front lawn. When he was clear of it, he gazed for a moment at the erratic pattern of cedars marking the woods' edge, then he lowered the mowing bar and began cutting a path through the hip-high grass. I closed Logos into the run and followed along behind, grinning, circling, anticipating Tommy's line of travel. Like a great caterpillar, the tractor munched its way up the low incline, around to the left, the west, across what was once a farmed meadow, turning again to the east, lumbering along and yet carving out a path, a place for me to walk on ground that had become all but impassable once the life of early summer rose ever upward out of the soil. On he went, down a small hill, through the barway in the stone wall, along the stone fence itself, and then around the entire clearing, the place in the woods where Logos loved best to jump over the stone walls to retrieve a stick or a ball. When Tommy turned to retrace his route, he widened the path wherever a tree didn't interrupt his forward movement all the way back to his starting point at my driveway.

"Tommy!" I yelled above the roaring motor. "Thanks!"

He did not pause except to check for traffic, then clanked onto the road, down the hill, around the curve, and was gone. He might have heard me. It didn't matter. He knew that those woods were an essential part of my every day. He knew how high the wild grasses grow in summer and the month in which they became a maximum impasse to me and Logos. He had seen the hand scythe I had bought a few days earlier, and he had watched, seeming not to, saying no word, as I made mighty efforts to cut my own path, cautious of the blade but getting the knack of it. It can take fifteen minutes and a lot of sweat to clear only a few square feet of very high grass, but I kept working at the scything while Tommy went about his errand, unaware that he had even seen me. I was still too ignorant to know that the edge of my new tool could have been vastly improved, that its inexpensiveness should have been a clue to how dangerous it was, that a good tool is expensive exactly because knowledgeable hands can use it for its purpose safely and for a long time. I was also too new at understanding Tommy to realize that I had done everything necessary, including not asking, to have him hook the mowing bar onto his tractor, drive the quarter-mile to my house, and spend half an hour in my woods making a path for Logos and me for no reason other than that he knew I wanted it.

I discovered the unpaved road near my house within a few weeks of moving in. It was a mile or so long, and Logos and I walked its length at least twice a day for more than two years. I knew where all the puddles would form after a rain, I cherished the sweep of trees visible from a certain curve, the water of the millpond at its north end was familiar to me in every weather and every light, I drank up the undiluted peace of the natural pool, a perfect oval, at the bottom of a gentle slope along its grassy border. I knew that road as intimately as any of the rooms of my house. It was in fact a kind of dwelling place for me, and every change in it was as perceptible to me as though someone were to have moved a chair in my study during my absence.

The narrowness, the ruts, the dust ready to drift upward from the toss of a pebble during a dry spell, the rocks dislodged by cars and horses and perhaps by Logos and me, and even the loneliness of the road, made cautious drivers out of the few people whose regular route it was. I chose it for our walks because any automobile chancing along was so audible in advance that I could, almost at my leisure, get Logos off the road onto one of its edges where he knew to sit without budging until the car passed, even though its top speed was probably no more than twenty miles an hour.

Walking that road at the same time every day I came to know some of those drivers. In the beginning they tooted their horns lightly when they were approaching from behind, as though seconds earlier I hadn't heard the crunch of their wheels against the gravel. I'd call Logos to come to me and sit, and I'd wave to thank them as they passed. In time, I'd wave from a distance as soon as I recognized their cars. By the end of our first summer they were stopping to talk for a few minutes, usually about Logos or their own dogs, before they went on their way again.

Once for several weeks an illness hospitalized me. The morning after I returned home, Logos and I were halfway down the road when a car I suddenly recognized as Olive's pulled alongside.

"What are you doing here?" she demanded.

"Well, walking. Why not?"

"I took some breakfast to your house. I couldn't believe you weren't there, and then I thought you must be here."

A smile started on my face and grew and wouldn't stop. She had thought to bring me breakfast. And when I wasn't at home she had thought to look for me on my road.

"What's so funny?" she asked, getting out of her car.

"Are you going to walk with us?"

"You should be in bed. I'm going to make sure you get back there."

In her company we walked only a little farther before turning back. Over the next few days Logos and I resumed our usual pace and distance, and the drivers whose names I never knew stopped to ask why they hadn't seen us on the road.

New people I met in that town would say to me: "I see you with your dog on the Newtown Turnpike," or, "You're the woman who walks her dog on the dirt road."

"You've seen me?" I'd ask, startled more by that fact than that my essence was being summed up by a single one of my activities. I had thought myself unseen, if I thought about it at all. No one was awake that early when Logos and I ambled along the road. Of course there were the drivers each day. But I had assumed they were simply passing through. And there were the people in the scattering of houses on the road. But weren't they still asleep at six in the morning? And it was true that, when I returned from my office and scrambled out of my city clothes into jeans for our walk before dinner, cars were streaming past on the state highway at the road's north end. Who would have thought that in their hurry to get home they'd look up long enough to see me walking with Logos down what I continued to think of as a lonely road?

Equally startled was I to discover, when I resigned the job that required my daily presence in an organization miles away, that I had offended almost every person in the company by closing the door to my office. To me, I was preserving my silence against the typewriters, the ringing phones, the walking back and forth, the hallway conversations about medical problems or Maine weekends. But to my co-workers, I was announcing that I was not one of them. They could work with their doors open: their concentration was interruptible by any passerby who, seeing them bent over the papers on their desks, might return another time or, if the matter couldn't wait, might simply tap at the open door. Before my closed door (so I learned afterward), people hesitated to knock, turned away, let the matter wait until I myself opened the door on my way elsewhere.

I did not notice either of these groups of noticers of me as I walked with Logos or did the job I was being paid to do. I had not connected to any of them, and so I was astonished at their having connected to me, even so transiently as to have noticed me in my habitude.

For my early dealings with other people I appropriated a principle that was already a functioning part of my kip for buying the objects I was then acquiring: if I could pay the price, I could have the thing. Otherwise not. Or not then. Not that I paid only in cash: Bloomingdale's and Saks were willing enough to have me as a charge customer. Even so, I paid my bills the month they arrived, buying only what I could pay for that way.

I could have it if I could pay. I extended the principle almost unchanged from collecting objects to connecting with human beings.

I found Harold Wooster in the course of scouring the federal government for an agency that would support some (it didn't matter what) research project so that I'd no longer have to work with the now-petulant associate I had rebuffed at the contract research company in Stamford. Harold Wooster is a big man but carries too much weight, even for his six feet two. His speaking voice approaches basso, and his sentences, deliberately matter-of-fact, are perfectly formed in advance. He was bearded when no one else was, always first with the newest saying, the newest doing.

Four days after locating him at the Information Systems Directorate of the Air Force Office of Scientific Research, I was sitting across from him in Washington and being instructed from his matchless knowledge about the workings of the federal government.

"You're too late for this year," he said.

"But it's only September."

"Calendar years don't matter in Washington," he replied. "You have to think in fiscal years." That long ago the federal fiscal year began on July 1 and ended June 30. "We're into the first quarter of FY 64 already. And that's just the day the authorization begins. Appropriations are voted months earlier."

I must have looked puzzled.

"Were you out sick the day they taught civics? Before Congress can set money aside to run the country, agencies have to tell them how much we want and what we want it for. We don't actually get the money until the fiscal year begins. So you have to think about research funds a year in advance."

I'd have to put up with office politics for another year.

"But I like your project. It amuses me to think of what would happen if I were to let you loose among the flock of pompous pigeons already working in machine translation. Write me a proposal and assure me that the outcome will be something more than pot-pies and feathers. Just understand that the government moves without visible speed. Even if I funded you, you wouldn't have money until FY 65."

"July 1964, then?"

"Probably closer to October."

The grant began November 1, 1964. It let me leave the company that failed to give me the raise it had promised.

Although the grant money matched my former biweekly salary, it was in fact worth more because I no longer had the daily expenses of commuting, lunch, clothes. In exchange, all I had to do was write a report about the extent to which the factor of meaning had illicitly crept into the supposedly purely formal, syntactical rules of the linguists and other researchers who had been receiving federal money for years without yet having delivered a resolution to the problem of effectively and efficiently translating natural languages using only computers.

At that level, the exchange with Harold made no uncommon demands on me. I certainly knew how to write research papers: I had done it throughout graduate school without being paid.

But the federal grant was giving me more than money: I was free to work on a schedule of my own devising. I could be at home with Logos in the country every day, walking in the woods or working at my desk or at libraries whenever I chose. I could awaken when I finished sleeping, and I could go to bed when I was tired. And if I were ill or wanted to drive to Boston in the middle of the week or entertain a guest for a few days, I didn't have to plead with anyone for the time off.

I did not deliberately try to repay Harold for this total freedom, but I did in fact do so in terms he himself recognized.

By not having nattering restraints on my physical activities, I soon began to discard the leftover restraints on my thinking, my creativity. Beginning to describe for linguists the distinction logicians make between syntactic problems and semantic ones, I soon understood that I had proposed to do only one very small part of what needed doing: the researchers whose work I was analyzing were unknowingly dealing with philosophical problems. As though playing checkers using the rules for chess, they would play neither game properly.

Exploring the breathtaking scope of what I wanted to do, what I had already begun to do, I remembered Washington. They were paying me to do one project but I was now irrevocably doing another. Channeling the grant funds into the new path would require a year's extension. I'd ask for two. Weekends I could write about Nantucket. The prospect was almost unbearably intoxicating. How to get Harold's approval?

Harold said, "When we invest money in a piece of research, it's as much because of the person as the project the person proposes to do. The person who's really earning our money uses the proposal only as a jumping-off place. So you've already proved you were worth betting on. This new tack sounds more than just plausible: people might actually read your final report. Just write us another proposal for next year and call what you're doing now the results of the research you did under the first grant."

"You mean you'll fund me to write the *Primer*?"

"Is that what you call it?"

"*A Philosophical Primer for Grammarians.*"

On principle Harold doesn't laugh out loud. But the pipe that was always in his mouth moved over to the far side of his face.

"Neat," he allowed. "I can't promise that will be its name by the time you finish, because congressmen have to understand what we hand out the taxpayers' money for. But it will do for a kennel name. And yes, we'll give you money for next year."

I amazed myself at how calmly I nodded, when whooping around inside me was the full-bodied certainty of another year, two, exactly like the one I was then living: the country silence and beauty, being with Logos most of each day, writing, thinking.

The renewal didn't go through unhindered. Harold's assistant changed my title without consulting me. She also decided that one year, not two, would be "more realistic." Furious, I blistered a page of stationery to Harold, who quickly informed me that my proposal was approved unchanged and assigned another staff member to be my project monitor. Having retained his long tenure as a bureaucrat by learning all the rules for playing the game so that he could work without impediment in pursuit of the deeper purposes for which he believed governments exist, Harold gave me a few lessons. "When Captain What's-His-Name gets in touch with you, let him win some smaller points so that you can walk off with the big ones. And let him win first. That obligates him to you. He'll be anxious to be rid of the debt, so close quickly. Let him think he won more than you. And, for God's sake, smile when you put that rapier in."

I would have kissed him if we hadn't been talking on the phone.

For three years I flourished in this abundance. Harold met my household and I his. We spoke at length by phone and interspersed funny letters among the official ones. I kept him apprized of my progress and he kept the money coming in and let me alone. And when his office circulated the final report I sent him, the research community he oversaw considered it first-rate and of lasting value. Both of us shaped that outcome: I by writing and thinking, and Harold by his professionalism, his essential understanding of the job he was paid to do and his refusal to allow even friendship to intrude.

As such things go in Washington, Harold's office was in time closed down, he was transferred, and then he retired. During these two decades and more, we have remained in touch. Last month he was seventy.

"How can you be seventy?" I asked when we talked by phone on New Year's Day.

"Easy," he answered. "Wait till it happens to you."

I can have it if I can pay.

During all the years I was borrowing money until the next job came along, I kept meticulous records of what I owed to whom and for how long. And if, when I borrowed, I said I'd repay the money in two months or four months, and then the time passed without my being able to repay it, I'd call or write my friend-creditors so they'd know I wasn't buying stereo equipment with money they'd otherwise be able to invest for double-digit interest. One friend voluntarily opened her wallet almost every time we met for lunch or for one of our long walks, placing twenty-dollar bills on my lap, five or ten or fifteen at a time. Sometimes at my house she'd leave cash in the pages of the open books on my desk. I know she didn't keep track of how much she had given me, and I think she didn't expect me to repay her, but I wrote it all down. And when I was finally able to send her a check a few weeks before one Christmas, she was startled by the accumulated sum.

If buying is relevant when I want something but don't have the money, I offer something else instead. I can offer anything so long as it meets a single criterion: it must be as valuable to you as the money I'm asking you to forego. If you have some object I want, or if you know how to do something I want to know how to do, or if you can perform some task that I need done but can't give you money for, I start thinking very hard about you. What object do I have that you might want? What do I know how to do that I could teach you? What skill do I possess that I could turn to your needs? Because the money you want for that object, that skill, that task, is only one of the ways, the easiest way, the common way, to value it. But money is no more than solidified chunks of time: the time it took you to acquire the sum you give up when you buy; the time it took you to acquire the skill, the object, the knowledge when you sell. I simply have to discover one of the things you want but, like me, can't afford. Or hadn't thought to buy until I propose the exchange of our time.

I'm all but convinced that connections between human beings would be nearly perfect if people were to deal with one another in accordance with this principle, which gives close heed to the equivalent value of one another's time. It's really no more than the principle of barter, but I'm touting it for sustaining personal relationships as well as economic ones. Or rather: I'm construing personal relationships as economic ones.

Some people want only the money, and that's the end of the matter. Some are open to creative financing.

Bonnie is head swimming coach at the women's college where I for the time being have a peculiar affiliation: I have a title but no salary. Hence, none of the other perquisites of being on the payroll: health insurance at low or no cost, long-term loans for various worthwhile purchases. What I have is a college ID that gives me a parking sticker, use of the library and of the computers at whose keyboards I input onto floppy disks the complete text of this very book, and (for a fee) access to the spanking new and beautiful sports center.

Before the academic year began last September I examined the schedule for swimming classes and marched over to present myself as a student. Persons at the three levels of authority whose permissions I needed eyed me curiously, I being somewhat beyond the age of the entering freshwomen who enroll for beginners' swimming.

The reason I wanted to learn how to swim is that I held an abiding fear of deep water. When I was a child of three or four, and therefore not much more than two feet high, I sat at the top of a sliding board just offshore of a lake where my father stood chest-high in the water, encouraging me to slide down.

"Come on, honey." He smiled up at me, inviting me into his arms. "I'll catch you."

In the moment my slide began, someone called to my father and he looked away. In the next moment I was in the water unsupported by my father's arms and going down. How deep could the water have been if he were standing in it? How long could I have been beneath the surface before he scooped me up? Only deep enough, only long enough, to take precedence over every other fact about water in all subsequent years. Half a dozen times I tried to learn how to swim, but the day we'd go into deep water I'd sink, and that would end those lessons. Once, in my thirties, I did learn; I was even diving. When that good instructor went on vacation, I enrolled in a class at the nearest YWCA so that I wouldn't lose what had been so difficult to attain. At the first lesson the instructor asked me to demonstrate a stroke. I did.

"That's not how we do the sidestroke here," she said.

"That's how I was taught," I answered, suddenly apprehensive.

"Well, you're here now, and you'll do it this way." For twenty minutes she compelled me to unlearn the stroke on which my new confidence rested, the stroke I relied on to get me across deep water. At the end of the class I showered, dressed, and never returned.

Bonnie listened to the whole story and admitted me to the beginners' class. For three weeks I attended faithfully, amazed to rediscover, in the shallow end of the pool, that human bodies float. Then some business kept me away for two lessons, and when I returned, the rest of the class was ahead of me.

I approached Bonnie. "I'm a professional writer. Does your job require you to write anything?"

Bonnie is in her early thirties, a Vermonter, cool. In her spare time she volunteers for ambulance duty as an emergency medical technician. She regarded me calmly. "Occasional reports."

"Do you like doing them?"

She shrugged. My gambit didn't look promising.

"I thought that if you needed something written, I'd help you write it. Or I'd teach you how to write better, so that writing the next thing would be easier. I was hoping we could exchange skills: you'd teach me how to swim."

There *was* something she was writing. Not a report, not something for her job, but something that mattered to her. She had been planning to do it by enduring the doing. It had not occurred to her that it could be done otherwise.

We struck a deal. I knew her hourly rate for private lessons. Mine was higher, but I was willing to call it even, hour for hour. At first I kept track of each hour, and so did she. And then she understood, as I knew she would, that she'd be as satisfied by the outcome of my efforts as I'd be by hers.

Bonnie never talked about my fear. She merely hacked away at it by teaching me ways to handle myself in the water. A moveable bulkhead separates the college pool's diving well from the eight lanes for swimming at the other end. I now do laps, twenty-five-yard lengths, in the swimming end, eighteen or twenty consecutively, freestyle. The deepest water in the swimming end is exactly my height: I can keep my head above water only by standing on tiptoe. By the time this manuscript is in print, I may be diving. The second time I swam freestyle in the diving well, rolling my face back into the water to exhale each time I drew a breath, I looked down at the floor of the pool, fourteen feet and eight inches beneath me, and I thought, "Why, it's just like the floor of the pool at the other end."

The thing Bonnie and I are writing will be finished soon. Sooner than I'll be able to swim in the diving well without any vestige of fear. But each of us has removed the pain for the other from something important to the other. Each of us has received something of equivalent value to the thing we gave.

My connecting to other human beings occurs across a lengthy continuum. At one end, the connection is a mere brush, a moment's contiguity, a registering of the bare fact that we, the person I address and I, coexist. At the other, I give my full attention to the concerns of a friend who may not yet even have voiced his need for me.

Because I do not connect to one specific man, have not borne children, I explore all the other ways there are to connect to people. Instead of having an exclusive link to one other person, to a few other persons, I have a multitude of open-ended hooks on my being that can fasten me, sometimes lightly, sometimes searingly, to a stranger in an encounter that fleetingly connects us.

When I leave my house I'm out on the world. Not only, or not primarily, open to whatever entertainment might offer itself, but open to any incident, any person with whom my interest, my words, might connect, some happening that catches me up, stopping my normal forward haste long enough to try to figure out how it began, how it will end. I am open to any person, any creature, any fallen tree, that might conceivably need my attention: my hand, my car, my information, my phone call, my reassurance. I see the need because I've set myself to be perpetually alert to it. I do it because it's there needing to be done, not because some reward will accrue to me. In fact the very doing rewards me. I do not keep a balance sheet when I am on the giving end.

The woman was walking along a stretch of highway where everyone else was driving a car. She was black, while almost everyone was white in the town toward which she was walking. And she wore a short, tight skirt and high heels, spike heels. I took only a moment to register all this, to wonder about her, because I too was driving, hurrying home at the end of a hot day to take Kairos for our walk, sit quietly with him on the grass of a small park I knew, be free again after eight hours of moneying.

At home I changed out of office clothes and into jeans and sneakers, and, with Kai in the car, reentered the highway. And saw the woman again. She wasn't heading toward any of the stores and gas stations and low office buildings that studded both sides of the road, and she wasn't hitchhiking: she was facing traffic. I was heading in the same direction, south, and I glanced quickly at her across the highway as I passed, then went on my way.

I walked Kai, bought gas at a station farther down the road, then headed home again, north on the same highway. And saw the woman again. In the twenty to thirty minutes since I had first seen her, she had covered about a mile.

On impulse I drove into a parking area, left Kai in the rear seat with the windows open, and dodged rush-hour traffic to cross to her side of the highway.

"Miss!"

She turned. She was younger than I had first guessed her to

be: no more than twenty, which meant she was probably eighteen. Until I saw her face, her eyes, I had not decided what I would say to her, a stranger. But in that moment I found the words.

"Are you in trouble?" It is a magic question.

She did not hesitate, did not wonder whether to talk with me. She said at once, "My boyfriend . . ." and then she held out her right arm. A thin streak of blood ran from her forearm to her wrist. He had cut her, taken her purse, thrown her out of her own car, and driven off. She lived in Stamford, twenty miles away. I had the distinct impression that walking there was the only thing she knew to do.

"My car is across the road." I pointed to it. She looked only because I was pointing: she seemed to have no wish to initiate anything at all. "Please let me take you to the police station. They'll get you home. They'll try to get your car back. You can't walk to Stamford."

This time she hesitated.

"Look at me," I said to her quietly, by my voice alone making her eyes connect with mine. "Can you see that I want to help you?" Her head nodded slightly. "Come on, then."

We crossed the road. I opened the passenger door for her. She was halfway into the seat when Kairos leaned forward to get a whiff of the new person.

She leaped backward out of the car. "No," she said, trembling, tears suddenly streaming down her face. "I'll wait."

"Please get in the car," I said, taking her hand to calm her. "My dog is very gentle. He simply wanted to see who you are. He'll stay in the backseat. I promise you he won't hurt you."

She would not look at me. "I'll wait," she said. She did not know she was saying the words. She glanced at the other side of the road, perhaps thinking that she could have walked a few dozen more steps if I had let her alone.

"Look, I'll take my dog home. I live just a few blocks away. Will you wait for me to come back?"

"I'll wait. I'll wait." She didn't hear me: they were the only words she had.

I knew she'd cross the road, start walking again, wouldn't enter my car when I came back for her. At that moment a VW driven by a couple who might have been on their way to church stopped at the corner where we stood, and I pounced on them, quickly told them the story. They agreed to help. I went back to the woman.

"Miss, the people in this car will drive you to the police station. Will you let them?"

She looked beyond me at them. No monstrous dog lurked in their backseat. She climbed into the car and they drove off.

I can still hear her, seeming not to know that she's uttering words: "I'll wait. I'll wait."

On the common in a New England town a woman whose path would in a few steps cross mine was carrying a reed basket, its handle spanning one forearm, its bottom supported by the other. Gleaming apples, red and perfect, lay nestled next to one another, open to the general view.

"How beautiful they are!" I called out as she drew nearer.

"I grew them," she answered, surprised, smiling, and kept walking.

I did not want an apple: I was not hungry. And yet the moment she passed I knew that I would have said: "Here, take one." I hold the Greek view about hospitality, recognizing it as my own the first time I read classical literature. Any guest in my household is all but royal: you shall want for nothing if I can in any way provide it. Whatever of mine you admire is in that moment yours. I will not give you myself or Kairos, but I will hand you almost any other thing.

I've thought about giving for a very long time, and I'm now

willing to stand here and say that there's only one kind of gift worth giving: a thing the other person wants or needs. What you'd like to give him, do for her, are irrelevant unless you know he wants the thing, she needs the doing. To know that, you have only to listen. But to listen, you can't get in your own way: you can't insert your needs, your wants, some expectation of gain into the gift.

Not getting in your own way is one of the outcomes of discovering what your purposes are. Thereafter, no matter how opaque the motives of other human beings had seemed to you before, they become transparent. Everything a person wants or needs or likes or dislikes lies among his words, his tone of voice, the way she holds her head, shakes your hand, orients her body toward yours, listens to your words, fixes her gaze with yours. What people mean to say leaps out into audibility as sharply as though they had said it. It does not matter that they may take abundant pains to conceal what they want or need or like or mean. That they are concealing emerges too, riding the need, the liking, the meaning. You may not know the reason for the concealing until you think about it later, gather some independent evidence elsewhere, but the fact of it will be there in front of you.

To give truly, you simply cut through all this. And it *is* simple. You have only to tuck away the knowledge people gratuitously offer about themselves, what they prefer and when and how, then give them the thing when a birthday or giftday arises. Or at any moment of your choosing. If you've a mind to it.

When I have a mind to it, I get inside the head of someone who matters to me, all but think his thoughts, sense her purposes.

A friend's mother, aged ninety-two, lay ill of many causes in a nursing home three states away. Periodically my friend spent a few days with her. She had to arrange with others to handle her professional obligations while she was gone, flew round trip, rented a car on arrival, stayed in a motel, and carried expensive gifts to her mother. My friend returned from these visits complaining that her brother-in-law, who lived locally, wasn't seeing her mother as often as he had promised, wasn't looking after the small things that would make her mother more comfortable, couldn't be counted on.

I listened as long as I could hold my tongue. Then: "If you were ninety-two years old, would you want to be lying in a nursing home?"

"No."

"If you were sick, would you want to see your daughter only for a couple of days four times a year?"

"No."

"If you were to combine the money you spend on your trips with whatever the nursing home costs, you could keep your mother in your own house. She wants to see you, not your brother-in-law. She's your concern, not his."

It took a few months to work out all the details.

Giving is easy. Receiving is hard. I am in fact always surprised to be on the receiving end. I keep very strict accounts in the matter of receiving: I stand on my head to give something in return. It's a failing of mine, one that displays a certain lack of generosity. Since I give something simply because someone needs it or wants it, I should be willing to let another person give something to me without prospect of gain. But I'm not willing. The principle I apply instead is: "I can have it if I can pay."

Weck is a designer of jewelry, immensely knowledgeable about the properties of all metals: silver, steel, titanium, gold. She melts and casts, anneals, solders, anodizes, rivets, folds, saws, pierces, polishes, forges, sands, makes settings and molds, fabricates jigs, invents the tools she needs, and works with fiberoptics, electronics, acrylics, and precious stones. You could mistake her studio for a metallurgist's, for a tool and die shop. It is both and more.

Before her work became known throughout the world, before she became one of only three women ever initiated into the six-hundred-year-old international society of goldsmiths, before she received her doctorate of humane letters for her development of electronic body-monitoring jewelry, before Nantucket, I used to sit in her shop watching her at her craft, her art. Earlier, in some private hour, she would have designed the piece, and although she kept refining the design as she kept working the metal, concentrating primarily on what lay beneath her hands, we often talked about other things. When I knew she had a deadline, I'd simply watch her. Sometimes I'd ask questions.

"Why did you do that?"

"Here." And she'd show me what would have happened if she hadn't.

"You closed those links so fast. How did you do that?"

"You clamp one end of the link in this pliers, and the other end in another pliers. See? Then you twist the ends back and forth all the while you bring them toward one another, and then they're together. You try it."

I did. It worked. "But I'd have thought you could hold the open link between the jaws of just one pair of pliers. And then bring the jaws together."

"Well, try it that way, then."

I did. It didn't work. Weck grinned.

A decade passed. In the yard of my house in the hills of western Massachusetts I was working with Logos on leash one afternoon, as I did with Ousia too, for five minutes every few weeks to sharpen the speed with which they responded to important commands off leash. "Come!" is an important command. When I say, "Come!" I mean that in that instant Logos is to begin racing to me, not stopping until he is sitting squarely in front of me. No moment must pass between my uttering the command and his swiftly and without thought obeying it. If I saw a car approaching him on the road and shouted "Come!" I wouldn't mean: "Look around. See that car coming? Would you consider getting out of the way?"

On this day Logos was annoyed that I had taken him away from the games we had just been playing. He responded without enthusiasm. I tried again.

"Logos, come!"

Pause, then a slow amble toward me.

I attached the leash to his collar. "No." I snapped the leash. "Come!"

A standard chain collar consists of stainless steel links, with a large ring at either end. Each link is polished and rounded so that no flat side can catch and pull a dog's neck hair; each is twisted, fitting loosely into the next; and the ends of each link are welded together so that the chain will not break if the dog lunges forward unexpectedly. You make the length of chain into a collar by holding one of the large rings in one hand and dropping the links through it until their fall is stopped by the other large ring. The ring through which the chain fell, the inactive ring, will now slip easily along the chain. The other ring now hangs free. To put your dog on leash, you hook the steel snap at the end of your leash into the free ring.

The standard way to correct a dog's slow or improper response is to snap the leash. The free ring thereby draws the chain upward through the inactive ring, tightening the collar momentarily at the dog's neck, then immediately releasing it. It is correction, not punishment. It merely reminds the dog that he is now messing up the thing he knows very well how to do. The musculature of a dog's neck is stronger by far than that of a human neck. Putting a chain collar on any of us and snapping it might send some of us reeling to the ground, but to a dog it feels like the flick of a finger.

That day in Massachusetts I snapped and released the leash to correct Logos. This time the inactive ring somehow locked into the link nearest Logos' neck, and he began choking to death. Instantly I remembered Weck's two pliers: if they could bring the ends of a ring together they could also break them apart. But the two pairs of pliers in my tool drawer were ordinary pliers, and my arms had only the ordinary strength of my hundred and five pounds. While I was pitting puny instruments against welded steel in my futile attempts to free Logos, I was losing time. I needed two men's hands, powerful equipment. Fifteen miles away from my isolated house and down a winding road were the barracks of the state police. I half-carried, half-dragged Logos, now gasping and pawing at his neck, into my station wagon.

It takes too many minutes to drive twelve miles down a curving two-lane hill, too many more minutes to speed three miles farther to the long driveway of the police station. I pulled in, leaning on my horn. A trooper came out of the office door as I flung open mine.

"My dog is choking! I need heavy tools!"

"Around to the back." He pointed.

I guided the car toward the tool shed. The officer ran ahead and was waiting to open my rear door when I pulled up. Logos jumped out.

First the trooper sliced through the inactive ring with heavy wire cutters. We had to tighten the already taut chain in order to move the ring a sixteenth of an inch farther away from Logos' neck to let the cutters do the work. When we released the chain again, the now-opened ring still lay tightly against Logos' neck. The man reached for a pair of long-handled pliers and, with one handle in each hand, turned toward Logos. He began fastening the pincers around one of the ends of the newly opened ring.

"You need two!" I said loudly, as though he weren't next to me. "Get another pliers!"

For a second the officer stared at me stupidly.

"You have to twist the ends of the ring *away from* each other!" I shouted. "You need another pair of pliers, goddamn it!"

Another trooper coming toward us understood in a flash what needed doing, grabbed a second pair of pliers, and, with each man twisting in the opposite direction, broke apart the death-dealing ring, then snaked it away from the chain. The collar dropped from Logos' neck and he drew his first unconfined breath in nearly twenty minutes. I laid my head against his face. I could not speak. The men stashed their tools and started down the driveway.

"Thanks," I called after them.

Only the second trooper half-turned toward me.

"I'm sorry for seeming rude," I said. "He was dying."

Both men nodded without saying a word, entered their office, and closed the door behind them. Logos jumped into the car next to Ousia, then I climbed behind the wheel, sitting there for a long time, thanking Weck, before I switched on the ignition.

It's one of the few times I'll never be able to repay someone's giving.

Having to ask is hardest of all. People who have families or colleagues are able to turn to one another in ways that I cannot. Because I do for myself most of the things that affiliated people do for each other, on the rare occasions when I *must* ask, I am like a beached whale thrashing about on shore, out of my element, casting an apprehensive eye on the curious onlookers from among whom one or none may step forward to assist me. At such times the thought crosses my mind that it's folly to circuit the stations of solitude, or at least that the full circuit must not be attempted unless you have a great deal of money. You then simply buy assistance at whatever level of quality you require at the time.

When I need someone's effort, someone's interest, and can't buy them, my handicap is less being a woman than being the particular woman I am: I know what I need and how I want the assistance rendered. Sometimes acquaintances construe my clearly stated need as arrogance, as a demand I unwarrantedly impose on them, and they turn aside. (I never ask them again.) Oddly enough, strangers to whom I must thereby apply do what must be done with little or no discussion of my motives or purposes, acting effectively and with dispatch. At some point in the past perhaps they accepted the help of a stranger and are now handing it back through me. As I too, out on the world, hand it along.

Returning from an afternoon at a library last November, I opened our front door calling to Kairos. He rose from his mat, staggered toward me, then fell. I thought I had startled him awake, that he had gotten to his feet too fast.

Abruptly my heart began pounding. Was this the incipient paralysis that had been diagnosed two years earlier as lying in wait for him, for me? I had to see him move again.

"Kairos, come!"

He struggled to his feet: you could not say he stood. His gait uncoordinated, his legs going every which way, he headed toward the kitchen, slipped on the tractionless linoleum, then fell again, half-on, half-off his mat in the corner.

It was Sunday afternoon. At such times it is always Sunday afternoon, unless it is Saturday evening. I phoned Todd Friedland, my vet a state away. He had just gone off weekend duty. I begged his answer service to find him, but he was in transit to Hartford, could not be reached until nearly midnight. I phoned two vets nearby, but on Sundays they refer even faithful clients to emergency clinics miles away where you will be dealt with by someone you've never laid eyes on before, where you must entrust your creature to someone whose qualifications you have no way of examining, whose special concern you cannot expect, when all along you had been building a relationship of trust with your veterinarian precisely so that you could call on him or her in an emergency. By the time I completed my futile phone calls, the vet on standby duty returned the message I had left for Todd. I described Kairos' symptoms.

"Don't wait until midnight," he said. "If there's a crushed disk in the spine, Kairos will need surgery at once. You have Angell Memorial in Boston. Go there."

Where I too would be compelled to rely on someone whose concern and qualifications I could not be certain of.

To help carry Kairos' ninety sprawling pounds, I phoned a neighbor. The three sturdy men in her household came at once. Somehow we lifted Kairos into the rear seat of my car. By then it was dark and had begun to rain, but there is only one way to drive in such circumstances: take deep breaths often, stay in the right-hand lane, be cautious about other drivers, reach one hand around to touch Kairos from time to time, and talk to him about good things as often as the exigencies of the roadway did not fully preempt my care. Next day Kairos required another trip to the same hospital, and I, requiring another pair of hands, called on another neighbor.

Within days of having asked for their help, I baked breads for both neighbors. The cranberry loaf was for Bill Sullivan, the second pair of hands, and I phoned to ask whether I could drop by.

"I have something I want you to see," I said. The something was Kairos, all but well again.

"Come on over," he replied.

I walked Kairos around the corner on the sunny December day, my leash guiding his occasionally wobbly walk only five days after his emergency, my other hand holding the wrapped bread.

Bill came to the door. "He's walking!" he exclaimed, his eyes following Kairos frisking about, sniffing all the new scents.

I handed him the loaf.

"You didn't have to do this."

"You didn't have to help me, either."

"Wait," he said. "I'll be right out." In moments he reappeared carrying a box of grahams identical to that which I had used to divert Kairos the day Bill lent his hands. Marveling at Kai's recovery, he slipped one cracker after another to my willing friend whose jaws barely closed on each before he swallowed it, then stood ready for the next, knowing that such a good thing doesn't last too long: he has by heart the list of the limited number of occasions when I allow him only one.

"Here, take the box," Bill said. "They're for him."

"Keep them for the next time we come over," I said, and led the reluctant Kairos home.

New Year's Day Bill knocked on my door with some pickles he himself had canned. "Happy New Year," he said. "You liked these when I brought you some last fall."

"Dear heaven, Bill!" I invited him in but he had other errands. He is a difficult person to stay even with. He is like me, giving where he sees the need, giving the thing I casually mention. Since I don't tally my givings, I can't tally his. My page on him is torn to pieces.

A few years ago some negotiations for a piece of my writing abruptly hit a wall. After my attorney's call, I marched around my house battling aloud the editor's treachery, Kairos following me from room to room before settling onto one of his mats to contemplate the goings-on. Then I went to the phone. The friend I called held a very high position in a major Boston institution, and her days were packed with responsibility that she honored. She listened attentively.

"I'll be there by noon," she said. And when she arrived, having driven nearly an hour, she carried a basket of expensive groceries. We sat down to the sandwiches and tea I had prepared, and for nearly two hours we talked as though her time were as unappointed as mine.

"I have to get back," she said then, and because up till that moment she had not mentioned how long she could stay, I knew she meant it. We put our arms around one another for a close minute and then I went outdoors with her to wave her off for her long drive back to Boston.

She had not walked into my house saying, "I can stay only an hour." She had said nothing about the extra time she had spent at the fancy grocery store, looking for treats to beguile me. She had said nothing about the complex arrangements she must have put in place so that she could walk out of her office late in the morning only a short while before the daily demands of her organization would accumulate at her door. She had come to me because I needed her. Not her costly food but her costly time was her gift to me. The extravagant groceries were merely incremental to that.

The land mass of the United States separates me from another friend I see only every few years or so, although we're in touch irregularly by lengthy phone calls. We save up stories that we know will make the other laugh. We trade notes on our current reading. He has an astute eye into his motives and purposes. I can't remember ever thinking of him, "He's fooling himself."

He was the husband of a long-ago friend of mine. Their apartment had been my hotel for uncounted weekends whenever the pressures of Cambridge had pushed me toward my limits. I knew the household habits well. In her search for some reality to cling to, my friend became involved with a religiously oriented group not at all to my taste, and I recognized that we could no longer speak to one another.

More than a year passed without my seeing her. Then, the evening before I was to sail for France on a yearlong fellowship, I found myself unexpectedly free. I called my friend.

"She's not here," said Bill. "We're separated."

"Then *you* have dinner with me. I'm leaving for Paris tomorrow. How many times will you have a chance to say good-bye to someone who's going to Paris?"

We ate in a diner whose finest hour was the lunchtime trade. Bill hadn't yet come into his money then, and the place was his discovery for an evening meal under four dollars. I think we split the check. When I returned from Europe I still had to get away to New York from time to time, and I still spent weekend nights on Bill's couch. Saturday nights four or five of his friends, all men, would arrive around nine o'clock, play chamber music till midnight, then push back their chairs and set up the poker table in the music room. I'd close the door to the living room, fall asleep watching television, awaken to turn it off at two or three in the morning, still hearing the laughter and shouting of male voices.

Next day around noon I'd spare Bill the pain of getting up to make his own coffee. I knew enough not to say a word until I brought him a second cup, and even then I'd wait for him to call out to me in the living room where I sat reading.

"You know, Tim," he'd say on an occasional Sunday, "these guys can't believe that you and I aren't getting it on."

"My God," I'd answer, "who'd have anything to do with you?"

He never made a pass. I never expected him to. We simply liked one another, understood the way one another's minds worked. For several years we weren't in touch, and then one day I called him from Washington. His phone had been disconnected. What calamity could have made him leave the apartment he had lived in for two decades? I tried to find him through one of his poker-playing-musician friends, and in a few days I had his address in California. His second mugging had convinced him that Manhattan was uninhabitable.

I owe him an enormous sum of money that began accumulating six years ago when the music stopped. It does not require great profundity to understand that royalties falling off by the end of one accounting period will rarely do other than continue to fall off by the end of the next, and so I started to write another book. But what seemed a book of a certain sort to me seemed a book of a different sort to the people who were considering buying its rights, who in fact offered to buy them, and so, after we disagreed, I, having no money for the book I wanted to write, stopped writing it. When I ran out of money for other things as well, ran out of ideas for obtaining it, I wrote Bill. The day he received my note he called to say he had just mailed a check. It arrived larger than I had asked for.

I called to thank him. It was hard to find something funny to say. "I don't know when I can repay it, Bill."

"When you can. What the hell? I had it, and you needed it."

During the next few years we were to go around that circle several times: my request, his call, his check, my call. Sometimes there wasn't time to write. And at the other end of the phone he'd say, "I can't let you be without money," and he'd arrange for a wire transfer through a bank near wherever I happened to be roosting, my belongings stored, Kai and I living in motels, waiting for a bite on one of the dozen lines I had out.

Then from one day to the next I had the money with which I now write this book. I learned of it on a Saturday morning near seven o'clock. I wanted to call Bill, but he'd have been asleep only two hours, and he'd be just as glad to hear my news fully awake. I waited out my estimate of how soon he'd initiate his day.

"Hot damn!" he yelled, among other congratulatory sounds.

"Bill," I began, "I have to live off this until I complete the manuscript. It'll be at least another year before I . . ."

"I don't need it now, Tim. Just write your fucking book."

We've known one another forty years, so I ought not to have been stunned by the fact of his seventieth birthday. I phoned him on the actual day, which he celebrated with friends, students, family, caterers, and a birthday cake costing one hundred dollars.

"I got your present, Tslim," he said. "Just right for California. Thanks."

I had sent him a pair of slacks, breton red, a purple turtleneck, and a lemon yellow sweater. "Wear them all at the same time."

"You kidding?"

"Fuck seventy," I said.

"Agreed." And he returned to his guests.

Sometimes I connect with other people after first colliding.

An oral surgeon to whom I had been sent for emergency care explained his procedure before he anesthetized my jaw. He worked with exquisite care, his concentration on what he was doing was unbreachable, his orders for the hygiene of the matter afterward were clear. When it was over, I stopped at the reception desk to talk about the bill.

"Today's fee is two hundred seventy-five dollars," the secretary said.

"I don't have it now, but I'll send it to you as soon as I'm able to."

The receptionist pointed to a sign: "Payment is expected on the day of service."

"I have every intention of paying Dr. Reinbold, but I can't do it today."

The secretary went off to confer with the surgeon and returned. "I'll need a definite schedule of payments from you, and I must have twenty dollars today."

We worked out a schedule. I left behind a check for which I had had equally urgent plans. I tried to make payments as I had promised, but I often failed.

In two months my jaw ached again, and I returned to Dr. Reinbold. Before he even looked into my mouth, he spent five minutes pointing out to me that I still owed him a large sum of money. I acknowledged the debt and explained my circumstances for the fourth time.

My fury at his onslaught did not make me a relaxed patient as he undertook surgery far more extensive than before. Again his attention to the task at hand was total. At the end he told me how to deal with what he thought might be severe pain when the anesthesia wore off. Then he said, "There will be no charge for today."

I couldn't piece together this sentence with the tongue-lashing he had handed me an hour earlier. "What do you mean?"

"The earlier surgery didn't work. It was my responsibility to deal with your problem, and the method I used was ineffective. Therefore, I did what would be effective, as I assure you today's

work will be. I can't charge you for correcting my own work."
He wheeled and left.

To his assistant, unhooking the last towel from my neck, I said,
"I'm very impressed by the way Dr. Reinbold works and by his
sense of professional responsibility. But his bedside manner leaves
a great deal to be desired." She smiled, then handed me his pre-
scription for a codeine analgesic.

At home I went straight to bed. When the anesthesia wore off,
pain surrounded my whole being, but I was not to take a tablet
until four hours had passed. Before the next four hours elapsed,
the pain returned, and it kept returning sooner each time.

The phone rang. "This is Dr. Reinbold. The surgery you had
involves the worst possible pain. I want to know how you're doing.
Does the codeine last four hours?"

"No," I answered, and then, because there was no one else to
talk to and because he knew what was happening to me better than
anyone, I talked to him for a long time.

"Try this," he said. "Just before the third hour, take two acet-
aminophen. They'll tide you over the fourth hour and probably
into the fifth. It extends the effect of the narcotic, so you end up
using less. You'll feel a little better by morning, but if the pain
isn't gone the following day, call me. And be sure to come back
in two days for me to have a look at you." He was silent a moment,
and then: "I couldn't help thinking about you."

I who belong no specific where make my home wherever I
happen to live. For the eight months, or year, or five years I might
remain in that place, I come upon people in the course of going
about my day with whom I can be companionable. We have lunch,
go to a movie, attend a gallery opening. Very soon it emerges that
the other person's interest lies only here or only there. A retired
couple whose year turns on their garden let me visit it whenever I

wished, gave me plants that still keep my rooms green, told me the history of each of their growing things, indoors and out, sometimes accompanied me to flower shows. With them my passion for gardens could spill out, but we could not have discussed literature. Other people walked with me in the woods but could not talk politics. Those with whom I worked politically would never have come with me to a lecture in philosophy. I, out on the world, am willing to let only that small part of me be caught up, if only for a few hours every now and then. I think of Bazarov in *Fathers and Sons*: "One wants to have to do with people if only to abuse them." I do not abuse them, but from time to time I want to have to do with them.

Connectings may settle into only one compartment of my life and only for a short time, but I don't begin them with that in mind. No, I begin a connecting in the hope that in time the person will be with me at the far end of the continuum. A man I see for an hour or two every five years or so connects to me and I to him as do the opposite poles of magnets. We meet in a public place. We do not decide on an agenda, how the talk will go. Neither of us bothers to bring the other up to date. From our first words we plunge into our most profound concerns, talking in a closeness I do not attempt with anyone else. We are fully clothed in the dully lighted café, but it is a wonder to me that we are not arrested as we sip our drinks: no barriers exist between us. One of us brings up a topic that would require two years to explore, except that we talk shorthand, a single sentence compressing hours of words. Dusk arrives. He is expected elsewhere. We walk out onto the sidewalk, even in these last moments not talking of inconsequential things. Then we must part. His lips graze my cheek. I turn and walk away. Not many five-year intervals are left.

With each new woman I meet, each new man, our coming to know one another raises the prospect of our becoming friends in one degree or another, of our inhabiting some segment of that far end. By then I have made clear a single demand: you must be willing to hear me speak to you in all candor, and you must be able to speak so to me. I don't hand out printed cards announcing the policy, and I don't expect it in every conversation each time we meet, but whenever it becomes necessary to talk to one another that way, I won't settle for anything less. Rather than continue the relationship on a basis I could never again trust, I'll end it.

A woman I approached to hire for her professional skills quickly began to seem likely to become a friend. A certain matter arose that we disagreed about, and I knew we'd soon have to talk plainly about it. I wrote suggesting that we arrange a time to meet to talk. Over the next two months the woman phoned several times, talking about many things but not about meeting. She drove a long way to attend one of my public readings, surprising me by appearing in the audience, but she did not mention our talking together. Slowly I disconnected myself from her. A month or so later she phoned to say hello. I reminded her of my request, by then four months old. She became upset, and then abruptly her voice lifted. "Well, let's talk about other things," she said, as though we had just polished off the weather.

"Until we talk about that, there's nothing else to talk about," I replied.

The phone call came to a rapid end. The potential friendship had dissipated long before.

I find people wherever I go, fewer in some places than in others. Rarely are they for the long haul: the connection almost never survives my moving elsewhere. Anyone who expects to stay in touch with me by writing letters fails to understand that I spend hours every day with the fingers of one hand around a pen or with all my fingertips on typewriter keys trying to precipitate my thinking onto sheets of papers. By the time I push my chair back for the day, the last thing I want to do is confront cool silence again with paper and pen. What I want then is the rushing sound of a human voice, preferably one well-disposed toward me. More than the voice: I want the presence of someone familiar, someone dear and familiar. I want to watch the play of light on his face, to intercept the sudden interest in his eyes as I begin a story, to observe her pride in recounting some incident in her daughter's career, to laugh together, to tease, to lend a hand preparing the evening meal.

The peripatetic life that is the unanticipated consequence of the route I designed carries a consequence of its own: good friends are not nearby. All the persons I remain connected to are in other parts of the country, the world. Bill in California, and Marilyn. Tommy and Olive in Connecticut. Another Tommy in Virginia. Harold in Maryland. Cindy outside of New York. Edward in Washington. Our long distance calls stave off my being far more solitary than I already am. It is one of my great pleasures: to answer a ringing phone and find a friend calling from the distance. For the five minutes or twenty or forty that we talk, I am immersed in familiarity. The strange town I temporarily inhabit falls away and I am in the place where he and I, she and I, last saw one another, spent most of our long ago time together. When the call ends the voice pulses in my ear long after the sound waves flatten out. Then silence returns.

I've learned how to endure most defeats, all physical pain, antagonism of a high order, without turning to other people, even though more than a few times the thing was unendurable. It is when the prizes, the triumphs, the stroke of great fortune, come my way, that I most miss not having a good friend at hand. I make the round of long distance calls so that this handful of people, accustomed to hearing from me in a different vein, can be in on the news. I love their joying with me, each in the way I know so well. But when the call is over, my exuberance is just getting under way. It needs an hour or two of bursting out, of scattering around in the streets, of minutely discussing the events that led to the goal achieved, of having my shortcomings teased to keep my head the proper size. Not just anyone will do: if I cannot have a friend in on my joy, I will not have anyone at all. But the rooms of my house, the ordinary routine of the day, cannot contain it. I gather up Kairos and we go off in search of fierce beauty.

Dear as they are to me and I to them, the people who are my friends are married, have children, or if not now married, not any longer married, have very close families. If any of them were to have a serious accident, become extremely ill, inherit great wealth, win a trip to Italy or Sweden, I wouldn't be the first person to be told. Most people, I suppose, have in place a ranking of the persons nearest them, and I think my name is not among the very few at the top of any list. I, on the other hand, when confronted by some form or other that requires me to name a next of kin, simply enter one of the names of my friends. No harm is done by my fanciful act: I don't expect any of them to be called on to do whatever next of kin must sometimes do, and it pleases the hospital admission's office or the bank or the insurance company to have all the blank spaces filled in.

In high school I had a best friend, another in dramatic school, someone else in college, yet another in graduate school. By then everyone I knew was marrying and having children, although some also stayed in their careers. I went to Nantucket. Since then, one or another person has presented himself, herself, as someone perhaps to be a best friend. But it takes time to become friends, and more time to become a best friend. You have to wait out her staying ability when you're ill or have little money, when your expectations crash to earth. And you have to wait out learning whether you're willing to give her these things in turn. You have to discover whether she disappears behind a big bubble of words or, worse, silence, when you say, "I need two hours of your time on Thursday." These are the credentials of best friendship, distinguishing it from others that are good but lesser. The small daily cementings are equally essential: trading news, giving her one of my sweaters because its color becomes her, her phone call just to tell me a funny story.

There is a space as well as a time requirement for best friendship: best friends must be nearby. Aristotle said that good friends will want to live together, but he could not have guessed at the ways telephones and automobiles collapse distances between people. I think nothing of calling someone long distance every now and then: it's one of my entertainments, and it's far cheaper than going there. But a best friend is, ought to be, a sustaining element in one's day. She's the person with whom one is most current, the person capable of detecting the slightest alteration in the tenor of one's voice. A best friend would cajole me out of a rotten mood, delight with me in not letting the bastards grind me down. She'd be on my side, no matter what, and if she thought me wrong in something I did or said, she'd tell me so and she'd find the proper time for doing it. She'd talk plainly to me in that way that is essential to me, and she'd inquire no further in matters that I'm not now, perhaps not ever, prepared to talk about. She'd mark my birthday in some special way as the holiday it still is to me. She'd see something that would remind her of me and she'd immediately buy it for me. Sometimes the thing wouldn't need to be bought: I'd prize the first reddening oak leaf of autumn. We'd try new restaurants, meet to go for long walks just to be outdoors and in motion and talking together. And from me this best friend would receive all these things and others I'd continuously think of.

A best friend cannot be sustained over long distances because the drop of water endlessly falling on our foreheads day after day compels each human being to change the angle at which we hold our heads to try to evade it. If we do not keep up with one another's attempts to ward off disaster, with the drifting standpoint from which each of us views the world, sorts out the happenings sig- nificant to each of us, recounting it all becomes impossible. Or rather: possible, but too great a burden of time, too heavy a demand that we think it through again, speak of it carefully and openly. The ongoing events themselves demand that kind of attention.

It took too much of my time: finding the living that would let me work. Had I been stably located somewhere, there might have been a man close to me in the intimacy of man and woman, a woman close to me in the intimacy of best friend. But few hours have passed during any day of the preceding two and a half decades without my considering what person to write to, what person to phone, then in fact writing, in fact phoning, to try to set in motion whatever events would have precisely that outcome: that by my work I would earn my living. You cannot live that way, your powers of practical reason consumed by that purpose (not just being single-minded by any purpose but by that particular purpose) for an almost unbroken thread of hours during nearly ten thousand days without the stamp of the endeavor being laid on everything else you do. It is not inherent in finding one's work, but one of its implications for me is that the very farthest arc of the continuum of my connectings is not occupied. I am quite without other human beings.

People who are immersed in human relationships from the moment they awaken until they climb back into bed at night tell me they'd give anything for an hour all to themselves during the course of their day, even once a week. That I awaken, work, walk in the woods, shop for food or blouses or a book on a schedule of my own devising, not having to accommodate my time to any one else's (they forget Kairos), except for occasionally appointing to repair my car or my teeth, strikes them as highly enviable. Not that they'd give up that interlocking network that is their lives, that they themselves wove so long ago they have forgotten it was all their own doing.

In contrast, my days are almost totally devoid of other human beings. And by now I wouldn't have it any other way. I thrive until about four o'clock in the afternoon. It is the dividing line of my day. I begin then to savor anticipating the few hours that remain when someone is to have dinner with me, see a film, hear a lecture, walk with me licking ice cream cones of a summer evening. Sometimes the hours until my bed invites me for the night slip by without my even thinking of other people. But some evenings I have very much wanted to be with someone close and cannot: he or she is too far away, forever gone, not yet found. It is the sometimes costly price of my way. I balance that longing on the proper scale, not contrasting this acute loneliness and what it would have been like to have him or her with me, but comparing these few difficult hours of this infrequent evening with the breadth of my freedom during all the other hours of all the other days.

11

COLLIDING

BY HAVING FORTUNATELY come upon or with exquisite care chosen the overarching purposes that guide your days, you do not necessarily collide with the purposes of others: your purpose may even be to mediate their conflicting purposes. On the other hand, the world is now less full of a number of things, and the contest for them quickens sooner.

Sometimes, having a purpose that matters deeply to you can serve as a lightning rod to others, can draw them to you to help you forward it: you have articulated some matter they cared about but did not know others cared about or did not know that or how the thing could be done. I think of Greenpeace (but the very essence of its purpose is to collide).

Sometimes your purpose will draw the attention of others invidiously: you are pursuing some end you've thought about and committed yourself to, while they're merely jogging in place or have not yet explored and chosen the way they want their lives to go, or they've locked their purposes into a bottom drawer until the time will be appropriate for pursuing them. Sometimes they may not like the way you wear your hair.

You can collide in one great continuing impact or in intermittent small scuffles. You can collide head-on, or you can orient yourself toward your opponents so that their blows land only on one unshielded part of you, albeit unendingly. You can conceal your purposes to postpone colliding with those of others, but this is a difficult option that requires a temperament I don't possess. Most difficult of all is to avoid colliding entirely: you are giving up your considered purpose for the purpose of another. Beware. Someone who forces you to keep the peace will not be content with winning once. Someone so implacable about defeating your purposes, so contemptuous of things dear to you, is an enemy you will do well to recognize, no matter the nature of your connection to one another heretofore. What is at issue with such a person is not this problem, dated and located, an irrelevant solution to which you have accepted only to avoid discord. To that other person, those others persons, what is at issue between you is whether her purposes or yours will prevail, his or yours, theirs or yours. Neither temporal nor spatial boundaries can confine it. Not reason but only power will resolve it.

At this station, you choose when to collide and how, or whether to collide at all. Whether to fight at all costs. Whether to keep the peace at all costs. Whether to keep the peace on this ground but to take up arms later if the front merely shifts elsewhere. The matter may not seem to you as one requiring you to unbind again, but it will surely cycle you back to constructing, to choosing all over again your wantings and even the principles in accordance with which you incorporate them into your days.

Nothing wrong with that. All of us encounter unanticipated circumstances that make us consider modifying our purposes while we attempt to put them into effect. But modify how? Do you let the circumstance annihilate the purpose? Do you in the light of events try to recast it? Or do you plunge ahead because your commitment is immutable? Whichever you choose, you will be colliding: with yourself, in the first instance; probably with others, in the second; almost certainly with others, in the third.

A man who earns a handsome living as a negotiator says, "You can negotiate anything." When he is asked to intervene between the opposing purposes of two people or groups, he sets out to discover what each of them must absolutely retain or gain in order to be satisfied, what each of them cares less about, what each cares least about. Then he whittles away at the low end where purposes are not so tenaciously held, gradually approaches the high end where the swords are crossed, gives to both opponents something each is glad to have that matters less to the other, and everyone walks away with something desirable. The outcome isn't what they started by wanting, but it's more than they would have netted if they had both remained locked in their battle positions.

If you know far enough in advance that your confederate will become your antagonist, that negotiating of some sort will eventually be necessary, it's worth setting up some dummy purpose that you'll then reluctantly give way on, conceding it, presenting your real purpose to your opponent as something of little value that you're willing to accept so that each of you will have won something of at least some importance. But if you make plain your real purpose from the start, not even attempting to conceal how important it is to you, you cut off the possibility of negotiating: there is nothing of lesser importance that you will accept in its stead.

Within my house I arrange my belongings in any pattern that pleases me, allocating them to whichever room I choose. And if, after a time, I decide to realign my desk so that the columbine are in full view whenever I raise my head, I undertake the move in the moment that suits me. I need not negotiate with anyone for use of the bathroom. When I buy fresh asparagus in spring, steaming them tender, still their own green, I know that exactly the quantity I store in the refrigerator will be on the very same shelf the following day when I whisk up a vinaigrette for them. Whatever I want to do. Whenever I want to do it.

Sometimes for good friends, always for Kairos, as before for

Logos, for Ousia, I accommodate my purposes, which is to say 'my schedule.' The polished hardwood floors in our current house became a hazard for Kairos the day we moved in. I had no rug for the long front hallway that descends one lovely broad step into the living room, and he, now thirteen, his rear legs already displaying the muscle-wasting that preluded the paralysis of Ousia's late years, lost his footing too often for me to bear watching. Before I finished unpacking, I bought, cut, and tacked down carpeting the length of the hall, curving it down and around the single step, which he can now skip up or down without sliding backward to sprawl on his haunches, looking up at me puzzled, unable to rise to his feet without my supporting arms.

It is a way of living that can set up a certain habit of mind in you. What are all these cars doing on the road, slowing me down? The appliance service can't come to my house to repair the refrigerator until *Tuesday*?

Daily I teach myself to remember that almost none of the other people in the world knows anything about my purposes, and that, even if they did, only a few would care. All the rest are not interested, having doings enough of their own to interest them; would not help me forward mine, being busy enough with their own.

But some among the people I come upon in the course of my day collide with me without even knowing me. If I have only minor dealings with them—a surly checkout cashier at my supermarket, say—I let the unpleasantness roll over me and go on my way.

Occasionally I attempt to beguile the churlish one. A woman of undisguised and indiscriminate ill humor managed the only copying center in the small town nearest my house in the hills. After weeks of putting up with her bad temper because I needed her services, needed her suggestions for some of the complicated pages I was paying her to copy, I decided I'd have no more of it. Driving there one day I tried to see the world from her point of view. She was probably earning no more than minimum wages: after all, the job was only to take pieces of paper from a customer, lay them on the reproducing surface, press the button for the correct number of copies, then hand back the old with the new pages. Perhaps she considered herself, perhaps she was, capable of far more than the job demanded. She was quite fat, though, and you barely noticed her pretty face, which her sourness was beginning to etch permanently.

That day I walked up to the counter with my pages. "Hello!" I said, even though I knew she would not return the greeting.

"How many?" It was her usual response. She looked only at the papers in my hand.

"Lovely sweater you're wearing," I said. "Did you knit it yourself?"

Startled, she looked at her own clothing. But she answered me: "No."

"Very becoming," I went on. "Good color for you."

She looked me full in the face for the first time. She didn't smile. She didn't thank me. I didn't wait for her to respond in either way.

"I need three copies of this, collated, please. And one copy of this long piece. Do you have time to do it while I wait?"

"Oh, sure," she said, dismissing with a gesture the piles of boxes and folders that had been occupying her when I entered.

We didn't speak while she did my work. But when she handed it back to me she thanked me. She had never thanked me before.

I made a point of saying good-bye. "I'll be back. Thanks for your help."

She almost smiled.

Thereafter, every time I entered the shop and stood in line, her eyes caught mine and she smiled. Other people in line turned to look at me: who was I to make her smile? And by the time I left that town, I was receiving the best copying service available, shortcuts and all, for the best price, and I was telling her my secret recipe for getting rid of a cold overnight.

She was not my enemy: her hostility had no determinate focus, and so I had only to show her that I, at least, carried no weapons.

Sometimes I encounter people who actively oppose my purposes. They are not so easily converted. Indeed, I rarely convert an enemy. Not because I'm not good at converting, but because converting is irrelevant: once someone becomes my enemy, there is good reason for the discord between us. We may both want the same thing, of which there is only one. Or our purposes clash in some joint undertaking we cannot, except at great cost, walk away from, and one of us is in a position of power over the other. So far, the person with power has always been the other. Here no number of remarks about comely sweaters will do. Only understanding the nature of power and then using it will do.

Sometimes I have not heeded the warning signs of future enmity. My ignorance of the field, no doubt. For more than a dozen years the book I had tried to get published carried the title I had given it. The editor who bought its rights for her house chose another title, and that became its name. Who would have guessed that anyone but I would have the right to name my own book? I did not guess. I simply found myself colliding with my editor.

"Forget about the title," my then-agent advised me. "Take her title. Just get the book published."

I swallowed the new title. The editor did not thereby become my comrade. We merely moved to higher ground with a new issue. Who would have dreamed that anyone but I would have the right to approve the final version of my book, the one that would be printed on real paper, bound between real covers, sold in bookstores, circulated from libraries, my name permanently attached to it? I did not dream. My editor sent on to me the copy editor's proposed changes, which laid rough hands on my book's language, its punctuation, the connections and disconnections between its sentences and paragraphs, and my editor concurred. To her my book was merely one of two dozen she assisted toward the marketplace each year. To me, it was my book: I had sustained its life for fourteen years until it could take up residence in minds, in lives, other than mine. What *is* a piece of writing if it is not a making that one's loving attention shapes by selecting from among all the details that come to hand in the course of bringing it forth? She would not give, nor would I.

I made use of my understanding of power: I went to my editor's editor. "It is my book," I said.

He agreed.

"Before the manuscript went into galleys, I spent three weeks responding to nearly three thousand queries from your copy editor."

Oh, my (or something similar), he said.

"Now I have the galleys," I went on, "and almost all of the copy editor's changes I had refused have been reinstated. Something amounting to ninety percent of those changes were attempts to alter my style. I wonder what book you would be publishing if your house so thoroughly rejects my way of writing?"

He was certainly happy to be publishing my book, he said, and he was sorry I was so unhappy. He would look into the matter at once and call me within the following day or so.

"She has agreed to let the galleys go to press as you have corrected them," he said when he phoned. "I hope now that we can all look forward to the great success of your book." My request for another editor was turned aside by the simple device of ignoring it.

What I won was the publication of my manuscript as the book I had years-long longed for. Some small changes were made without my consent: I was never sent page proofs. But in the abrupt and lengthy lull from all this flurry until publication, I began to realize that my editor could heavily weight the decision about how much money would be spent promoting my book. That, after all, is what a publisher does: make known a book's existence to the world. And she decided that she really needed very little.

The array of people I sent to her to try to persuade her otherwise! After I myself failed, two attorneys, an agent, and one of the publisher's own representatives approached her. "But it's just a little book," she told him.

I'd have preferred not to collide with her. If we had been working together on some project I hustled for money, I'd probably have tossed my objections into the pot at some point, but then I'd have stepped aside. We were, however, dealing with my book. Even though I won, initially and ultimately, the cost of opposing her in the time between was very high. The alternative would have been even costlier: it would have set me in opposition to myself.

When someone has more power than you, enough power to blunt your important purposes, seek out the person's constituency, the source from which her power, his power, derives. My editor's power wasn't born in her, like the color of her eyes: her superior granted it to her, just as his superior granted his to him, and so on back to the owners of the company. She held her power from her superior because he expected her to achieve certain purposes: those of an editor in a publishing house. She was answerable to him in fulfilling those purposes, as he in turn was answerable to his superiors, and his to his, and so on back to the owners, and even they were answerable to shareholders. His position as her superior carried sanctions, some capability for enforcing his wishes. Not to enforce his wishes as John Jones, private person, but as John Jones, editor's editor in this publishing house. The power delegated to him by his superior had the teeth of these sanctions (else how could the purposes for which his position was created ever be achieved?), just as the power delegated to her carried sanctions enabling her to enforce her wishes as holder of her position. His sanctions ranged from the mere fact of interceding, of questioning her actions, perhaps of admonishing her; from these mild gestures to firing her, to withdrawing the power he had granted her for the use of her position.

I turned to him because I knew that the power he granted her was rooted in the power granted him (and so on back), and that that power was not for her private use but for the use of her position. He knew that I knew that the power relationship is brought into existence not by the holder of power but by the grantors of power, that grantors can withdraw it, that grantors can render the powerful powerless. He acted on my appeal to him because he knew that I knew it was his job to do so. He knew that I knew that I could go to his superior, and then to his and to his, and so on back, if he did not satisfy me. Rather than be admonished by his superior for not doing his job, he admonished the editor for not doing hers.

Through the power of my position, I used the power of the editor's position against her. To retain her position, she submitted to the superior from whom her power derived: she restored to me the authority over my own work that she had arrogated. But force is forceful. The force I exerted against her was too great for her to contain, to absorb, so she expelled the overflow against me. It was a natural sequence of events, power being what it is. Because power, once exerted, will spring back at you. Sensing this, few people are willing to deploy even the small amount of power they possess in each relationship in which they are involved.

My editor did not direct the excess force back at me in a rush of violence: she simply sat on her hands rather than act in a way that might have benefited me. But I have also used power against men, and I have been stunned by the intensity of the force sent crashing back at me. After an encounter with a man against whom I've used power, I've slumped in a chair trembling for up to half an hour, simply letting the wave of force he aimed at me wash over me. This is not a figure of speech. My shaking body immobilizes me: I wait out the time until my hands, my arms, my torso, become their own competent selves again. But all the while I compel my wayward mind to recognize that I've exerted power effectively: the force that has just been hurled against me is an accurate indicator of the success of my action. When I can stand again, I leap into the air and laugh and shout.

Do men react so violently to other men who use power against them? I think not. Men expect other men to be rivals for power. When a man does another man in, it's all part of the game. Lying low until the next time, the loser acknowledges that the outcome would have been the same in a hands-down fistfight, so why not avoid the mayhem now? There will always be another day, and next time he could be on the other end. But a man doesn't expect a woman to be in the arena with him when the issue between them will be resolved in favor of the one who most aptly uses power. A man's sense of who deserves to be his rival is affronted when a woman shows that she's fully as competent as he in using power, so he releases in a yelling fury the force he failed to bring successfully against her.

I use power for my authentic purposes, as do some other women I know, as do most men. Perhaps when enough women use it as it can be used, as men have always used it, men will treat women as they now treat other men: as potential rivals who will sometimes defeat them and whom they will sometimes defeat, rather than as charming big-eyed creatures full of nasty surprises.

———

The wood of white oak is nearly impermeable. Makers of whiskey use it for kegs to hold the precious liquid within. Colonial shipbuilders used it to keep the sustaining liquid without. It is also nearly impenetrable. The close grain of the wood can flatten the tip of every nail that is not the sharpest steel, can withstand the point of any screw unless a drill initiates its bite. You will exhaust the muscles of your hammering or torquing arm unless you first prepare the wood for entry.

Just so did my close-grained days during August of 1966 resist the early facts of the war in Vietnam. My head was full of perhaps having to spay Ousia in case she had hip dysplasia, of discharging my obligation to my federal sponsor who, by extending my grant for six months, expected a smashingly fine piece of work in return.

But by Christmas week of that year, my reading in out-of-the-way periodicals and my deepening attention to the scatterings of protest convinced me that the United States did not belong in Vietnam, and I joined my voice to what was then the minority. I sought out a Quaker whose name I had been hearing as the person who could most swiftly connect me to the full sweep of national activity, and for the next eight years I committed time, thought, passion, and money to opposing the war.

I will not rehearse that struggle against our own government that we were perpetually made to feel was hopeless. Like everyone else, I marched in New York, marched on the Pentagon, marched wherever an undifferentiated mass of bodies was needed. I wrote letters, sitting down to my typewriter yet another time to say the same things to yet another person whose mind, once changed, could *eo ipso* change thousands. I was arrested, along with a hundred others, demonstrating at a military embarkation point. But while the arrest was real, the imprisonment was only *pro forma*: we were closed off into the cell area of the county jail but the cell doors themselves were left open, and in a few hours the attorney who the day before had advised us about our rights and described the arresting procedure secured our release and, later, dismissal of the charges against us.

Yet all these doings were familiar from earlier political activity. Only one confrontation drew a new edge out of me.

Specifically to fund the war, Congress had levied a federal tax on long distance phone service, and I refused to pay it. To put myself on record, I so notified the telephone company in writing. I pointed out that, since the phone company was merely collecting the tax for the federal government, my not paying it was unrelated to my paying for telephone service itself, which I certainly intended to do. Each month before mailing off my check I deducted the 6 percent tax, which by statute was scheduled to decline over time and to vanish when the war ended (it remains, twenty years later, at 3 percent, although now for a different reason).

Nearly two years of tax refusal passed before the early evening in April when I returned home to discover an IRS calling card slipped between door and jamb precisely where it would catch my attention as I inserted my key into the lock. A week later I looked up from mowing the back lawn to see a strange man crossing the grass toward me. Logos and Ousia, safely closed into the house away from the mower, had undoubtedly been warning me of his approaching presence, but the distinctive music of the mechanically rotating blades had lured my attention elsewhere. I stopped mowing and in the instant knew exactly who he was.

Yes, I was Alice Koller. Yes, I had written the letter he held out for me to examine. Yes, I was still refusing the phone tax. Yes, I'd be glad to explain why, although my carefully written letter had surely clarified the matter?

He stayed for half an hour, pleasant, never threatening, agreeing at certain points, disagreeing at others. It was a period when Americans were inserting flowers into the barrels of guns being pointed at them by other Americans who happened to be soldiers. Every supporter of the war, of the status quo, was a potential convert. No person, not even the police during your arrest, was to be passed up as a yet-to-be ally. Keep talking. Explain. Each new person who knows the facts will help end the war that much sooner. The agent was uninterested in my facts. He left without extracting the promise he had traveled so far to win.

I skipped up the three stairs to the back door and let the dogs out. They rushed past me and curved around to the wire mesh fence that prevented their racing out to the road. Their inquiring noses told them that someone had been here, someone they had not been given an opportunity to check out for me. To compensate them for the lost novelty I took them deep into the woods to their favorite stone fence, and I kept them leaping back and forth over it for one of the sticks lying there waiting to be thrown.

If that agent ever returned to Weston to renew his persuasion on me, he missed me again. Because a few months later we were living in Canada. Not, as young men did, to protest the war, but to accept the only teaching appointment in philosophy I ever held after Nantucket. The following year I returned to the United States, then over the next two years I moved twice within that New England that I even now believe holds a home for me somewhere. And still I withheld the tax each month.

By 1971 there were too many of us for the IRS to continue letting us courteously disagree. Wages were garnisheed. Bank accounts were attached. Property real and personal was confiscated, then auctioned off to whatever bidder would pay the delinquent tax. Some resisters, braver than I, refused to pay income tax as well, to pay any tax that could conceivably be used to support the war. Their friends and families would gather at the IRS auction, and they'd buy back the seized car or house for whatever pitiable sum was owed, then return it to its rightful owner who, while grateful for their concern, promptly began tax refusal again. Some tax resisters spent time in jail. Not the few hours I had been detained in a holding cell but months and years in real prisons. There is never a time for taking the IRS lightly, but it was most particularly not a time for doing so then.

The sun was already setting the mid-November afternoon I drove into the garage of the house I was renting at the edge of a hundred acres of wildness in western Massachusetts. I opened the rear doors to let the dogs out of the car first. That day, as always, Logos led the chase back into the woods, Ousia half a length behind, nipping his flanks. A grocery bag in one arm, my keys in hand, I was heading toward the house when a slowly moving car stopped at the entrance to my driveway. The sky was still bright enough not to require headlights, but the sun was low and a November dusk moves in quickly. At the car's unexpected appearance in my isolation—the woods behind me, the lake across the road, no other houses for half a mile in either direction—I shouted, "Logos! Ousia!" A man had stepped out of his car but quickly returned to its protection as the dogs made their noisy presence visible at my back. He unrolled his window a slit.

"I'm from the Internal Revenue Service," he called out. He had to repeat it several times before I heard him because I made no effort to silence the roaring dogs who were by then standing on their hind legs, front paws against his car window, trying to see the stranger within. They had raced out of the woods less because of my call than because they had heard a car's motor switched off. Although I had done a good job of training Ousia, I had failed badly with Logos, and she, noticing the way he thumbed his nose at my commands, soon paid little heed to my requests except when he was not nearby. Standing alone next to that country road in the receding light, I didn't call the dogs away from the car because I knew they wouldn't come until they had exhausted their curiosity. The interval of their uproar let me gather my thoughts, and then I placed my grocery bag on the ground, walked toward them, closed a hand around each of their collars and took a few steps backward.

"I'll put the dogs in the house," was my only response to the IRS identification card the man was holding up for me to see through his window. In the few moments of unlocking the front door and hustling Logos and Ousia inside, I overcame my unpreparedness for the discussion that I knew would be less cordial than the last one.

"Damn them," I muttered as I shut the house door. "How clever to keep trapping me at this time of day."

I stood quietly at the bottom of the front steps. I did not smile as the man approached, but neither would I let my face give away my whirling thoughts.

He set the tone without preliminaries. To the same three questions of three years ago I uttered the same "Yes." This time there was no attempt to persuade me out of my beliefs.

"You owe the IRS . . ."

I don't now recall the figure he recited from the piece of paper he pulled out of his coat pocket. Even after five years of not paying 6 percent of my long distance phone bill, it couldn't have been much higher than thirty dollars. I held back the whoop of laughter rising in my throat. In that cold air it issued forth to the man's ear as an intake of breath, and he heard it as though I had said, "You've caught me."

The little game we had barely begun ended at once.

"I'm here to collect that money." The voice of a man robbing you at gunpoint must carry the identical menace that abruptly filled the darkening air. "I'll accept cash or a check, and I'll write you a receipt on IRS forms. And here's my card so that you can verify my identification."

I looked quickly at the card he handed me. His office was forty miles away. It was then past five o'clock.

"I don't suppose anyone would still be in the office at this time of day," I said, on a rising inflection.

It was not that he had forgotten the time. It was the commonsense ordinariness of my question that surprised him: he thought I had already capitulated. In the silence I waited.

"Call in the morning, then," he said. "And I'll expect to have your check in my hand the following day." He turned, crossed the pebbled driveway toward his car, and then stopped. He was standing directly in line with the doorway of my garage, and the rear of my new orange station wagon, heavily subsidized by a friend, gleamed in what little light was ambient. He walked a few steps toward the garage, and suddenly I understood what he had the authority to do.

My mouth must have fallen open because this time when he turned to look at me he knew he had me.

"I'll impound your car," he said again, shaking his finger at it, as though it, not I, would be punished. Two decades earlier while I was studying for my first driver's license examination, I learned that a police officer's orders take precedence over any traffic light, any traffic sign, any rule of the road that would otherwise control a driver's actions. A police officer *is* the law, *is* its embodiment. And here, before me, in the person of a man speaking in anger and pointing to my car next to a lonely road as darkness descended was the full power of the United States government.

"I want your check on my desk the day after tomorrow," he said again, striding to his car, opening his door, getting in, and then, through the half-open window one last time: "I'll take your car. You know I can." He raced his engine through first and second gears, and then his angry motor heading east on that hilly road was the only sound audible as the November evening began.

The grocery bag upright in the driveway reminded me that I had not yet emptied the car of my other purchases. When I slammed the car door before my final trip into the house, its satisfying thud broke through my distraction. I'd have to make the car unmovable. I set the emergency brake and slipped the clutch into first gear. I checked the hood latch (it held), then locked the four passenger doors and the cargo door. If the IRS showed up with a tow truck the day after tomorrow, they'd get the car rolling only by first destroying the transmission and the entire braking system, and then who'd buy it at their auction? Yet as I stood contemplating the barrier I had made, there came to mind the image of a child I long ago watched build his sandcastle too near the ocean: when the tide began to creep onto the beach the little boy ran to the water's edge and held his arms out in front of him, palms facing the water, to keep it back.

Because there were no doors on that garage. The owner, thinking to save money, had built it to face west into the prevailing winds. An inch of snow might be blown around into the entry, but by and large it was safe against the weather. Who could ever have supposed that it would have to be made safe against an enforcement arm of an agency of the federal government?

I did not sleep well that night. Not because I was considering whether to pay the tax but because I was thinking of ways to safeguard my car. The one solution that kept coming to mind contained an element of deep uncertainty: the man I needed had two sons who knew everything about cars, but I had never discussed the war with him. He himself was a countryman whose long years of improvising, first as a farmer, then as the owner of an agricultural service, had taught him more than a trick or two. Turning to Harry for help carried a high risk because I was involved in a business relationship with him. Had he been merely an acquaintance, the possibility that my tax refusal might have angered him would have been unpleasant but one that I could walk away from. That our connection was through my livelihood meant that I might endanger even the minimal level of stability on which my days then rested.

At the earliest decent hour next morning I phoned him.

"Yes, come over," he answered immediately, hearing the urgency in my voice. "What's it about?"

"I'll tell you when I get there," I said, then drove the twenty miles into the bordering state as fast as the sloping curving road would allow, one eye on my rearview mirror for the prospect of being followed. Once I abruptly focused on the dogs in the rear seat. Might the IRS consider them "property" too?

I told my long story to the family around their breakfast table. I had to begin with the war, tossing my high card into play right at the start. There was a little squirming, a little getting up and walking around, but no one seemed ready to throw me out, so I kept talking.

One of the sons demolished my belief that I had immobilized my car. "A coat hanger can be slipped into the space between the window and the door. You fish around with the hooked end until you catch onto a bar that holds the lock button down, and then you just lift it up. They won't have to break a window to release the brake for towing."

"How about fastening a heavy chain across the garage doorway?" I asked.

"They could saw through it, or cut it."

Those were my only two ideas. I looked at the men in dismay.

"You can't leave the car in the garage." Harry was speaking. Listening to him propose the plan, his sons embroidering it, I realized that we were all talking about ways to protect the car, that we had plunged at once into discussing means, that no one had done more than lift an eyebrow about the end I was serving. Only then did I accept a cup of coffee and some freshly baked rolls, safe finally in asking whether they opposed the war.

One son was of draft age and more quickly on my side than the other, who was leaning toward opposition but would wait to vote for different representatives. The mother gave that shrug that still says: "My husband makes all those decisions." But then she went on:

"Harry hates the IRS."

I turned to him and smiled for the first time in fifteen hours. Harry told a story that every taxpayer who has ever been audited knows by heart. So: not for my reasons but for his.

I took him up on his offer anyway, and for the next several weeks I put his idea into effect. He owned some property a few miles away. I could garage the car there, lock the doors behind it (he gave me a key), and walk home. Since I was working in my own study, I could arrange my errands and appointments in town on one or two days a week. My erratic schedule would be difficult to track and if, returning from town, I thought I was being followed, I'd drive past the safe garage and circle until the road behind me was clear. The overwhelming advantage of the elaborate procedure was that it displayed my garage as empty to any car that happened to pass by.

By the time winter set in and the agent had not reappeared, I was parking in my own garage again. Partly I was relying on the snows of western Massachusetts to render travel from far away undesirable. Partly I was guessing that the IRS had found other ways of using its time for a greater return.

———

I am to meet the attorney very early this May morning at the elegant hotel on Fourteenth Street. In Washington, early morning is the only way a May day is tolerable. Even midmorning the dreadful humidity turns every moment outdoors into an encounter with a physical force that cannot be mastered but only evaded, and then only temporarily.

The attorney's "very early" is three hours later than mine. To meet him for breakfast I do certain things differently, but awakening early is not among them.

Wearing makeup is. This morning I smoothed on a light foundation and lipstick. I wear makeup now only when I deal with someone who is helping, who might help, with my case. The attorney this morning might. Anyone who will give me a writing or editing assignment that will let me pay for the case might. No one else, not even I, can make me care how I look. What I need from these two categories of people is so monstrously important that I place no irrelevant obstacles in the way of their giving it to me. Wearing makeup, I implicitly woo them, I open the way along familiar paths. We get to the business faster.

It is the same with my clothes. At home I wear a friend's cast-off sweaters and jeans the patches of which I patch. In summer I change to cotton shirts a dozen years old, some of which began life with long sleeves, now cut off above the elbow and hemmed. One of the laws of poverty is that you can't mend holes in cotton as easily as in wool. My other clothes have escaped the devastation of time because I so rarely wear them. A few blouses, a couple of pants, two pairs of shoes with moderate heels: I haul them out of the closet for meetings with attorneys and moneyers. For seeing everyone else I wear jeans.

I present myself to the eyes of others with the barest minimum of courtesy: I am clothed; the garments are clean. But there is no ornament of any kind. No jewelry. No scent. The makeup is my only concession to custom, to old habits. For two months after Logos' death I did not look into a mirror at all. It was not a policy I followed: it was my instinct. I could not look into my own eyes. Putting makeup on without looking into a mirror is not difficult. You look at the cheek, the chin, the nose, the lips, and you're through. You do not look at the eyes.

I am almost alone on the drive from McLean: Georgetown Turnpike to Dolley Madison Boulevard to George Washington Parkway to Constitution Avenue Bridge, the Lincoln Memorial in my direct line of vision as I cross. East on Constitution Avenue, the south side of the White House visible from the Ellipse, north on Fourteenth Street to a few blocks beyond Pennsylvania Avenue. All this in eighteen minutes, when in daytime traffic I'd allow twice as long. In less than a hour those Virginia highways, these capital streets, will be nearly impassable. Now they are conduits along which I flow.

I am earlier than the attorney's half past seven. I park close to the hotel but with due regard to whether the space will be legal by the time our breakfast meeting is over. I pass some old buildings, some new, all expensively maintained, annuals planted at the base of flowering trees. In this neighborhood on an early May morning you can put up with Washington.

I linger on the semicircular drive in front of the hotel, examining the slender pendulous branches of the weeping cherry near the sidewalk. I used to believe that only willows wept, for all the thought I ever gave the matter. But in the past few years I have undertaken my own education in botany and I have discovered the weeping European beech, the weeping Deodar cedar, the weeping Nootka false-cypress, the weeping Sargent hemlock. In the Gotelli Collection of conifers at the National Arboretum in northeast Washington there is a forty-year-old specimen of weeping blue spruce, so grief-struck that it is nearly prostrate. It stands only six or seven feet high, but the diameter of its falling branches measures more than fifteen feet. If you stoop beneath the weeping crown to look at the underside, you find lengths of galvanized pipe tied to and propping up branches that might otherwise recumbently spread along the ground.

I consider entering the hotel in the same moment that the doorman sees me and holds open the door. The dark wood of the lobby reflects discreet artificial lighting that augments the subdued daylight from west-facing windows. I sit in a chair deeper and softer than it had seemed to my eye. I concentrate on the doorway to make the attorney appear.

Before too long he is here. He guides me toward the dining room, where the maître d' greets him by name and immediately leads us to the table regularly reserved for him. No one else is in the room.

He does not look at the menu. "What fresh fruit do you have this morning?" he asks the waiter. It is a simple question and yet it dazzles me. I know the price of fresh pineapple, melon, blueberries in the market. I buy it anyway from time to time, not because I can that day afford it but because I buy less of something else I need.

But I am dazzled too by my surroundings. The heavy white napery on the tables, the perfect china, crystal, silver. The upholstered chairs. The waiters at their distant stations alert to a head slightly raised or a hand, then quickly, quietly, attending.

I used to be at home in such places with such people: Chicago, Boston, New York, Los Angeles. Blithely I'd enter on someone's arm, be entertained, and leave, never wondering when I'd return, knowing it would be the next day or the next week. But I abandoned that life after Nantucket. I could have reentered it in the years since: I chose not to. This morning in Washington, after long absence, I am here again.

I have had breakfast already: this morning at five when I returned from our daily walk in the woods a mile down Georgetown Pike with Ousia, soon to be fourteen, partially lame from a deteriorating spinal condition. And with Kairos, soon to be three, Ousia's companion, except that she more often sees him as her competitor. They wait for me at home in McLean, although they are certain that I shall never return.

To keep the attorney company, I order a croissant and coffee that I'll leave nearly untouched. We speak briefly of the weather and idle matters. I am ordinarily incapable of idle matters, but I am his guest. He will not charge me a fee while we talk informally here, and I know the fees Washington attorneys charge. I therefore wait for him to open the subject that brings us together.

He is kind: he reads my face, hears my voice, and he begins almost at once.

The strawberries arrive. The heavy cream. The croissants. The coffee. My disinterest in my meal does not stand in the way of his interest in his: he has listened to hundreds of people pleading for his help across breakfast tables, lunch tables, dinner tables. He has also started his day earlier by one hour in order to hear me out. He breakfasts but he listens while I outline the case as I have come to understand it from the small bits of evidence the defendants have grudgingly offered up in response to my attorneys' efforts to obtain them.

Attorneys. There have been four. Not one law firm of four but four in sequence. The fourth will be in court with me on Tuesday morning and I anticipate disaster. He will ask for a continuance because he needs more time to find a veterinarian who will agree to be my expert witness in the lawsuit I have been pressing for four years. The law requires that only persons as expert as the alleged malpracticers can testify that their actions have been inexpert. But collegiality has requirements that conflict with the law's. So far, no veterinarian we have approached is willing to testify that the two Maryland veterinarians in whose hospital Logos died malpracticed. Tuesday is only four days away.

Earlier this week when my host and I spoke on the phone, making these arrangements to meet, he warned me that extensive commitments would probably not let him take my case. He'd see me because I had his name from someone he knew, someone to whom I had been referred by someone I knew slightly through an animal rights organization that had written an amicus brief for me, one of three now filed with the court records. I watch him now for any sign of abiding interest as I condense the facts that almost never leave my consciousness. When I stop talking I do not know whether I have won him to me.

"More coffee?"

I shake my head: the level in my cup is down only two sips.

There is almost no pause. "I can't take your case, Alice," he says. "I wanted to meet you to see what you're like. To see what kind of person would try to do something that you must know is almost impossible. I also thought I might have some suggestions if I knew a little more than we had time to discuss on the phone."

I cannot speak for the surge of pain to his "No." There may be no case after Tuesday without him. Without someone.

"Have you considered representing yourself?"

I am drowning and he is offering me a wet dishcloth. I try to move my being up out of the deep well into which his "No" has flung me, to catch hold of the scrap he has tossed into our dying talk.

"I don't know what you mean," I say. I salt some interest into my voice. We are near the end of our time. I must carry something away from this talk so that my search for why Logos died, and when and how, will not be aborted on Tuesday.

"In the United States any person is entitled to represent himself, herself, in any court of law. It's called acting *pro se*."

I know the Latin: for oneself. In my own behalf.

From one instant to the next I am electrified. I am permitted to stand in a courtroom in my own behalf on behalf of Logos. The power I have given over to the parade of unsatisfactory attorneys during the past four years can be mine again.

"What do I have to do? How do I do it?"

He is smiling to see my excitement. "On Tuesday when your attorney asks for a continuance, the judge will ask the opposing attorney whether he objects."

"We've won our continuances over his objection. He'll object this time too."

"Pay close attention now. The judge may already be leaning one way or another from having read the file before going into court. Judges don't like to grant continuances. It keeps the court calendar cluttered with cases that should long since have gone to trial. So when the judge hears your attorney's reason for wanting a continuance, and the opposing attorney's objection, he may then immediately give his verdict: 'Continuance granted' or 'Continuance denied'."

I am memorizing his words as he speaks. I can be my own attorney.

"Now, suppose he grants the continuance. Your present attorney will still be the attorney of record."

"I don't want him. I thought I was hiring him last year, but apparently I merely hired his firm. He turned me over to a younger associate who worked hard, was very bright, even concerned, but a few months ago he was transferred to another case. The original attorney then assigned my case to someone I consider incompetent. If we win the continuance, I'm saddled with him."

"And if the judge denies the continuance, you'll have to go to trial on the assigned date. What you have to do is tell the court that you want to represent yourself *before* the judge decides about the continuance. The timing is absolutely essential."

He sketches quickly what will happen in the courtroom. I listen: how I listen!

We leave the dining room and stand talking for a moment on the sidewalk in the soft morning whose tempo and volume are now increasing swiftly. I am lightheaded with what lies before me.

"I'll help you when I can, Alice. I can't give you any priority, but if you call me at the right time I'll talk with you."

"What's the right time?" I know the answer before my words end. My interior concern makes me obtuse to even the smallest pleasantries.

"When I'm not busy doing something else." He smiles again, and we shake hands. I walk away only a few steps before I hear my name. I turn around.

"Alice, don't get bogged down in the details." He waves, and this time he's gone. I stand watching him, uncertain of his parting

words. The whole case is details. It is exactly details that I'm trying
to discover. He means something else, then. Something about this
new standpoint that he has opened out to me.

The drive home is almost as unhampered as the earlier drive
in: the heavy traffic is moving in the opposite direction.

Kairos waits a slither away on the other side of the door as I
turn the key in its lock. Our time of nuzzling is close, warm, but
only for a moment. I am thinking already of Ousia, and I call out
to her. Kai follows me down the entry hallway, then leaps ahead
across the living room, turns, rushes at me to let his nose brush
my calf, touching base, then leads the way straight to my bedroom
where Ousia rests on her mat in the corner formed by the foot of
my bed and the wall alongside.

I kneel to her as she raises her body up onto her elbow. I
encircle her in my arms and lay my face against hers. "Ooss Poos,"
I croon. All the names she has acquired during our years together
ripple off my tongue, and then I simply become silent, holding
her. I know that Kai is watching us, soundless, a little way behind
me. I know that he knows I say Hello to Ousia differently from
the way I greet him. She and I have been together thirteen years
almost without interruption. The hours of her day now bear pain
that I try all means to assuage. This morning I let her set her own
pace: I time my activities around her sense of how long she must
lie quietly, when she needs to go outdoors, when she is willing to
play, whether she will eat the food I prepare.

"I'm going to change my clothes," I say, loosing my arms from
around her neck, waiting for her to lower her head to the mat
again. But she rests on her elbows, regarding me as I peel off
blouse, pants, shoes. Halfway into my jeans I watch her struggle
to a partial sitting position, then lie down again. She does not want
me to help her. I busy myself in the closet and find the cotton shirt

that will see me through the muggy morning. Ousia is sitting now, leaning against the wall for support. Her soft black eyes have not left me, but she knows now that I am here to stay for a while, and so, in stages, she will in time move herself off her mat and come to find me in whatever room I'll light in.

With Kairos racketing behind me, ahead of me, not sure whether to lead me to the kitchen or my study, I leave Ousia in the bedroom and turn into the adjacent doorway where phone, desk, chair, typewriter, paper, files, books will ease my way into the newest path in the labyrinth of trying to learn how and when and why Logos died.

An hour before I am to appear at the courthouse I sit at my desk, dressed but not ready. This morning I awakened uncertain of the exact sequence of events, and so I have allotted extra time for a call to the Washington attorney. His secretary hands him the phone just as he walks through his doorway.

"I understand that I have to wait until both attorneys make their arguments, but how do I enter into all of that? My attorney won't know what I plan to do."

"Alice, just tell the judge there's something you want to say. When you're on the stand, tell him that you're dismissing your attorney and that you're representing yourself. It will be over before you know it, and then you can get down to work. Good luck." We hang up.

I inhale deeply, then expel the air. Out with the old. In with me.

I pick up my purse from the desk, stoop to stroke Ousia's silky fur. "I'll see you later, my girl." She knows what that means. She does not get off her mat to follow me to the outside door. Kairos does.

I slip through the space I hold purposely narrow, but Kairos inserts his nose into the last few inches as I try to close the door.

"Kai, I can't take you with me. I'll be back. I'll see you later."
The last phrase is almost a song. Confronted by the finality, he
withdraws his nose and now the door stands closed between us.

The Montgomery County Courthouse is only half an hour's
drive away, but I cross the highways of two jurisdictions to reach
it. 'Jurisdiction' is Washington-talk I learned quickly when I arrived here five years ago. The District of Columbia is a diamond-
shaped piece of geography carved out of Maryland on the northern
shore of the Potomac River. The southern shore of the Potomac is
Virginia. Northern Virginia. Everybody who works in the Washington area lives in one of these three places. Maryland is a state.
Virginia is a state. The District of Columbia wants to be a state
but the Congress, which governs the District in addition to gov-
erning the whole rest of the United States, refuses to give up that
privilege. Residents of the District regularly petition Congress to
let them have a referendum on whether the District should be a
state, but members of Congress regularly refuse to let the matter
be put to the vote. So a country based on the belief that no one
should be taxed without being represented taxes the residents of its
capital but lets them have only a nonvoting representative. Since
you can't talk about the "states" of Virginia, Maryland, and D.C.,
you talk about the "jurisdictions."

From my garage in McLean, which is in northern Virginia, I
head due west toward the circumferential route around Washington,
the Beltway. An interstate route and thus federal land. At first I
travel on Virginia territory, but within two miles the highway
crosses the Potomac and I am in Maryland. In a mile I choose the
left fork in the road, now a differently numbered interstate highway,
that will carry me to within a block of the courthouse, where I may
park for an indeterminate number of hours at no cost.

And why am I, a resident of Virginia, driving toward a Maryland courthouse?

Mr. Kay, Attorney Number Three, explained it all to me in his expensive northern Virginia office stuffed with furniture not to my taste. "We can file the suit in Maryland, because that's where the matters at issue happened. Or we can file in federal court. That's the advantage of your being a Virginia resident. If you lived in Maryland, we could file only in Maryland. But you live in one jurisdiction and the veterinary hospital is in another, so you have the additional alternative of federal court."

I was bewildered. On what basis could I make such a decision? "What are the advantages of federal court?" I asked.

"Some of the judges take a broader view than those in the state courts, particularly at the circuit level, which is where we'd be in Maryland." He paused, then called out to his younger associate: "Get me a list of the judges in federal court."

We neared the end of our discussion before the other attorney brought Kay the list. Swiftly they both considered the names.

"We're better off in Maryland," Kay decided. "Some of the judges in Baltimore are good, but they may be tied up with other cases by the time we get into court."

"Baltimore?" I was puzzled.

"Yes, federal court is in Baltimore. The circuit court where we'd file in Maryland is in Rockville."

"That's something to consider, too, isn't it?" A one-hour drive each way to Baltimore. Less than thirty minutes to Rockville.

"Yes." He said it casually, his head bent over papers, deciding which to photocopy, which to return to me. Then he looked up at me. "It's your decision, of course."

"But I have to rely on you. I have no understanding whatever of the consequences of doing one or the other."

"Then we'll file in Maryland. We have a better chance there."

But I've been observing attorneys for two years now, and I think the hour's drive to Baltimore was too far for him.

And that is why I am driving to a Maryland courthouse. To a

courtroom where I, by saying a few words, need no longer wait for other people to do things for me.

Courtroom 10 on the second floor is missing only one actor by the time I enter. The defendants' attorney and an aide are standing casually, talking at their table on the far side of the room. Mr. Gee, Attorney Number Four, and an associate are huddled over files at the table nearer me. A bailiff lounges against the judge's bench, and the court reporter unpacks her stenotype machine. Apart from the judge, all the essential performers are present.

Court and theatre: mirror images of one another. Actors, directors, scripts, costumes. Beginning, middle, and end. There is even a curtain in a courtroom: the bailiff draws it with words rather than hands. "All rise," he'll soon say. "In the Circuit Court for Montgomery County in the State of Maryland this court will come to order. Judge Edward Edwards, presiding." The formula begins its sweep the instant the judge opens the door from his chambers and it ends as he takes his seat at the bench.

The way you know you're in a courtroom, not a theatre, is that here there is no audience. In the theatre, if no one is out in front you're only rehearsing. Long ago I studied acting professionally, lived acting, thought of and wanted nothing other than acting, but I must shake off the belief that misleads me. It is a deadly error to think that we are only rehearsing because no one is in the audience. Here the audience is not the final ingredient, necessary as are all the others, perhaps more necessary than some, seemingly unaware that it can either inspire or shatter a performance whose parameters the actors thought they already had in hand. There are seats here for an audience, just as in a theatre, but these seats are not a constant feature that actors, director, lighting, makeup, sound, and crew keep in mind through all the weeks of rehearsal, the hoped-for months, years, of performance. These seats are only symbolic. They say: the courts in the United States may be entered by anyone at any time during any proceeding. Without explaining anything to, without asking permission from, any authority, you may simply sit in these seats, listen, observe. The symbolic seats are real benches: wooden, smoothly polished, but hard. Count on changing your position frequently if you remain.

My attorney looks around the room, sees me, and nods. The gesture acknowledges my presence, no more. He knows my dissatisfaction with the attorney he assigned to me. I know his dissatisfaction with my having fallen behind in the monthly retainer fee he had required me to agree (in writing) to pay. He has lectured me about it several times, but my delinquency would give him a good reason to ask the court to relieve him of representing me.

I know that I may, am permitted to, sit at the plaintiff's table with him. Instead, I take a position on a bench from which I may view the entire performance. Fifth row center. Today I am the audience.

The defendants' attorney, Attorney Ess, is now alone. The person with him a few moments ago was only a messenger from his office bringing him some papers to sign. Compared with mine, his route to the courthouse is almost instantaneous. He simply crosses the street and walks a few steps to the entrance.

My first summer in Connecticut, my country backyard was surrounded by woods and rock fences. From someone at my then-office, I bought four young tomato plants, carried them home carefully in my car, then spent the rest of the daylight digging holes, fertilizing, planting, and watering them. For maximum sun but also to protect them from Logos' racing after a ball, I planted them out of the way, next to the stone fence that separated my yard from the swale beyond. When Logos and I tumbled out of the house first thing each morning for our dawn walk, I'd go straight to the plants to check on their progress. Returning home after work, I'd change clothes as fast as a very close German shepherd nose would let me, then we'd rush outside and I'd inspect the plants before we walked into the woods. I'd have a last look just before we went into the house after our evening stroil. With all that looking and tending, they thrived for about two weeks. One morning one plant was a few inches shorter than the others. By evening a second plant had also minimized. Over the next several days both plants and now a third seemed to be evaporating into the air. The following morning from my window I saw a dark brown furry creature walking along the rock fence, then suddenly disappearing.

I described him to one of my office-mates.

"A woodchuck, probably," he said.

"Maybe you can also tell me what's been happening to my tomato plants," I said. Almost as I began the story he burst into laughter.

"The woodchuck lives in that fence," he said.

I had set the tomatoes to grow directly outside the woodchuck's front door. He had only to pop out of the ground, chomp on a leaf or two when it suited his fancy, then go on about his business until he was hungry again.

By filing suit in Maryland I had planted the tomatoes outside this woodchuck's door. No, not woodchuck, not any nonhuman animal. The qualities this man displays are solely human ones: he says nothing plainly, openly, but only evades.

"The vets must have looked very hard under a lot of stones to find him," I said to Attorney Kay the first time we all appeared in court together.

His baby face turned toward me with some surprise. "The vets didn't hire him," he said. "He's the insurance company's attorney."

"Insurance company?" I sometimes thought that almost every word I spoke during the early months of this years-long struggle betrayed my ignorance. But then, my advanced degrees are not in law.

"Vets carry malpractice insurance, just as doctors do. When someone sues them, their insurance company defends them."

"So he works for the insurance company? He's on their staff and they sent him here?"

"No," said Kay, not taking kindly to his role as instructor. "He practices here in Rockville. When the vets contacted their insurance company to tell them you filed suit against them, the company looked for an attorney they believed would prevent them from having to pay the damages we're asking. They also wanted someone convenient to the court so they wouldn't be socked for travel time as well."

I remember how my stomach felt, curling into itself. "They pay all his fees? The vets pay nothing?"

"The vets paid when they bought their insurance policy. They pay an annual premium, just like you do for car insurance." He was tired of the line of questioning.

"I hope it costs them a fortune," I muttered.

"It doesn't," Kay said. The subject was at an end.

At home that same day I riffled the Washington phone directory. What would an organization that lobbies for the insurance industry call itself?

I started with the Insurance Institute. Quite a few companies write malpractice policies, I am told. In Maryland? In Maryland. And how about veterinary malpractice policies? Long pause. Only two companies. Baltimore, both of them. The woman had no idea about costs. However, if I wanted the names of the companies to contact directly? I took down their phone numbers.

The first company sold both kinds of insurance. At first they thought I was inquiring about buying a policy. The manufactured affability jelled a little when I said I was writing a report for a college course. There were a lot of "depending upons" in their information. Depending upon whether the vet was in a city or a suburb or the country, depending upon whether he had previous claims, depending upon his own choice of coverage. Surely there's a general range you recommend, I asked. Well, she said.

Four pointed questions later, I had it. A veterinary malpractice policy is written for about a million dollars. It costs about fifty dollars a year.

Kay's fee was eighty dollars an hour. An hour. Every phone call I made to him or he to me. Every letter he wrote me or I him. Every phone call he made to the court, to the defendants' attorney. Every time he opened a law book to refer to some precedent. Every minute, bar none, accumulated with other minutes to form an hour, and every hour took eighty dollars out of my pocket.

The vets were each paying fifty dollars a year. Probably only the vet who owned the hospital paid the premium, since the other vet merely worked for him. So one was paying nothing, the other was paying less than two dollars a week. In exchange, they had an attorney with access to unlimited resources. They didn't care how long their phone calls to him were, or how much time he spent on briefs responding to ours. And his instructions from the insurance company were: win. Whatever your fees are, they'll be lower than the damages we'd have to pay if we lose. Win, they must have told him, however you can: if not by hand-to-hand combat, then by whatever trickery you can conceive. Or maybe they merely looked for a man (they would think only of a man) who understood, without being guided, that those were the rules.

There he sits now, at his full ease. No shadow of concern or tension on his face. He expects to win this motion: he expects the trial to begin three weeks from now. As finally scheduled.

Because he himself moved for a continuance last year. The vets, he said, wanted to attend the annual meeting of their professional society. Not just wanted to, but needed to, in order to keep their professional skills well-polished, to learn the news of all the techniques, all the drugs, all the latest of everything. For evidence, he enclosed a flyer announcing the meetings. On the first page of the flyer was a line drawing of a cowboy on a bucking horse. Come on and have a good time in the far West, said the drawing, to anyone whose idea of fun was to lay a heavy strap across a horse's genitals, then tighten it around his back, so that the pain and nothing else would make him fight the strap, leaping into the air, whirling around, kicking with the whole rear half of his body. As though all that, and not the vicious men who placed it there, would get it removed. Broncobusting, it's called. A sport, it's called. But veterinarians are committed to the well-being of nonhuman animals, aren't they? Ah, but what they're really committed to is the owner: his wishes, his check; her wishes, her check.

The judge was not upset that the decorum of the legal system was being ridiculed by the flyer. Amused, no doubt, instead. He knew, from his own professional society, that almost no new knowledge gets passed around at annual meetings. Abstracts of the papers to be read are distributed in advance with the announcement. You may call the person who has written a paper that interests you and ask for a copy before the meeting. No, it's not knowledge that's exchanged: it's conviviality. Whoever designed the flyer was conveying a truer sense of what happens at annual professional meetings than the ponderous titles of the papers.

Yet the judge wrote: "Motion granted." And in those few squiggles of his pen another year of my life slipped by. Because postponing a date for a trial isn't like postponing a date for lunch: you can't just set it for next Thursday at the same time. A trial lasts a certain number of days. The opposing attorneys themselves estimate its length: three days, five days, a month. The appointments office in the courthouse has charge of the court calendar. The judge's clerk phones downstairs: "When do you have three days?" Or, "Five days?" There might not be a block of three days uninterrupted by half-day or one-day or two-hour trials for another fifteen months. In August she might say, "June 21 next year."

That's the continuance Attorney Ess won for the defendants.

Last August they decided (Ess suggested that they decide?) to attend the annual veterinary meeting in September. "Motion granted," said the judge. Trial rescheduled for next June 21.

Today it's my turn. My attorney will remind the court that last summer the defendants were granted a continuance. We, of course, have asked for continuances ourselves and had them granted. That, not his own continuance, is what Ess will emphasize.

My choice of seat allows my peripheral vision its widest scope. Without seeming to look at Ess I can watch every movement he makes. Files and papers and pens and notebooks spread out in careful order before him, he leans back in his chair. Not hard against his table, but a foot and more away from it. Not going back and forth from one yellow sheet to another, as my own attorney now does, head to head with his associate. It is part of Ess's ploy: to look so sure, to be so sure. To worry his opposition.

The judge enters. We rise. We sit.

The judge speaks. "I wish to advise the plaintiff that I have had dealings with the defendant Dr. Arr. Many years ago he took care of one of my family's animals. I have not had occasion to see or talk with him since. I am, however, willing to step down from this case if the plaintiff believes that I might not be able to offer an unprejudiced decision."

Attorney Gee rises. "Your Honor, I would like to discuss this with my client."

"Certainly." He waits only a moment, and then he declares a twenty-minute recess. Gavel. All rise. Chamber door closes behind him. Scraping of chairs. Movement. Noise in the courtroom.

I walk to the plaintiff's table as Gee turns to find me. "Do you want another judge?" he asks. He does not care, but he must ask me.

I have watched this judge in another courtroom. He is quiet and he is fair. Indeed, my heart leaped when he came through the door into this court: we would at last have someone judicious.

"If you don't want this judge," counsels my counsel, "we'll have to get another court date for this motion. It might be a month. Or more." The irritation in his voice tells me that he did not like driving all the way out to Rockville from D.C., would like even less doing it again a month from now. Nothing in his voice tells me that the uncertainty I'd have to bear for the intervening weeks is of any importance to him.

"I don't want to wait," I tell my attorney. "Let's just go on as we are."

"You're sure?" He barely attends to my response. He is simply covering his tracks.

I return to my seat. Gee arranges files in his briefcase. Ess has now moved his chair a few inches farther back from his table. The sprawl covers a wider area. The ease is more apparent. We have used up only four of the recess's twenty minutes. I do not have a book with me to pass the time: this morning was to be too extraordinary for me to think in terms of passing the time.

All rise. We do. Be seated. We are.

My attorney stands behind his table to address the court. His voice carries tones I do not hear when he addresses me. Earnest. Concerned. The judge listens carefully. Not untowardly serious, not bending backward to show me anything at all. Simply serious enough for the occasion. It is a good sign of fair.

"This case has already been continued several times," he says, glancing at the record stapled to the inside back of the file folder. Then he looks up at my attorney. "Are you prepared for trial?"

"We are, Your Honor. But the veterinarian we've been consulting as our expert witness has a schedule conflict that he has so far been unable to resolve." He sits.

The judge nods toward Ess, who rises to make his argument. He is sincere too. "My clients are anxious to have the trial take place as scheduled. They have arranged their time so that they can appear in court on the day now set. Your honor, the reputations of these two excellent veterinarians are at stake in this case. They want to do everything possible as quickly as possible to show that Dr. Koller's charges are totally unfounded."

I gloat. Their reputations have been soiled. In this tiny moment I taste one fleeting drop of justice. It will have to last me a long time.

The judge asks Ess the same question. "You are prepared to go to trial?"

"We are, Your Honor." Abruptly he moves close to his table and leans over it, both hands spreading outward over it in a gesture designed to calm roiling waters. Palms down, arms encompassing tablets, notes, files, he speaks again, the assurance that he is winning seeping into his voice: "I have everything on hold."

On hold. The two vets can be brought to the courtroom in half an hour. His aide is only across the street and can deliver to him here all the rest of what he needs for trial. He himself could, without even straightening his tie, begin his opening remarks.

The judge now leaves off watching him. He turns his attention to the files in his hand. There is a silence.

Now, Alice.

I stand. "Your Honor, there is something I would like to say." I remember the correct words: "I would like to address the court."

My attorney wrenches his whole body around in his chair to stare at me. To my right, Ess's snake-charming hands fall to his sides. He is still standing but he seems abruptly shorter. The judge looks at my attorney, whose back now faces him, then turns toward me. None of what the others do or say matters. The court is the judge's.

"Please come forward to the witness stand." His voice is no more nor less kind to me, who have disrupted the flow of events, than it was to the two attorneys.

To reach the stand I must pass behind and around the side of the defendants' table. Ess steps backward to let me pass. I do not look at him. I am intent on carving my way toward the witness stand.

The bailiff approaches me, a Bible in his hand. Thinking about this moment during the last four days I have considered announcing that I am agnostic, that I will not swear on a Bible, but that I will swear. But since I am agnostic, I could swear on a heap of colored ribbons, for all the difference it makes. I intend to speak the truth, no matter the form of words I am required to use.

"Raise your right hand." I do. "Repeat after me." I do. I am sworn.

The judge rests his chin in his left hand and contemplates me. My attorney half-rises as though uncertain whether to lead me through he-knows-not-what. The judge waves him back into his chair.

"For the record, tell the court your name. Spell your last name for the court reporter." I do so.

"Your complete current address. Spell any names that are un-usual." I do so.

"What is it you wish to say to the court?"

From the witness stand I see suddenly that there *is* an audience: it is all the people whose eyes are on me now. I am writing the script even as I speak the words.

"I wish to dismiss my attorney." I look at Gee for only an instant: his face is reddening, his mouth is tight, his whole bearing is angry.

The judge is now examining my face. It is there, and in my voice, that he will see his decision.

"And have you chosen another attorney?"

"I have, Your Honor. I wish to represent myself."

My attorney is now closing his books, folding his long yellow tablets, gathering his file folders, and throwing everything into the briefcase he will no longer need in this case. It is the last time I look in his direction.

The judge asks me the question he has already put to the two attorneys. This time there is a very slight smile on his face but I understand that he is not mocking me. "Are you prepared to go to trial at the scheduled time?"

"No, Your Honor. But if you grant the continuance we have requested, I'll be ready on whatever day the trial is rescheduled for."

Convince him, Alice, said the Washington attorney, that you are not frivolous, that your cause is not frivolous. He can't refuse to let you act *pro se*, but he can refuse the continuance.

It has come down to this one man and these few minutes. I begin to talk. I do not know what my next words will be, nor where they come from, but I find them, or they me. I talk, calling on the years I have spent studying and teaching reasoning, the years I have spent writing my thinking, the years long ago of having learned the impact of my voice and my eyes and my way of sitting in a chair. I tell this man who has it in his power to close the door on my ever knowing how and when and why Logos died who Logos was and what he meant to me and I to him. I tell him of the four years that I have been committing myself to this search for the truth by the only means I believed accessible to me, how I have supported this lawsuit by whatever writing and editing assignments I could find, that I am capable of learning whatever I must learn in order to represent myself, to be Logos' voice, until I learn what I have set myself to learn.

For long minutes I do not stop talking. I have the sense that if I stop talking, the judge will think that I have nothing more to say, no further reason to lay before him. I do not keep my eyes steadily on him: I am thinking every moment as I talk, and as my thought rushes along one corridor after another, pursuing my purpose, I cannot be distracted by what I see, even though the judge is now within the essence of my purpose. From time to time my gaze sweeps the room and I, unwillingly, see that the defendants' attorney is no longer sitting three feet back from his table, one leg carelessly propped on the other knee, hands in pockets, the confident winner I saw before I took this stand. I do not want to attend to him at all, and yet my peripheral vision lets me see him as in almost constant motion. With every few words I speak, he hitches his chair forward, closer to his desk. In the instant that I allow even a speck of my attention to alight on him, I think: "He's scared!"

But then I'm back with the judge again, who himself has turned away from me. An aide has brought him a note that he, while I still talk, now reads. Why isn't what is happening in this courtroom important enough for him to give it his full attention? Is he simply humoring me, letting me run on, when he has already decided that the case will go to trial as scheduled?

I find one last argument in my armamentarium, and then I become silent. I look around the courtroom trying to gauge in advance of the verdict what I have accomplished. To my left in the middle of the room, Ess is now pasted up against his table, leaning forward, not smiling at all, staring at the judge's face.

"I am not inclined," the judge begins, "to grant continuances. This case in particular has been on and off the court calendar many times. The present circumstances, however . . ."

His voice drops slightly, pauses slightly, on the last syllable of 'circumstances,' and even before the 'however,' I know his decision.

". . . are sufficiently compelling for me to grant one today. I have already asked my clerk to find out for me the next open date for this trial."

The note!

"I hereby grant the continuance until May 12, 1980. Dr. Koller, I expect this to be the last request for a continuance. And I expect you to take your responsibility in this matter seriously."

"I will. I do, Your Honor."

I won. I won.

He taps his gavel, gathers his papers, stands. We stand. He leaves.

In the witness box I am a few steps above the courtroom floor. From this slightly elevated distance I see small clusters of activity break out. At his table the man who no longer represents me and his associate are methodically placing papers in files, files in briefcases, pens in pockets. From his former command station, Ess walks over to my former attorney. They talk as though they had not been former enemies. The court reporter is packing up her little machine. The bailiff and the judge's clerk are in earnest chat.

I wait. Are there some papers I must sign to make my new status official? Does someone here have some instructions for me?

No one even glances in my direction. Suddenly I understand that I have no connection whatever to anyone in this room. I step down from the stand. In three paces I am nearly opposite my former attorney's table. Neither he nor Ess interrupts their discussion at my approach. I walk around them and pass behind the plaintiff's table to the heavy courtroom door and leave.

Along the corridor. I am my own attorney. Down the stairs. Logos, I will learn the truth now. Out the mammoth door into the bright clear Maryland morning. The victory carries me like the wind all the long drive home.

12

MOURNING

IF THERE IS a person you love only because he is who he is, love him only for the sake of loving him, so that you commit yourself to him, valuing his well-being equally with your own, then you will mourn when he dies. And for each person you love this way you will mourn: five persons loved, five mournings are in store for you.

What is it to mourn? It is to be hurled into pain so vast that you cannot imagine it in advance of being incorporated by it, a pain that usurps all other thinking, all other feeling, a pain that occupies you as you occupy the house you live in. While the pain that is mourning appropriates you, making you identical with it, so that you do nothing but only mourn, you will cry out, "How have all the millions of people before me endured this?" Women have told me that if they had been able to remember the pain of childbirth they would not have had a second child. But birthing ends with a newborn. Mourning does not end.

Track 'mourning' through the dictionary and you'll come upon all these ideas. 'Mourn' from Greek for 'care,' in turn relating to 'memory,' 'remembering.' 'Pain' from Greek for 'payment,' 'penalty'; 'to pay,' 'to punish'; 'price.' 'Grief' from Latin and from Greek for 'heavy.' 'Grieve,' from Middle English, Old French, Latin for 'to burden,' from Latin for 'heavy,' 'grave,' like Gothic, Greek, Sanskrit for 'heavy.' 'Sorrow' from Middle English *sorow*, from Old English *sorg*. Like Old High German *sorga* 'sorrow,' and Old Slavic *sraga* 'sickness.' 'Anguish' from Latin for 'straits,' for 'narrow,' like Old English for 'narrow.' Philosophers warn against equating the etymology of a word with the word's uses in contemporary language, but these derivations from language to language carry living seed. Mourning is one of the prices of loving, the sorrow a permeating heaviness that constricts your doings to one single doing: trying to match the present absence with the past presence, and failing, remembering.

At eight minutes past eight o'clock on the morning of March 10, 1975, Ousia was asleep near me in the dining room of our house surrounded by woods in northern Virginia. I, having breakfast, was thinking ahead two hours to the time I'd be permitted to see Logos at the veterinary hospital, to try to feed him against his disinterest in food, to reassure him that he'd be back with me in a day or two in face of his clear wish not to be in a cage, catheterized, uncomfortable, lonely.

When the telephone rang, I glanced at my watch and thought, "After eight. So it can't be long distance." And then I lifted the receiver.

"Miss Koller," said the murdering voice, "I have bad news for you."

"Yes?"

Silence.

"What is it? Tell me!"

Silence still. Then: "Logos passed on a few minutes ago."

"Passed on"? Did he really say that? Or did he say, ". . . passed away"? I know he did not say ". . . died."

"I'll be there right away."

I hung up the phone. I stood where the telephone rested in the small hallway and I began to scream with the deliberate purpose of erupting into sound. But I could not bring forth the roar that was in me surging to burst the farthest limits of my lungs and vocal cords. My voice became a screech, narrowing the volume of sound instead of expanding it. Ousia appeared in the doorway, watching me in fear and wonder, and in between my shrieks I said the one word that you will say, that everyone says: "No." No, it is not true. No, it did not happen. No, I don't believe it. No, no, no, no. It is the only route open to you in that instant of hearing the word 'died,' or as the professional soothers, the thieves, say: 'passed on,' 'passed away.'

Only months later, thinking over and around and inside and from the underside and from above, hour after hour, minute following on minute, from the first moment you awaken until you lie down at evening, dozing, blurring the jagged, hazy time of waking up from dreams and nightmares two, three, four times a night, it is only during the course of an unending attempt to understand what 'dies' means that you begin to catch your earliest glimpse of it in all its concreteness.

Logos died. The two words do not go together: 'died' is the wrong verb. Logos runs. Logos wants to go for a walk. Logos eats. Logos chases the stick I throw. Logos jumps the rock fence. Logos swims. Logos teases me into trying to get his ball away from him. Logos skips out of my reach. Logos leads the way on our paths in the woods. Logos warns me of the approach of strangers. Logos comes to me during thunderstorms. All these verbs go with 'Logos.' But 'dies'? What does 'dies' mean?

'Dies' means 'nothings.' Logos nothings. No verb in the present tense can now be truthfully used in any sentence in which 'Logos' is the subject. Not even 'sleeps in the earth.' Logos *is* not. There is no place I can go where Logos will be. Even where Logos' body now lies buried, Logos *is* not.

Logos died. If I must use the words to someone I knew before March 10, I say 'Logos,' then I stop, and in those seconds of silence, 'died' appears to my mind's eye in whatever fullness of meaning I have thus far been able to extract from it, and I am unable to say it. Because Logos plays, Logos comes to me, Logos wants to go outside, but not: Logos nothings.

Dies. Does not exist. After six months and three days, it occurred to me that Russell's Theory of Descriptions, although invented to solve a technical problem in formal logic, was an incredible insight into the meaning of 'dies.' It is not possible to say that something exists, said Russell, because you have to be able to use the identical symbols, together with the negation sign, to declare that it does not exist. But the only way to say that something does not exist, he went on, is to say that no matter what you do, you will not encounter the thing in the course of your doing. However, the only way to say that something does exist is to specify at least one activity which, by your doing it, involves that thing. Just so, there is no activity such that, whatever I do, I shall be able to encounter Logos in the course of my doing that thing. 'Logos died' means that there is no place such that, if I go there, I shall find Logos playing, eating, sleeping, running, jumping, calling to me, rolling in the leaves. He is not upstairs or downstairs or in my car or in the woods or on the front lawn or on the side lawn or on the back lawn or walking down the road or swimming in the pond or at Whit's or at any vet's or hiding from me or out of the reach of my voice. Logos is not ill or in pain or well; he is not fat or thin or hungry or content or lying beneath my desk as I write. Nothing I can say of any creature who is still alive can be said, any longer, of Logos. Nevertheless, I keep having the feeling that he is somewhere waiting for me to pick him up, and if I could only remember where he is, I'd go to get him in the instant. It is the only way I seem able to account for why he is not here with me, as he was, almost without interruption, for twelve years and four months, to the day. Twelve years and four months was a quarter of my entire life. I did not spend more time with any human being. He was the most familiar being in the world to me, and now that he is no longer in the world, the world itself is not familiar.

'Dies' means that, however efficient you are at dealing with practical problems, with finding out what needs to be done and how to do it and who does it best or who can teach you how to do it and what you need in the way of tools or implements or materials to do it, your efficiency has no field in which to function. There is nothing to be done, so it does not matter how good you are at doing anything else. But how is that possible? How could there be nothing, not one single thing, to do? Your hands, your legs, your body, your perceptiveness, your ability to manage and direct other people's activities, your insight into the nature of some given problem, your freely ranging imagination that is ordinarily capable of projecting half a dozen solutions within minutes of being presented with a problem, which then becomes newly transformed and thus exhibits even more possible ways of being resolved, dealt with, abolished: none of this is even relevant. There is *nothing* to be done. There cannot be a problem, because no solution is necessary.

Yet, although there is nothing you can *do*, there *is* a problem. It is a problem so intractable that nothing that ever preceded it seems deserving of having been called a problem before. It is the problem of where Logos is and why he isn't here with me. I still do not know the answer to that problem.

In Bergman's *Seventh Seal*, an idealistic knight and his cynical squire are returning home from the crusade after many years away. Nearing the end of their journey, they have drawn to themselves an assorted group of pilgrims. A man who had tried to rape a young girl, now part of the group, is wandering in a forest nearby, about to die from the plague that has been sweeping Denmark. The man calls out for help from anyone who can hear him. The group stands by silently, then the young girl starts toward him to comfort him. The squire runs after her and catches her before she touches the man, draws her back, holds her arm tightly. "There's nothing you can do," he says to her in a low voice, and then, when she tries again to go toward the dying man, roughly: "Can't you hear that I'm consoling you?" I gasped, then wept when I first saw the film in my final year of graduate school. Later that evening I wept uncontrollably when I tried to tell a friend what had harrowed me. Now, all these years later, I see that what had caught my attention that evening was that the squire attempted to console the girl, that he even wanted to try. It was the lesser matter. The matter to be understood is that there is nothing I can do. But I do not see that as consolation.

For almost as long as Logos has been dead, I have found myself waiting to hear a certain idea voiced by someone. I know neither what idea I'm waiting to hear, nor who will say it to me. I don't even know what kind of person I'm expecting to hear it from. If I knew at least that much, I could begin to go to that kind of person, a doctor, say, or a poet, until I found the specific person who would be able to, who would in fact, say the thing I am aching to hear. But neither, of course, do I know what kind of idea I want to hear expressed. If I knew that, I could begin ranging among the ideas of that kind. It is not in philosophy. Do not look in philosophy. The idea I'm waiting to hear may well be a consolatory one, although that's not so much a category of knowledge as a use to which any category of knowledge may be put. But I don't even know that: I don't know whether the thing I'm waiting to hear is something which, when I grasp it, I'll use as consolation.

In fact, I think the idea will be one that will let me understand, will let me comprehend the meaning of 'dies.' Comprehend: take up within the web of all the other things one understands; make part of one's mind; fit in with the other ideas that one has, with immense effort over the years, brought to clarity.

Yes, that's it. I do not *understand* Logos' dying: it is not part of my mind yet. The events that began March 10, 1975, are so thoroughly foreign to me that I cannot mesh them with what was so familiar to me before. They subsume themselves in some category other than 'familiar.'

Other than. You find yourself doing almost everything in ways other than you did them only the instant before you hear the word 'died.' In that instant you start saying "No," and thereafter you say "No." And you do "No": you do other-than. It is the single feature common to all cultures in the otherwise protean confrontation of human beings with death.

> Peoples who wear their hair long cut or shave it;
> those who habitually cut or shave it allow it
> to grow. Those who paint omit the painting.
> Those who braid their hair unbind it and wear it
> loose. Those who wear clothing go naked, or wear
> scanty, coarse, or old worn-out clothes.
> Ornaments are laid aside or covered up. Those
> who habitually dress in gay clothing put on
> colourless—black or white—garments. Ainu
> mourners at a funeral wear their coats inside out
> or upside down. Among the Bangala a man sometimes
> wears a woman's dress in token of sorrow. Peoples
> who ordinarily cover their heads uncover them, and
> vice versa.

So writes E. S. Hartman in "Death and Disposal of the Dead," an article by many authors in Hastings' *Encyclopedia of Religion and Ethics*. Remember to read this article when you mourn, if you now mourn. These one hundred pages, a good third of which are set in diamond-point type, detail the customs and beliefs surrounding death in all religions, among all peoples, prehistoric, ancient, and modern. Reading a few pages at a time while your own wailing waits a breath away, you will not be surprised to learn that the "custom" of wailing is universal. The anthropologist merely remarks the fact, but of course it is not a custom, although customs have risen out of it, their patterns conforming to each society's beliefs about all other matters. Wailing is universal because human beings are equipped to cry, and death surpasses all other occasions for calling forth crying.

In the sixth century B.C. the otherwise great lawgiver Solon forbade Athenians from "excessive" manifestations of grief: striking their breasts, lacerating their faces, tearing at their clothes, pulling out their hair. But his fellow citizens continued to do these things despite the law. Plato himself considered it indecorous to weep for the dead, in his *Laws* prohibiting it, except perhaps inside one's own house. But he wrote the *Laws* a few years before he died at eighty. Fifty years earlier, at age twenty-eight, he was not present at Socrates' dying, as he tells us in the *Phaedo*. We know only that he was ill: we do not know what the illness was. Socrates' other friends watched him drain in one breath the cup of poison that was the Athenians' penalty for his "impiety," and when they saw that he had actually drunk it, everyone in the room except Socrates broke down. Plato would have known that Socrates would not weep, and he would not have wanted Socrates to see him weep. That was his "illness," I think: weeping, and within his house, during Socrates' last hours.

'Excessive' and 'indecorous' are observers' words, not words of those who mourn. Observing my anguish, you shrink away from me, saying, "It is too loud. It goes on too long." And then your child, your lover, your friend, dies. Whose lamentation is excessive, indecorous, now?

I did not eat for three days. Only coffee, hot, and vodka, straight, passed my lips, and these only because, assaulting my mouth and throat, they let me register the fact of taking fluids in. I gave away my scarves. I could not consider looking into a mirror, and so I wore no makeup. For six years I did not touch my jewelry.

I did or forbore from doing these things not because some

religion, some social custom, dictated them to me: they were my spontaneous doings and forbearings. They are natural elements of mourning, and the human species has long taken note of them, then prescribed some version of them that thereafter became that tribe's, that nation's, that sect's, ritual to be performed in those circumstances. Tibetans wear no colored clothes, neither wash their faces nor comb their hair; the women wear no jewelry, the men shave their heads. Grave clothes for Muhammadan women are white or green or any color but blue, but mourning women dye their clothes and veils dark blue and wear blue headbands, smearing the same indigo dye on their hands and arms and on the walls of their rooms. Orthodox Jews fast for seven days, sit on the floor or on a low bench bareheaded and barefoot in ashes, with ashes on their heads. Each mourning practice of no matter what culture is a device, an accumulation of devices, for attempting to knit together that which cannot be understood with whatever paltry else is understood, to weave together the aberrant with the familiar without once losing sight of its anomaly.

That which is out of keeping, not consistent with the usual, is the body that does not move.

Living bodies are a constant source of human conversation. People normally speak of their own bodies at your first faint expression of interest in the state of their health. They allow one another almost unlimited leeway in describing current sickness or recovery from it, recent surgery or the prospect of it, every gain or loss of weight, every step in every building up of strength, of endurance, of flexibility. They speak of the health or illness of the bodies of their wives, their daughters, their husbands, their sons, in nearly equal detail. We know the bodies of those we love better indeed than our own: we can see and touch those bodies in places they themselves cannot see and touch. We know by heart the repertoire of movements distinctive to those bodies. Every shade of every motion of her child's body is familiar to a mother, so that the tiniest deviation serves as a clue to oncoming illness, a hint at a new stage of growth. You willingly, joyfully open yourself out to the fullest reaches of cherishing the body of someone you love, of nourishing it, of sustaining it in being.

And then that lover, that child, dies. In the next instant it is still his body, her body, but it is still. The chest does not rise up and lower, the eyelids do not flicker, the hands do not seek their most comfortable position, nor the legs, the shoulders do not shift to balance the weight of the lower limbs. Nothing else has changed, except that it does not move. Touch the body and your fingertips will find warmth; hold the body and it will fill your embrace; arms, legs, head, fingers will respond to your slightest pressure; the profile is the same to your eye; the hair still silky. All details except that single one remain unchanged. But that single detail has changed everything: starting now, he is dead, she is dead.

If in the instant of death bodies exploded or spontaneously combusted, it might—I say only 'might'—be possible to understand death. There would be no object continuing to look and smell and feel familiar and yet lacking in that one small detail. That is what sets the beginning of the problem for you. What words will you use?

Living, Logos and Logos' body are identical. Dead, Logos' body lies before me. I cannot say 'Logos lies before me,' because Logos *is* not. If this body *were* Logos, as it was when he was living—not just Logos' body but Logos himself—I would see, feel, hear, movement. Except for this one small detail, it is the same. In point of logic, however, it is either the same or it is not the same. And if not the same because of only one detail, then plainly, incontrovertibly, not the same. In point of logic again, the only thing that is identical with a thing is that thing itself. And so while Logos' body is identical with Logos alive, when Logos is not alive there is nothing for Logos to be identical with, even though Logos' body remains identical with Logos' body.

When you pursue the ideas, the reasoning is without flaw: you can understand the reasoning. It is the unmoving body of Logos that is no longer Logos and yet that is as close to Logos as I shall ever again be: that is what is incomprehensible. My hands, my eyes, my nose, controvert my reasoning. A thousand years ago in a different social stratum and having a different temperament, I might have said, "Logos' body is dead but his spirit lives." Because that word 'but' comes unbidden to you, whether you are religious or no. If religious, all the problems are solved for you: the set of beliefs to follow the 'but' is laid out in advance, as the body itself will be laid out in accordance with ritual already laid down. But if you are not religious, there is no "where" for Logos to be: Logos *is* not. And yet, here before me is Logos' body, so very like what it was until a moment ago. How can this body be Logos' without at the same time being Logos?

I did not envy the religious their consolation, if that's what their beliefs, their ceremonies, do: console them. I invented my own ceremony. I fought my way through, not to beliefs, but to my own ragged understanding. It remains my poorest effort.

Not then, not while Logos' body lay before me, but later, during months of calling out, screaming, weeping, shouting, I became aware that a door had opened: nothing concerning death would from that time forward be alien to me. The Hurons and other Native Americans formerly deposited the body on a scaffold or in the boughs of trees in the forest. In New Caledonia the dead were taken to the highest point of a cliff and left on a bed of leaves or dried grass. The Pueblo peoples of Arizona and New Mexico buried their dead in the farthest recesses of the caves they themselves inhabited. Navies even today bury at sea. Dynastic Egypt, with its dry climate, found ways to preserve the body artificially, and they did so for one reason only: so that *ikhu, ka*, and *ba*—intelligence, soul, and double—would in time rejoin the mummy, the whole person rising again from the dead. I could comprehend, find room in my mind, my feeling, for all of this. I could pity, not from a distance, but crossing time, crossing civilizations, to enter into the baffled seeing of all these human beings who, like me, had to find some way, found this way, to deal with that which mocks understanding: the body that does not move.

And the intricacy, the variety, the extensiveness of the ceremonies, the rituals, gave people something to do. Since there is nothing you can do that will let you have that person you love *be* again as that very person, but since you must do *something*, then do in this elaborate detail all the following things in the following order for the following period of time and do not omit any of them or their order or their duration. All of it is a triumph of the human imagination: that since prehistory numberless millions of people all over the world have found something to do where there is nothing to be done.

It is not my own death that I labored so to understand. As long ago as Nantucket I had stared at the prospect of dying, had nearly invited it during a long night. The knowledge that I by my own hand could die was the lesson of the first station of solitude, a lesson never needing to be learned again. It let me throw off the last of the cords that bound me to a life not of my making. It was the criterion against which I thereafter measured my days: "Is this, which I contemplate doing, worth staying alive for?" Until you confront, then answer, that question, you will not begin to design the life that is yours to tailor so that it fits you, only you. You will not understand that finding, then committing to and pursuing, your own purposes is a reason sufficiently powerful, perhaps the most powerful, for staying alive, unless you are already persuaded that you live to fulfill the purposes of some Supreme Being. But then, you will hardly have come so far with me.

Understanding that my own death will end everything at all for me, I began a journey that soon became one of integrating all my actions, all my beliefs, into a single unified whole, intentionally

and unendingly defying the final triumph of the disintegration that
awaits me.

Why, then, is there no illumination in this for understanding
Logos' death?

They gave him back to me dead, you see. I had driven him,
living, to their hospital during the morning rush hour. Because he
was so sick, I preempted the breakdown lane for my route through
the solid mass of cars on the Beltway at eight in the morning, my
emergency lights flashing, leaning on my horn as I wove in and
out, finding empty bits of roadway, then running red lights when
I turned off the highway into the streets that would take me to the
hospital.

A police car stopped me.

"Please," I begged the officer, "I have to get to the vet's. Follow
me there and talk to me there but let me get there first."

He looked into the rear seat where Logos lay breathing rapidly,
shallowly. "No," he said. "Go ahead."

But by the time I reached the hospital, two other police cars
were behind me, red and blue lights blazing, sirens blaring. One
left; the other waited. And only when the vet had Logos on the
examining table, only when I was certain I had done everything I
could do, having delivered him into the expert hands of those who
would make him well again, did I talk to the policeman, who
lectured me but let me go.

On Friday morning I brought Logos to them living. On Monday morning they gave him back to me dead. I was not with him
the moment before, the moment of, the moment following his
dying. I will tell you without equivocating that it is essential to be
present at the dying of a person you love. It is all but impossible
anyway to grasp the fact that the dead body lying before you *is* no
longer that person. But trying to comprehend it when you have not
been with him, with her, the moment before, the moment of, and
the moment following the dying will set you a problem the mag-

nitude of which will occupy you for a very long time. I understand very little about mourning, but I understand this.

At a specific moment Logos died. I am certain of that because I understand the English language. What I am not certain of, and what I shall never know, is what moment it was.

I did not know it that day but the "few minutes ago" of the veterinarian who phoned me with his practiced artificial sympathy at eight minutes past eight o'clock on the morning of March 10, 1975, was only the first version of a story. It was a fabric containing holes that did not cleanly fit together, this incutting margin matching that outreaching one, this long slash overlapping that one. It was a man-made fabric, a fabrication. The continuity between Logos' living and his dying was rent, and for the next five years I would be compelled to try to piece it together.

I rushed to the hospital, flung open the door, burst through the waiting room and into the hallway, passed the examining rooms. At the door leading to the cage area, Dr. Arr barred my way: "You can't go in there!"

"I'm here for Logos." It was his hospital but Logos was mine.

"We didn't expect you so soon. He's not ready."

It all registered only later. Didn't expect me? Did they think I'd stop for groceries? Go to a movie? And get him ready how? For what?

They made me wait ten minutes, and then two attendants came through the doorway I had been prevented from entering. One carried the mat I had brought two days earlier for Logos to lie on. The other carried a tan garbage bag with Logos inside, his head hanging out. It would be part of what my third attorney, the one who filed suit for me, called the tort of outrage.

They placed these objects in the cargo section of my station wagon, then they left. Dr. Arr remained.

"How did he die?" I asked, looking only at Logos. At Logos' body.

"It was uremia." He went on, as though already I did not believe him: "Miss Koller, there's only so much a body can take."

It was not an answer. It was only a bunch of words strung together into a sentence that was uttered following my question. It was of course intended to be an answer. And that day, because it came hard on the heels of my question, I heard it as an answer. That day, leaning over Logos' body in the rear of my station wagon, I was not a being whose life is asking questions, listening closely, pressing out the meaning, the truth, from bunches of words. Logos was dead, and I was only thirty minutes into beginning to take that in.

During the night that did not end, a small, a very small, tatter of the person I had been only twenty-four hours before began a just noticeable movement. To and fro. Stop. To and fro. Stop. How did Logos die?

His dying was not predicted.

On Sunday afternoon, March 9, Logos lay in pain, a urinary catheter held in place with tape, the tape directly on the fur of his right thigh. He was lying on his left side, on his arthritic left leg, the leg he never lay on because it hurt too much. He lay, not on my mat but on a towel on a metal grid an inch above the concrete floor onto which flowed his own urine. So much infection filled his left eye, an inch above his urine, that he could not see out of the eye, lying in the concrete cage with the smell of urine still in it, even though I had sopped up as much of it as I could reach without disturbing the catheter. I went then into the next room and stood talking with Dr. Tee while Logos lay in the cage calling to me to take him away from that horror in which I had been leaving him for three whole days, calling me to take him with me, and I did not take him with me. I went to him when I heard the special high-pitched note he used just for calling me, and I laughed with the young veterinarian, agreeing that it indicated he was getting better, that it was as much vitality as he had exhibited since before I had brought him there. I laughed, yes, I laughed, and I stroked Logos' head and lay my face next to his, and I said, "I'll see you later, Sweet Puppy," but I never did. He was begging me to take him away, because he knew (as only later I began learning) what they had been doing to him there, and he wanted no more of it. Wasn't I supposed to be with him when he was in pain and discomfort? Then why was I leaving him there, where those things were happening to him? He was saying all that in that call, but I did not hear him. What Logos was and wanted and needed and did and thought and felt were as much a part of what I was and wanted and needed and did and thought and felt as though I myself were the initiator. And yet I did not hear him. I knew, or thought I knew, that he had to remain hospitalized for two or three more days, and so I steeled myself against wanting to take him with me. I ought to have tried to listen exactly to what he was so exactly saying to me, but I failed him. If I had taken him home that night, and brought him in again the following day, wouldn't he have lived? If I had taken him home and called Whit in Connecticut to tell him what I had found, wouldn't I have driven him to Whit the next day, and wouldn't Whit have made him well?

But I went home without him, and when Whit called later in the afternoon to see how Logos was doing, I in my ignorance said he was coming along fine, that I'd have him home by Wednesday, that the level of urea nitrogen in his blood, his BUN, was down to 40 and that Dr. Tee had said his own BUN was only 40. I said that I had had a long talk with a sail maker who had described the kind of canvas I could use to build Logos a low cart so that I could wheel him through the door to take him outside until he could use his legs again. And Whit said it was fine that I had found such good care for Logos, and I, I was gloating to Whit to show him that I hadn't needed him after all, that, although he had turned away from me that Friday morning I called him, at the moment in my life, in Logos' life, when we had most needed him, I had found someone else who was helping me. And Whit said he'd call me the next day to see how Logos was getting along. But the next day there was no Logos to get along at all.

The morning following March 10 I phoned Dr. Tee. Not Dr. Arr, because I had heard in his voice the day before that I would not learn the truth from him.

"How did Logos die?"

"Gee, I don't know. It was a surprise to me," said Dr. Tee. "They were changing the catheter, and while he was there on the table he died. Sometimes when a dog is very sick, the most ordinary thing will be just too much stress."

"Did Dr. Arr attempt to revive him?"

"I don't know. I wasn't on duty. I'll ask him and let you know."

New questions thronged my mind. I wrote them down, talked to Whit, talked with my own doctor, who agreed to meet with Tee to ask him the medical questions I didn't know how to ask.

Twelve days later, not having heard from Tee, I phoned again. Initially pleasant, he became rude and hostile when I suggested he meet me and my doctor to answer my questions.

"What are you going to do with all this information?" he demanded.

"Do? What would there be to do?" And then I understood he was afraid of legal action. "I don't know what I'm going to do. I just need to understand what happened." Pleading for information to which I had a right.

"I'll think about it and let you know," he finally said.

In two days he called. "I want to know what you and your doctor are going to ask that you don't already know. Dr. Arr *told* you that he found Logos nearly comatose that Monday morning."

I could not help crying out: a whole new picture of Logos' last hours flashed before me. I covered the phone with my hand. When I could speak again: "He did *not* tell me that. If he said so, he's lying."

"Listen," said Tee, "there's nothing to understand. Logos was sick, he was old, and he died. But I'll meet your doctor. Call me when you arrange it."

For twenty minutes I raged through the house, shouting aloud the new questions that the new story prompted, imagining aloud the answers that would give me the sequence of events still unknown to me.

The phone rang. It was Arr. He launched into medical matters so technical that I kept interrupting to ask him to explain, and he kept the flow coming, detail piled onto detail. Since you're so damned smart, he was saying, keep up with me. "I'm telling you all this now because my wife is having surgery next week and I can't meet you."

I had not asked to meet him.

"I'll think about what you said," I answered.

Fifteen days had elapsed since his call announcing Logos' death. Three more years would pass before I saw him or Tee again. It would be in a conference room around a long table, and they, with their attorneys on either side, would be giving their depositions to my attorney. By then I had acquired two other versions of when Logos died.

I called Whit and asked him to explain to me what Tee had said, what Arr had said.

"Alice, I need to see their records. Ask them to send me their records on Logos."

I have to be grateful to Whit for telling me to obtain the hospital records, for studying them, for explaining to me as best he could what had happened. The records became a text to which I bent all my powers of exegesis. When I acted as my own attorney, I hired a handwriting expert to analyze them. He would have testified as an expert witness for me, telling the court about colors and kinds of inks, pressures of pens, thicknesses and thinnesses of straight and curving lines, times at which notations were written, whether before or on or after the dates inscribed. A laboratory technician I knew spent hours examining the laboratory reports, explaining how each test is conducted, how soon results are available, the usual procedures for testing when there is an emergency. I could not have collected the fattening file of inconsistencies if I had not had the hospital records.

Not knowing what Whit would do with the records but assuming that a fellow veterinarian would not misuse the collegiality of the profession, Dr. Arr sent him the outpatient cards, the hospital sheets, and the laboratory sheets on which they had scribbled their notes about what they had done.

The records were not written with a fellow veterinarian in mind, let alone a philosopher. They were not written in sentences, one following another, the way the records of human patients are written, so that a doctor on duty in the night, suddenly called to see a patient she had never seen before, would know exactly what had been done when, and what had to be done now, at once. They were abbreviations of abbreviations, the barest jottings minimally necessary for recall. Puzzling over them, Whit pointed out places where what the two vets had done was incomplete, places where they had omitted doing things they ought to have done, and places where why they had done this rather than that was unclear. All this was in the light of eight years of what Whit knew about Logos, of what I could tell him I had seen the vets do, of what they had told me they had done.

I phoned Randall, and we met at his office. He was not then practicing law but only lawyering on the staff of a federal agency. Once, long before, we had engaged ourselves to marry. It let me say, "I need your help. I want to sue them."

"Timmie," he said when I told him what they had told me and what I still needed to know, "go home to your typewriter and write down everything that happened. Write everything he said and they said and you said. Write every fact you can remember, no matter how small. Write all of it. Then stop for a while. It will let you remember more, so add that to the rest of it. When you finish, send it to me. That will be the basis of your suit. Of course I'll file it for you. I'll help any way I can."

I have to be grateful to Randall for making me write that narrative, forty-three pages it turned out to be. As with Whit, so with Randall: each gave me the best advice I could have received. Because those two sets of paper, the veterinary records and my written narrative, were invaluable to me and to all my succeeding attorneys during the next five years of trying to learn the truth. Each man advised me from within his own profession, and the two professions contained the knowledge I most needed. Both men were close friends.

When you take the actions that your commitments require, there are no rules about who will accompany you. Do not assume that those you honor will, in such a circumstance, continue to honor you. Because once you make plain the full extent of what you're prepared to do, you may touch too near your friend's commitment, nearer than either of you would have wished, could have anticipated. At close quarters, each of you may see the commitment of the other as an assault on yours. Will you then, at the price of the friend, retain the commitment? Or will you, at the price of the commitment, retain the friend?

It was Randall who, six months after Logos' death, found the attendant who provided the second version of the time of death.

On Sunday evening, March 9, 1975, I lay on my bed, too tired to undress for the night but not too tired to doze. And then Logos called me. I arose from my bed at once and called to him, called his name in all the directions in which he might be: kitchen, hallway, at the foot of the stairs, in a corner of my very room. I was fully awake calling him, looking for him, watching for him to appear. Where was he? Long minutes passed before I realized that Logos was not there.

I sat on the edge of my bed and glanced at my watch. Nine-thirty. I could call the hospital. No, he's fine. When I left him at four, he was improving.

Call.

The answering service said, "Everyone left at nine."

I hung up. So nothing is wrong, or they'd be there. I took Ousia outside for a few minutes, came in, locked up the house, and fell asleep wondering how a sick animal could be left alone in a hospital all night long.

But at nine-thirty the attendant called Dr. Tee at home to tell him that Logos was dying.

"And did he immediately come to the hospital?"

"No."

"What did he say?"

"He said he was tired, he had stayed an extra hour to finish everything that needed doing."

"So he did not return to the hospital?"

"He didn't come back."

"And when did you leave for the night?"

"Eleven. When my shift ended."

"And by then Logos was dead?"

"He was dead when I left."

Randall called me in Maine where I had moved with Ousia to start a life without Logos, except that he was equally present in his absence. This new version of when Logos died, the second, made me revise my first imagining of his dying, and it was not to be borne.

What Randall did not do was meet the man face-to-face; he did not prepare an affidavit for the man to sign in his, Randall's, presence. I did not know then that Randall had not done any of these things, or even that they were elementary things for an attorney to have done. Randall told my second attorney that he had made notes of his phone conversation with the man, but months later he had still not produced them, never produced them. My second attorney phoned the same man in February 1976. He remembered having talked with Randall in October, five months earlier, and repeated the same story. My attorney, in his notes to the file, remarked on the man's reluctance and defensiveness.

I'll get him on our side, I thought. Wasn't he the same attendant I had talked with at the hospital that Sunday afternoon while Tee was busy with other dogs? He had told me he was glad I was there because that day Logos seemed almost cheerful but that when I wasn't there Logos was very unhappy, wouldn't respond to anyone else. The man was no longer working at the hospital but I had his home phone number.

He set me straight immediately. "I never laid eyes on you," he said. "I wasn't there on Sunday. I worked the morning shift." At seven o'clock that Monday morning when he arrived for work, he found Logos dead.

"What did you do?"

"What was there to do? Dogs died there all the time. Dr. Arr would take care of it when he came in."

"When was he due?"

"Eight o'clock."

"And when Dr. Arr arrived at eight, did you call his attention to Logos, tell him Logos was dead?"

"No. He usually checked all the cages anyway when he first came in."

"And Logos? What did he do when he checked Logos?"

"I don't know. I wasn't watching him. I was doing my job."

It was the third version.

Not my second, but my third, attorney filed suit for veterinary malpractice against Tee, Arr, and their hospital. The third attorney, and the one following him, tried for two years but failed to find this man so they could obtain his sworn testimony. In the fourth year, when I became my own attorney, I found him.

I did not do it alone but with the assistance of someone in law enforcement who had access to information I could never, without her help, have obtained.

Although we knew where he worked, we planned to surprise him at home, giving him time to get there, to change, to relax. Six o'clock would be a good time. The day itself would have to be a last-minute decision, depending upon when Ingrid finished her other duties. I spent some afternoons in one of my law libraries reading the standard texts on interviewing hostile witnesses, as we by then knew the man would be. I understood the strategy, I memorized the format, I memorized the key questions, I memorized their most effective order. Late one afternoon Ingrid called. An hour later we met, driving to the man's house in her car.

"I'll handle it," I said. "I've been studying how. But come in with me."

It was dark when we arrived. We went up the steps of the small house and knocked. Through the window we could see the man sitting on a couch with a woman. He came to the door, opened it.

"Yes?" With the lighted room behind him, he was trying to adjust his vision to see us in the darkness.

"Are you Carl Carlson?" I asked.

"Yes. Who are you? What do you want?"

The doorway was a step up from the porch where Ingrid and I stood, and I was looking up at him instead of being able to look at him on my same level, look straight at him. I had a thousand words to speak, a hundred questions to ask. Here was the man who knew the truth about Logos' dying, the truth I had pursued for four years. I opened my mouth to ask him the first question in my memorized series, but all of it froze on my tongue.

In the instant, Ingrid took over, identifying both of us to him.

"We just want to ask you a few questions about the night Logos died at the hospital. May we come in?"

The man drew back as though Ingrid had struck him. "I don't know anything about it," he said, and his voice was hard.

I found a word to say. It was not part of the inquisitorial string I had misplaced: it was not demanding, not peremptory at all. "Please," I said.

"This is my house and you're intruding. If you don't leave right now, I'll call the police." He slammed the door.

I stood in disbelief. Ingrid took my arm and led me back to her car, then drove to the delicatessen where I had parked. We went inside and ordered sandwiches.

"All my studying, yet I stood there unable to utter a word."

"It didn't matter. He wasn't going to tell you anything."

I looked at Ingrid under the unsubtle lights of the deli, and suddenly I saw that her hair was concealing a large bandage.

"What's that?"

"Nothing. Line of duty."

"Are you refusing to answer my questions, too? Tell me."

A wounded dog she was rescuing had in his pain turned on her, gashed the whole left side of her head.

"When did it happen?"

"This afternoon."

"And you came with me anyway."

"You wouldn't have known how to get to his house."

"I would, if you had given me the address."

"I wouldn't have given you the address."

When we parted I put my arms around her, trying not to touch the bandaged side.

Whit behaved differently, but the effect was the same. When I became my own attorney and read through four years' worth of motions, depositions, interrogatories, affidavits, amicus briefs,

notes of phone conversations, and correspondence, I found a letter
he had written to the defendants enclosing his records on Logos'
medical history, together with his hope that the information would
be helpful. It was not a current letter. He had written it, airmail
special delivery, eleven months after March 10, 1975. It bore the
same date as the letter he had written my attorney saying that, for
confidential reasons, he was withdrawing as the expert witness in
my case.

If you have had no dealings with the law, you start by learning
the difference between criminal law and civil law.

In criminal law, when someone harms you by acting against
you in ways that the body politic, the state, classifies as a crime,
the state itself prosecutes the person. If he or she is convicted, the
punishment is a term in prison or, for lesser crimes, community
service that a court considers equivalent to a prison term. Although
you were harmed by the person's action, you neither pay for the
attorney nor do you receive recompense.

In civil law, when you are harmed you hire your own attorney.
If a jury finds the person who harmed you guilty, he or she is
penalized by being ordered to pay you a sum of money, the damages,
awarded in supposed proportion to the extent of your loss, the harm
done you. You pay for your attorney, but you receive recompense.

In a criminal matter, the decision whether to prosecute is out
of your hands, even though you were harmed. The state's attorneys
decide, and (if they're not overwhelmed by cases involving greater
harm than was done to you) they do so on the basis of the amount
and kind of evidence. If they have or can acquire evidence sufficient
to convict the wrongdoer, they will prosecute. The political or
economic status of the wrongdoer is not supposed to be a consideration.

In a civil matter, your attorney is less interested in whether you
have a case than in the potential amount of your damages. If your

attorney believes that your damages will be substantial, he or she will waive an hourly fee and will accept instead a percentage, usually a third to a half, of your damages. The difference to you is whether you pay now and keep paying as the case moves along, often for years, or whether you pay only after the case is decided and only if you win. So it is very easy to gauge your attorney's belief in your chances of winning a civil case by whether he quotes you his hourly fee or whether she agrees to take your case on contingency, contingent upon your winning. And he in turn, she in turn, makes that decision on the basis of the amount of damages courts customarily award in cases similar to yours.

Someone walks into your home and sprays black paint across an authentic Rembrandt hanging on your wall. If you find the person and can provide evidence at the civil law's level of probity, any attorney you approach will take your case on a contingency basis. The value of your loss is huge, it can be established as huge without question, and so a third of huge will be worth the attorney's time, even in advance of hearing a judge award the actual sum.

Logos was a dog. A purebred dog, but a dog. In the eyes of the law, a dog is a piece of property, like your kitchen table. No matter that a dog is, or was at one time, a living being. Slaves, too, living beings, were once legally property. Having thus classified dogs as chattel, and without inquiring impartially into the matter, the law arbitrarily assigned them a value. It was necessary that some value be assigned so that the law would have a criterion by which to establish damages that could be asked by someone foolish enough to go to court with a case involving the loss of a dog.

The law's assessment for damages in such a case can be summed up in two words: not much. For the loss of a dog, or of any domestic or companion animal, courts customarily award the market value of the animal at the time of the loss. Market value is the amount of money someone would have paid you for the animal had you sold him or her just before your loss.

The calculation works like this. Say your dog was the American Grand Victor, the top German shepherd in the United States. Everyone wanted a puppy from his bloodline and willingly paid top prices in breeding fees. Had you decided to sell him, any breeder would gladly have paid you $50,000. Give or take a few dollars, the respected shepherd breeders in the country would agree he was worth that sum. Then, through the fault of someone you relied on—a handler, a vet—the dog dies, aged three. He was at his peak: there is no question of his value. The court will award you $50,000. Perhaps even court costs and attorneys' fees (and triple damages, if you can prove that the handler, the vet, acted with malice).

Now sit as the attorney approached by the person who has lost this valuable dog. One-third of $50,000 is $16,666. If the case were open-and-shut, so that only about a month's worth of your time would be required from filing to judgment (or to settlement out of court), even though it stretched over a year, you might take the case on contingency. Might. It would be borderline whether your share of the damages would be worth a month of your time: 160 hours to net you $16,666. Ninety percent of the American public would consider that a handsome sum for a month's work, but to an attorney it's only a hundred dollars an hour. Still, you, the attorney, would at least consider taking the case on contingency. Perhaps if the client upped your share to one-half, you'd do it. But if you thought it would take more than a month, even with these damages you'd ask for your hourly fee.

Logos was twelve years, eight months, and thirteen (or was it fourteen?) days old when he died. I paid $75 for him as a four-month-old puppy. Would you have bought him, nearly thirteen, lame from arthritis? A court would not even have divided $75 by thirteen years in order to set Logos' market value. A court would have decided that his value at death was zero dollars. And his value would have been set at zero even though, in the year he died, 1975, Americans spent $1 billion for veterinary care. For their legally valueless animals, Americans also spent four times that sum on food, collars, leashes, doghouses, clipping, grooming, and license fees. Not to mention the original purchase price.

And so no attorney would represent me on contingency. For an attorney's time, I would have to pay, I in fact paid, his hourly fee for each and every hour. After the first hour and a half of my second attorney's time (Randall did not charge me a fee), I had used up the total value of the sum I might have been awarded if Logos had arranged to die at the age of three. Because he was so careless of my purse as to die at the age of twelve and some, every dollar I paid out in attorney's fees was a dollar I would never see again.

Each of my four attorneys subsequent to Randall, and Randall first of all, explained all this to me. They'd pause then, and lean back in their chairs, or lean forward, or get up and walk around, and then they'd ask, one after the other, "Why are you doing this?"

"Alice, why are you doing this?" Over and over, people asked me the same question.

Over and over I gave the same answer: "Because I have to know when Logos died, and why and how."

It is not difficult to teach someone the difference between understanding something and not understanding it. You understand it when your thinking flows smoothly over the whole of it, taking it all in, fitting it all together with everything else already smoothly present. You do not understand when some jagged item stops the onward rush. It can be exceedingly tiny, that point that interrupts the swirl of thinking. It is the point around which you will ask a question, or several questions. The questions you at first raise may not be the question you ultimately want to ask, but you will discover what that question is only by formulating and reformulating all these other questions until you slice through all of them to your real question. When you've undertaken this process a few hundred thousand times, the upward thrusting point that stops you, the question you really want to ask, emerges faster, and then a few hundred thousand times after that you recognize the question immediately.

The point jutting out of the law's doctrine of damages in my civil matter, and malpractice falls within the civil law, was the value of a (nonhuman) animal.

Randall began my education about damages soon after he read my narrative.

"How much money was Logos worth?"

"Money?"

"Yes. If I had wanted to buy him, what would you have taken for him?"

"You can't believe I'd have sold him."

"I know that, Tim. But we're trying to decide what damages to ask. So we have to have a figure."

When Randall understood at last that he was asking a question I was incapable of answering, he became my voice. "We'll ask for a sum that will exhaust the limits of their insurance policy. We'll ask for a million dollars: half a million from each of them." He sat back in his chair and grinned.

Months passed without Randall's finding time to draw up the legal papers. Then he became ill and took a leave of absence from his job. After more weeks, I found another attorney.

My second attorney, after an initial flurry, developed digititis. Digititis is a severe inflammation of the forefinger (left or right) that renders lawyers incapable of dialing a client's telephone number. I have dealt with people in a wide range of professions, and I can confidently say that digititis is exclusive to the practice of law. Exclusive and exhaustive: all and only lawyers firmly believe that it is not necessary, that it is never necessary, to return a client's calls. No doubt it is a required course in law school: all lawyers exhibit the ailment in canonical form.

It was my third attorney who, eighteen months after March 10, 1975, filed suit for me. The reason that television cameras were at the courthouse that day, the reason that one crew came to my house that evening, lighting up my living room to look and feel like noon, was that my suit asked for damages of half a million dollars: $250,000 in compensatory damages and $250,000 in punitive damages. The declaration still called Logos my "property," but, to the standard charges of medical negligence and of misrepresentation of the facts surrounding his death, it added the tort of outrage, then newly recognized in Maryland. I was claiming compensation for the outrageous conduct of the two veterinarians in their mistreatment of my property.

Outrage. There is something to be said for the law, after all, if it has the insight to choose this word to name a tort, a civil wrong. Of course the law uses the term to characterize only certain discernible conduct, not certain indiscernible feelings. Outrageous conduct, in law, is an act or acts violating accepted standards of behavior or taste. No matter that the word also described an indeterminately large portion of my consciousness, beginning with the moment I answered the ringing telephone in my house in northern Virginia and not ending for five, six, seven years.

"My suit," I said, looking straight into the television cameras, "concerns the value an individual animal has, both in his own right and to the person who is his friend. The very particular animal who was my friend Logos had the right to be respected for his own sake as the individual he was, rather than being dealt with as an object that can be replaced because it is of little value. The outcome of this lawsuit will, I hope, make new law that other persons can then use to assert the value and rights of other individual animals."

Reporters who came prepared to do a funny little story about the kooky lady from Virginia who wanted half a million dollars for the loss of her dog (a dog, for God's sake!) stopped using the word 'pet' after talking with me for only a few minutes. They listened closely to me before they turned on their cameras, so that when they began filming they were asking me serious questions and recording my serious answers. And when the tape, which their editors barely touched, was played on the eleven o'clock news, it was part of the news, not the flip final piece that sends you away laughing.

When the defendants received our declaration they demurred to both its counts, and they kept on demurring at every opportunity for more than a year. They were trying to persuade the court that I had no case.

I asked for help from national organizations that worked in behalf of animals. The Humane Society of the United States submitted a brief supporting our opposition to the defendants' demurrer. HSUS argued that the court should view my case "as one primarily compensating the plaintiff—as opposed to injuries to her property—and as one having overwhelmingly important public policy implications." The Friends of Animals, jointly with the Committee for Humane Legislation, filed a motion to intervene and a memorandum of law supporting our opposition to a new demurrer from the defendants. The Friends' brief provided an early outline of the legal precedents, citing *Levine* v. *Knowles*, a Florida case only ten years earlier, in which the District Court of Appeals wrote that an owner may sue to recover compensatory damages for a dog wrongfully destroyed, just as for "any other property wrongfully destroyed"; and that punitive damages might also be recoverable if the destruction was caused "in such an outrageous manner as to amount to a willful, wanton, reckless, or malicious disregard of the owner's rights." The Society for Animal Rights wrote a brief amicus curiae, twenty pages of close reasoning, precedent piled on precedent: the *Levine* case again, which relied on the *LaPorte* decision rejecting "market value" as determining the value of a dog; the Texas Appeals court affirming the trial court's award of $200 for pain and suffering to the owner of a dog deliberately and unlawfully killed by local police; *Brown* v. *Frontier Theatres*, allowing to stand the award of several thousand dollars for the "sentimental value" of family heirlooms having no market value but that had been burned in a fire due to defendants' negligence; and, most tellingly, *Southern Express Co.* v. *Owens*, in which the Supreme Court of Alabama held that damages are not limited to the market value of a property when the market value cannot be proved and may have been negligible. The court wrote:

> Where the article or thing is so unusual in its character
> that market value cannot be predicated of it, its value, or
> plaintiff's damages, must be ascertained in some other rational
> way, and from such elements as are attainable. . . . Where the
> article lost has no market value, the rule of damages seems then
> to be its value to the plaintiff.

No precedent in any of this, of course, for damages of half a million dollars, but then the Texas court's award in *Garland* was two hundred dollars more than the zero dollars the defendants expected to pay, and the *Brown* award was several thousand dollars higher than zero too. The law moves on square wheels. If I had won, the court would not have awarded the full damages I asked, but I might have received the thirty thousand dollars I spent in attorneys' fees and court costs. And thereafter others could use my award as precedent for their claim of damages. And market value would have vanished as the criterion for the value of an individual (nonhuman) animal.

Attorneys for the veterinarians understood all this and fought me every inch of the way. There is a court paper filed almost every

two weeks for three and a half years, four court jackets full of
documents.

The brilliant amicus brief of the Society for Animal Rights was
written by Henry Mark Holzer, a professor at Brooklyn Law
School. During the seventh of the nine months I was my own
attorney, learning both the law and veterinary medicine, bringing
to bear on the only thing that mattered to me everything I knew
about reasoning, writing, teaching, studying, locating facts and
people, and endlessly trying to persuade a blind court system that
I, a woman, existed, and that I needed to know why Logos did
not, my head began to break apart. I phoned Holzer to ask him
to represent me.

"Your case has laid out all the issues concerning the value of
an individual animal for the next decade," he said.

"Very gratifying to hear that from an attorney. From you. I
wanted to make new law."

"You're doing it."

"Will you be my attorney, then?"

"No, I'm teaching and I don't have time."

"But you believe my case is important."

There was a silence on the line. I thought we had been disconnected. "Are you still there?"

"Alice, I can't take your case because you and I are writing
about the same thing. I can't join you: you're my competition."

When we hung up I stared out the window for a long time.
People do have, do work for, more than one purpose. I had believed
his purpose was to move the law forward in everything having to
do with the rights of nonhuman animals. I did not understand until
he said so that his way of achieving that purpose was to write of it
rather than to teach it, to argue for it in court.

Ousia called me from the next room. I rolled back my chair
to go to her. Before I was on my feet it came to me that I had just

been given not one but two compliments. I remember the moment, because I almost smiled.

While my civil suit limped along I was also working to bring criminal charges against the two veterinarians. Cruelty to animals is a crime and, like all crimes, attorneys for the state prosecute it. But mysterious things kept happening: files were mislaid and not found for a long time; reports of interviews with important witnesses were lost; jurisdiction was bandied back and forth between the county attorney and the state's attorney, one wanting to call a grand jury, the other refusing to approve the request. This too went on for years. If it hadn't been for people within the system who unofficially helped me in spite of official opposition, I would not have had the inside information that let me keep the state's attorneys' office off-balance for so long. When they finally refused to file criminal charges against Arr and Tee, I phoned a state legislator who asked the state's attorney for Montgomery County to meet with me to explain the reasons for his office's decision. They were enraged that I had gone over their heads to compel them to talk with me in person, and so not only the state's attorney but several of his colleagues were waiting for me the day I walked into his office, I alone, no reporter, no attorney, no friend accompanying me. They wiped the floor with me. When I left I had exactly as much information as when I entered: the decision to prosecute was theirs, and they were not going to prosecute. Driving home, I realized that it had taken all of them to deal with just me, but my hands did not stop shaking until I turned into my driveway.

Early on, while I waited for Randall to file my suit, I went into the public files of the Maryland Board of Veterinary Medical Examiners, who not only licensed all vets in the state but also heard complaints against them. Dr. Arr was a member of the board and was in fact up for reappointment the following summer. In the board's files I discovered that seven persons had found it worthwhile to complain against Arr, to go through the time-consuming but

ultimately futile procedure of asking veterinarians to condemn a
fellow veterinarian for mishandling the animals left in his or her
care. I called each of these people, listened with anguish to their
anguished stories, then asked whether they'd help me petition the
governor to remove Arr from the board.

To my lengthy meeting with the state's secretary of agriculture,
I carried copies of all their complaints, together with the names
and addresses of nine others who had not bothered to go to the
board about Arr. One of the secretary's duties was to recommend
veterinarians to be members of the board, and one of the governor's
duties was to approve the secretary's recommendations.

"If Arr has done all these things, he should be removed," the
secretary told me. He was an unlikely ally, a white Southern male,
courtly to a white woman, a farmer born and reared. But he also
understood that I understood power.

"Even though the board has taken no significant action against
him," the secretary said, "the number and nature of these complaints
could taint the board's activities in the public's eyes."

To ensure that the governor himself knew what we wanted,
three of us carried our petition to his office in Annapolis. Sheets
of rain slowed my driving that day, and my car almost stalled on
a roadway that lay four inches under water. Even so, we met at
the agreed time at the State House, then tramped up an imposing
stairway to the office of the governor's assistant who would accept
the petition in his behalf.

The assistant was not there. Yes, the appointment was marked
on his calendar, but no, we do not know where he is.

We regrouped in a corridor, discussing what we might do.
And then I saw the governor himself walking in our direction,
flanked by bodyguards two heads taller than he. Without hesitating
I walked straight toward him, and in the same instant the bodyguards occupied the floor between us. I ignored them.

"Governor Mandel," I said, "your assistant failed to keep his appointment with us this morning, and so I would like to hand our petition directly to you."

You could not say that the governor greeted us warmly, but he waved the two men aside and stood waiting to hear me out. He was, after all, a politician, and petitions come from people who vote.

I began. "This petition urges you to remove Dr. Arr from the Veterinary Board. In support, we have the following documents." It did not take long for me to have my say: all of it was in writing in the papers I placed into his hands.

"Thank you for accepting our petition," I said. "I appreciate your spending these few minutes with us."

He nodded. I reached out to shake hands, and even the bodyguards saw that my palm was empty.

That morning Marvin Mandel had other matters on his mind. Later the same day a grand jury indicted him on charges of racketeering and mail fraud, and in time he was tried, convicted, and served a term in prison.

But not before the secretary of agriculture recommended that Dr. Arr not be reappointed to the Veterinary Board. Publicly, Arr announced that, in accordance with a new Maryland law, his seat on the board was one of two that from then on would be filled by laypersons.

For twelve years Logos lived with me, in the open air of the country, free. They left him to die alone, at night, in a cage. He did everything with me, but he did this last thing without me. He was beyond price to me. They were not blind to that: they were contemptuous of it. Although his death occurred in darkness, I blazed every imaginable light onto it. I had found something to do.

☐   ☐   ☐

A sequence of events had occurred when I was not present. When I could not obtain the truth about that sequence of events by asking the persons who *were* present, the ones having expert knowledge of the medical events but also the ones, same or different, having expert knowledge by having seen and heard what Logos did and what was done for Logos, I sued for malpractice the veterinarians into whose care I had entrusted him. It was so clear to me: through my lawsuit I was going to learn the truth. I, who had saved my own life by learning how to tell myself the truth, thereby becoming able to recognize when others were being truthful with me, was merely continuing my journey on the exceedingly narrow path I had worn by my own use.

I needed to know how and when and why Logos died. Needed: as I needed air, as I needed water.

I had not changed. Just as on Nantucket in 1962 I had to know the truth, so in northern Virginia in 1975 I had to know the truth. More so than on Nantucket, because by 1975 I had been seeking out and looking at what was true for thirteen years. On Nantucket the truth lay only within me, to be lifted out using the hard discipline that had become my mind during the years I studied for and earned my doctorate in philosophy. In suburban Washington, however, the truth lay in the hands of others.

It did not seem to me then that the truths I was setting myself to discover in court would match in severity the truths I had learned on Nantucket, the ones that had let me begin a whole new life carved to my own contours. What I would learn would be painful because I would be acquiring the facts about Logos' pain, but those facts would also—might also—let me let him die.

That was to be the outcome of my lawsuit. We would get into court, all of us, and I would learn the truth, and then I could let Logos die.

It takes a very long time to learn that a courtroom is the last place in the world for learning the truth. In courtrooms people do not tell the truth, if the truth is the whole truth: they only do not lie. Even then, they do not lie only if they know you possess irrefutable evidence that could prove they are lying. The reason they do not lie when you have such evidence is that, in addition to whatever civil wrong you have charged them with, the state will thereupon charge them with the criminal wrong of perjury. Furthermore, their attorneys are officers of the court who, if they tell their clients to lie, can be criminally charged with suborning perjury and, if convicted, can be jailed and disbarred. So it is only the prospect of severe punishment that prevents lying in court. Nothing prevents not telling the truth. I had misconstrued the whole endeavor.

My lawsuit never went to trial.

In cases involving injury caused by someone having expert knowledge who failed to exercise the knowledge and skill of his profession in accordance with his profession's standards, the law requires that another member of the same profession testify in behalf of the plaintiff on two key matters. The first is to set forth the acknowledged standards of the profession: that under this circumstance, that action is customarily taken, while under another circumstance, the same action is never undertaken. The second matter is to respond to questions the cumulative essence of which will inform the court that the person(s) charged with injuring the plaintiff acted contrary to the standards in this instance and in that and that, and also that they failed to act when the standards required them to act in that instance and in this and this.

For bridges that collapse, plaintiffs need an engineer as expert witness. For dogs who die in veterinary hospitals, plaintiffs need a veterinarian. No veterinarian would serve as my expert witness, sitting at my table in court, the plaintiff's table, while two fellow

veterinarians sat across the room as defendants charged with injuring me.

And so, eighteen days short of five years after the telephone
began ringing in my almost empty house in northern Virginia, five
houses later, five attorneys later (six, counting me), thirty thousand
dollars poorer, still not knowing the truth about Logos' dying, I
had to ask the court to dismiss my case.

That night of February 20, 1980, when I called Doug Breg-
man, my last attorney who should have been my first, to tell him
to go ahead and do the only thing the law permitted me to do,
Ousia died.

I mourned Logos with private tears and a public action that
was directed also at establishing new law on the issue of the value
of an individual nonhuman animal. But I mourned Ousia by closing
her death into myself: sealed her death into the last moments of the
bitterly cold grey day when I walked away from the frozen ground
on the hill next to where Logos was buried, where the hired diggers
buried Ousia for me.

I have mourned, I mourn, both ways. I have spent hours, days,
crying, yelling, raging, punching walls, floors, calling out Logos's
name, all his names that he will never again hear. And I have
forborne tears, roaring, hitting hard objects with my fists, voicing
Ousia's name, all her names. I took the second way because I could
not endure continuing the first, extending the first to contain this
new grief. But the second way is equally bad. The carapace I flung
around myself to stave off Ousia's death is an inadequate shield.
When I have pressed myself beyond my own awareness of being
tired, when I have fought and lost some mean battle, when I have
sought and failed to find some course of action that would let me
slice through a tangled path, Ousia's dying is with me in each
detail, moment following moment, and effortlessly with me, as
though I were not exerting fathomless effort to hold it back.

To everyone else, the death of that being you love for his own sake, for her own sake, is an event that occurs on a certain day. For you, the death only begins that day. It is not an event: it is only the first moment in a process that lives in you, springing up into the present, engulfing you years, decades, later, as though it were the first moment again.

Do not look for consolation. Consolation is a little thing, small change in the hands of others, easily dispensed. What you want is a big thing, a thing so big that no matter how hard anyone might try, might even want to try, to give it to you, he cannot succeed, she cannot succeed. What you want is to be again with that being you love, and even you cannot bring that about.

The most you can hope for is that while you are crying a good friend will be with you, will hold you while you cry, will not tell you to stop crying, will listen to you each time you try to speak, will let you talk when you can talk, will do all this for some indeterminate segment of time simply because it is necessary to do. You will not often, perhaps not even a second time, call on that friend for his arms, for her arms. But you will remember the gift and you will offer it in turn to that friend, or to another, or perhaps one day even to a stranger. That holding, that listening, may be the most generous gift adult human beings can give one another: I am letting you observe my sorrowing, and what you are observing as you hold me is my love for someone else.

You break a bone in your leg. You go to a doctor to have her reduce the fracture, to give you something for pain. In time the bone will heal, the pain will go away. To whom can you go when your life breaks? You mourn because you love: there is no other reason. So there is nothing to be healed of. Would you be healed of your loving? Well, then, stop loving. Better still: do not love at all this way. Or, if you love, arrange to die before he dies, before she dies. These are the only ways to avoid mourning.

There are those who would cure you of your mourning. Since

they also claim to be able to cure you of your loving in circumstances when your loving harms you, it is quite consistent for them to claim to cure your mourning. They will tell you that you must accept his death, her death, and get on with your life.

It is an odd word to use in connection with dying: 'accept.' You accept a gift, an offer, a job, but death is none of these. You accept the obligation of paying your debts, but death is not a duty. A group accepts you as a member, but there can be no welcoming of you into the midst of those already dead. Scientists accept properly confirmed hypotheses, but what is the hypothesis deserving acceptance from the knowledgeable when someone you love dies? You accept a reprimand when you've done something incorrectly, particularly when the person correcting you has more power than you, so that you decide not to challenge him, but what have you done incorrectly when someone you love dies? In fact, you ask yourself that question unceasingly (the curers call it "guilt"), and you would eagerly acknowledge the correction if you were able to make it, but those who speak of accepting a death are not concerned with correcting anything. Cotton cloth accepts ink while oilskins repel it: the cotton absorbs the ink, wicking it up, making it part of the cloth. Ah, here we are coming closer to the relevant sense of 'accept.' And yet, the ink and the cotton interact in this way, becoming inseparably inked cotton, because they have certain well-known characteristics. Why do the curers assume that human beings are more like cotton than oilskin when the substance to be wicked up into ourselves is not palpable ink but the palpable death of someone we love? We are in fact more like oilskins: we repel that death; we all say "No."

The curers can intend only the remaining sense of 'accept': "to receive into the mind (see UNDERSTAND)," says my dictionary. So we are back to the starting place. But that dying cannot be understood, be woven into the fabric of all the other things you understand. I hereby contradict outright the curers and the soothers: the dying of someone you love is not to be *understood* at all. No part of it resembles in any smallest detail anything you already understand. It is surd, from Latin for 'deaf,' 'stupid.' It cannot be heard: you are deaf to it. You cannot take it up into yourself: it renders you stupid. More, it is *ab*surd: beyond surd, away from surd, ridiculously unreasonable, having no rational or orderly relationship to human life.

The curers are wrong. The dying of someone we love is so far from being natural to us that we repel it. It cannot enter our ears, our minds: no part of it can be taken into ourselves.

You are running along a country road. The day is clear, perhaps a few clouds pass overhead, it may even be raining. But you are in your stride, breathing evenly, sweating easily. Your course lies along your familiar route, three more miles, eight miles, well within your powers. With the next striking of the ball of your foot on the roadway, your body crashes into the concrete wall that in that moment rises up out of the ground. How is that to be understood?

"Must get on with your life," they also say, those who would cure you, those who would soothe you. But 'must' is another slippery word. It carries a burden far heavier than its meaning can support. Young children hear 'must' uttered in a severe tone of voice by their parents. Long after they grow up and know that they can always ask "Why?" they often forget to ask, hearing only the long-ago tone of voice. Subordinates in military service hear the same tone of voice from their superiors, but by now they understand why without asking: they will be court-martialed if they disobey. To a child, to a soldier, 'must' carries an implicit threat of punishment: the person who says 'must' has the power to enforce his will, her will.

Usually of course there *is* a reason for the imperative, and that's how its true colors are seen. It is a hypothetical imperative, an imperative only under a condition: "Do this (unless you want that to happen)." Categorical imperatives are imperatives without a condition: "Do this." So when someone can provide a reason for a 'must,' you're being commanded with a hypothetical imperative, one that you can in point of logic disobey. You have this logical alternative even though there will be consequences, usually painful, for disobeying. With a categorical imperative, the hearer has no choice in point of logic but to obey. But since disobeying a categorical imperative is logically impossible, there will be no consequences of any kind, since there will have been no action from which a consequence can ensue.

Categorical imperatives are difficult to find: I cannot give you one example. The condition is there but merely unstated in the 'must'-statements you usually hear. People who use 'must' rely on you not to ask for the reason, the consequences that will ensue if you disobey. They expect you to hear only the severe tone of voice of your childhood.

When someone tells you that you must end your mourning, end that which does not end, that you must get on with your life, what is the painful consequence that will accrue to you if you disobey? Listen to the pitiably few, pitiably innocuous, consequences you will face if you do not stop mourning (as though you can, as though it is in your power to stop). Compare the pain of those consequences with the pain now living in you. Then ask yourself how reliable a guide that curer is, promising you a pain greater than mourning if you do not stop mourning.

Those who would cure you might as well have said, "You must stop loving." Because that is what you do when you mourn: you still love. Mourning is the other face of loving. How can there be a coin with only one side?

But of course they don't mean that you should stop loving. They simply mean that loving is not for-its-own-sake. They mean that people love only for some benefit to themselves. Since you should only benefit from loving, you won't really mourn when your benefactor dies: you'll merely, for some not too long period, feel the loss of your benefit. Still, many other people can confer benefits, even the very benefits you lost. So, after an interval has elapsed, the interval decreed by the community whose rules you follow, you should look around for someone else. If you look, you will find him for however long he lives, find her for the rest of her life. You can keep that up until you yourself die.

Or so they might say, if you press them very hard.

I have no doubt that more people believe that view of loving than mine: that loving is for no benefit, for no reason other than the person's being who he is, who she is. But what loving is is not decided by counting heads. When you love someone for his own sake, the loving is as distinctive as you are, as he is, as the pair you both lovingly create and sustain. No one on the outside of your pair is either qualified to utter or justified in uttering a single 'must' to you: you yourselves make your choices, committing yourself to them, bearing in mind their consequences. And a consequence of your loving is that when one of you dies, the other mourns. If no one outside of your pair had either the knowledge or the right to command you before, how has such a person gained the knowledge or the right to say 'must' to you now?

The only 'must' in mourning is one that rises up out of you, out of your loving. Having to know what's true was one of only two principles I carried with me, along with Logos, when I left Nantucket. For the next twelve years, both that principle and Logos were hourly at the center of my life. How, then, could Logos die and I not need to know the truth about his dying? Everything else that happened was only a next step, and a next, in my being who I am and in Logos' having been who he was.

The circumstances of the dying of someone you love may not lay a comparable demand on you. You may be present at the dying, and it may occur in such a way that it crowns the life.

Marvin Goody, a Boston architect greatly admired, a man who loved to sail, died on the new sailboat he himself had meticulously

outfitted, died of a heart attack in the very moment he switched off
its engine and invited the wind. Only Joan Goody, his partner in
his architectural firm, his wife, his best friend, was with him.
Except that it came too soon, you cannot have a better death than
that. To Joan Goody in her mourning, the Parks Department of
the City of Boston and the Friends of the Public Garden gave
something to do: design a memorial that would remind all the
people who came to the Garden of the many things Marvin had
done, out of his own pocket and with his own time, to take care
of the Garden, to preserve it for everyone, simply because he
cherished it. Joan did not design a statue: Marvin would not have
liked a statue. She designed something that is quite like him: something graceful but enduring, something integral to the Garden and
yet slightly apart from the main way. During his life Marvin had
designed and overseen the construction of a certain area of the
Garden: a broad circle of rose-grey granite paving stones at the
base of a flagpole he had also erected. Joan's memorial is a broken
circle of rose-grey granite benches placed around the perimeter of
that stonework. The granite benches will keep alive forever the
memory of the man who walked in the Public Garden every day
and whose artist's hand, eye, and mind sustain it still. You cannot
have a good mourning, but you cannot have a better one than Joan's.

I do not expect anyone to be present at my dying. I will not
be in a hospital; there will be no nurse, no doctor. If I cannot be
in the one place where I wish to be, I'll at least try to be in my
own bed in my own house. But if, *per impossibile*, some friend is
with me, he will see, she will see, that I am in tears. If you are
that friend, know that, like Socrates although not for his reason, I
will not be weeping for my own death. At my very last I will
unstop at last all the mourning that lives in me for those I loved,
still love: my father, my Logos, my Ousia.

Somewhere in all the useless books and articles I read about
mourning someone wrote: "Have I used up my despair?" As though

you have only a limited amount. Or as though the person you're mourning could be allocated only, deserved only, a certain share. But mourning cannot be used up. My mourning will end only when I end. As so as I lie dying I'll unlock all the tears that still remain in me for Andrew Koller, and for Logos. For Ousia's death that I did not let begin, I'll rip out the seal that has stopped it up, a death enormous enough in its own right but compounded for coming at the very moment I was forced to end my search for the truth about Logos'.

As I lie dying I won't be writing, since I would not be dying if I still had the strength to write. I won't be asking questions because I'll understand that I'm dying, and nothing about it will puzzle me. I won't be collecting fierce beauty because almost certainly I won't be in an art museum or out among the trees under the sky. The circumstances will not let me do any of these things I chose to do, spent my life doing. But there is one other thing I did while I lived, committed myself to, accepted the consequences of: I loved for no reason other than that those I loved were who they were. And that's what I'll be doing as I die: loving them. I'll call out to them one by one, or in pairs, or all together, calling them all the names they had when they were with me, calling them not because I expect to be with them again in another world but because I don't, because their lives as beloved will end with my end. Mourning, loving, Alice, Andrew, Logos, Ousia, all: all will end.

"And what of Kairos?"

I think there is no third way to mourn, but if I do not have the good fortune to die before Kairos, he may teach me otherwise.

13

RECESSING

ALONE AMONG ALL the stations of solitude, at this station choosing is not demanded of you. It is in fact a recess from choosing.

And yet of course you choose when to arrive and when to depart, arriving here after any station at all in whatever sequence you are now following, or even midway during your stay elsewhere. You need not stop at all. But neither can you stay too long, on pain of obviating whatever segments of the circuit you made before you arrived: a recess is only taking time out.

It is a peculiarity of this station that if you have not yet found your work at its own station, you may find it here, since the best of you is in play when you work, making new rules out of sheer playfulness and thereby extending the former boundaries of the field in which your play freewheels, able to make new rules because the old ones are so familiar a functioning part of you. Here you are most like a child at play, as children still, in some parts of the country, run and tumble in their schoolyards at recess, swinging on the swings, serious about their games because games are the only things adults let them be serious about. Just so, at this station you are at serious play, absorbed in some doing for no reason beyond the doing. Suddenly, that which you are doing out of your exuberance may make itself known to you as your work.

Should you then come here looking for your work? If you have not encountered the feeling of doing something for its own sake at any other place doing any other thing, then come here. Sit on the shore. Watch the water in motion on the surface of the lake. Take off your shoes, roll up the legs of your trousers, tie your skirt behind you, wade in knee-deep, and let the water's warmth or coolness quiet your skin, quiet you. It can be a version of standing open, another place to stand open, after you know what standing open is.

If you find your work here, do not stay. Go where the work is to be done and do it. Only take away with you the feeling of the place: time out from choosing, being at play.

If you've already found your work, recessing may nevertheless puzzle you.

Do you garden? I have never seen anyone plant seeds or bulbs or rooted cuttings who does not also tend the plants until they flower or fruit, fertilizing them at the proper time, watering them, weeding them, deadheading the blooms to encourage continued flowering or to allow the bulbs to manufacture the nourishment they will contain within themselves during the long winter so that they will in early spring bloom again. All that is serious play.

Do you read to the blind? Ski cross-country? Hike the Appalachian Trail? Attend theatre openings? Go to baseball games to roar for your team, no matter that you swelter in the grandstand and are packed next to others of your kind in the subways coming and going? You are recessing.

Nothing comes to you yet? Sit. Look. Wait until you are no longer rehashing battles, figuring out someone else's motives, projecting future ploys. At a certain moment, you will inhale a deep breath, and the air you expel will carry it all away. Now you are at recess. It will be enough to bring you back another time. And another. And perhaps the time after that, you may find yourself doing something in play. And if not, doing nothing will do.

□   □   □

I collect fierce beauty, and I am curator of my own collection. I do not house it in a building: most of it cannot be housed at all, and some part of it is in me, in some sense of 'in' that philosophers still quarrel about.

A certain light precedes winter darkness by ten minutes or so. You see it only if the afternoon sky has not been overcast and only after you can no longer discern any trace of the pale yellow that is the final color of sunset. What remains is luminosity. Sometimes I'm almost willing to call that light 'silver,' except that I think of silver as a metal, not a color. And yet, it's the lustre of silver that lets even the least discriminating eye distinguish a silver spoon from a pewter one. An object has lustre when it reflects or radiates light evenly, glowing from without or within, when no area of its surface catches moving points of light to make it sparkle. Just so is this winter light: lustrous.

It needs a New England winter for the seeing, or wherever leaves fall from deciduous trees in their appointed seasons. Leaves fill the spaces between twig and branch, branch and trunk, tree and tree, obscuring the light. It is there, between the bare branches of trees standing together in the woods of winter, that I look for this light. With no color in the swiftly departing light for trees to reflect, they become black against it: narrow saplings near broad trunks, straight branches beyond sinuous ones, traceries of twigs. That interplay of lustre and line is fierce beauty for me.

I sustain the feel of a lute I more than once balanced on the four points of my left thigh just above my knee, the inside of my right forearm, the inside of my right thigh, and against my chest two inches to the right of my barely beating heart. Even now I still my breath, remembering the fragility my body cradled. I have held a newborn infant in my arms, and 'fragile' was not applicable to it: an infant *weighs*. But a lute is almost weightless: although a good part of your body all but encompasses it as you play it, it seems to hover just out of reach at the outermost edges of the tips of your fingers, of the cloth of your garments. Your speaking voice alone can set it quivering.

I did not expect to be so moved by the mere feel of the instrument. It was its sound that first ravished me, even though I was hearing it only from a recording being broadcast over public radio. I had to be in the presence of that sound instead of at two removes. And in time I beheld the making of the exquisite sound that transforms my body into a reverberating sound box, trembling with each stroke of each of the lutenist's fingers against the paired strings. I failed in my half-year's worth of lessons to produce that sound myself on my teacher's lute. I do not possess a lute of my own. But the sound of a lute is my sound: mine, of me. I single it out from among all other sounds, whether its source is one among the instruments of a consort or whether it suddenly emerges from my car radio as I drive among the noises of a city street.

And a lute is an amazement of beauty to the eye. Its neck hangs down at right angles to its flat belly. Its sound hole, the "rose," from which its hushing tone issues, is an intricacy of carving. Its great swelling back is composed of ribs, narrow strips of wood glued together, often as thin as the thirty-secondth part of an inch, dark heartwood alternating with light sapwood, as many as thirty-seven to a single instrument.

The triple beauty of the lute is almost unbearable to me. Its sound and feel and look are in my collection.

The leaves of jasmine are pinnately compound, each leaf in fact composed of seven leaflets, six in pairs opposite one another along the leafstalk, the seventh at its end. The leaflets are lance-shaped, the seventh longer than the others, and their edges are entire, neither toothed nor lobed. It grows as a vine in its native east Asia, and so in New England it cannot overwinter outdoors. But its vining habit means that its slender stems trail far beyond the rim of the pot that is its home, spilling downward in arching curves.

Jasmine does not bloom in summer but just after winter settles in. In early summer jasmine is only a mass of lengthening stems carrying their small lanceolate leaflets. By then you can suspend it outdoors in its pot, taking care to face it toward the sun, nurturing it with light and water and an eye watchful for its natural pests and sudden summer storms. In mid-October, when you bring it indoors again, you will wait another month or more before its filaments of buds appear, hundreds on each stem if you have served it well. And then one December morning three buds will have opened in the hour since you last examined them for the very possibility, and you will nearly faint from the intensity of the fragrance.

When I first stepped through the doorway of a greenhouse where jasmine climbed across the whole south-facing wall, I fell in love with it in the instant. I walked straight to it, standing as close as I dared without crushing the profusion of flowers, each white five-petaled blossom opening out flat at the end of its finely elongated tube, and I enveloped myself in the scent, inhaling to my left, my right, above my head. Five years passed while I sustained the fragrance in memory, and then, the January before last, wandering into a greenhouse in another state, I all at once felt as if I were being flung against the plant bench I was passing. Jasmine, not remembered now but gloriously present, cascaded from a pot an arm's length above my head. The plant was promised to someone else. The florist listened to my special pleading, then led me to a growing-on area not open to the public where a youngling rested on a windowsill. She had not planned to offer it for sale for another year, but I bought it at once, thereby breaking my own rule that beauty must be free. Still, at a few pennies under nine dollars, the rule had barely been breached. And if I were to divide that sum by the number of times I've drawn the jasmine's beauty into myself by nose and eye and fingertip since it has been in my household, the price per piece would run to five hundred zeroes following the decimal point.

In the beginning, beauty had to be free for me because I could not pay for it. But the world cooperated by offering it to me at no cost. Museums and many of the great gardens used to be free. And most of nature is there for the looking, hearing, smelling. Concerts are another matter. I traveled five hours by car and train into Manhattan to listen to Julian Bream play his lute for one hour in the salon of the Frick Collection that is the perfect size for hearing that perfect sound. None of that was free. There is little music in my collection.

Philosophers whose business is aesthetics talk about free beauty in another sense. They mean that your judgment about the excellence of a work of art cannot depend upon who owns it, that the judgment of beauty is a disinterested one, that the work exists for its own sake. There's something of that in my slippery rule. The status of an object that exists for its own sake is unaffected by whether it rests in my house or in a museum: I could not treasure it more in one place than the other. But I tell you that I would not decline the gift of a Tiepolo drawing. Not because it would be mine, mine, mine, but because it would become an intimate part of the hours of my day.

I should more carefully call my collection a collect*ing*. It is a continuous activity of gathering in, sometimes deliberately going in search of, always being open to. Rarely do I turn aside from it, and then only in extraordinary circumstances that also bring a halt to everything else I do.

Once a flock of Canada geese rose up from a pond a hundred feet behind someone I was talking to. In the next moment the rich orange light of the setting afternoon sun was suffusing the undersides of their bodies and wings with a color never otherwise theirs, and then they were gone. For those three seconds I was neither listening to my friend nor talking nor standing on the ground: I was only a pair of eyes and there was only the light from the west burnishing the slowly beating wings of eight geese moving in V-formation toward the south.

On a June day four years ago some galling news came my way, and, trying to make sense of it, untying one professional connection and beginning to tie into another, I had neither wit nor will to quiet my pounding heart, my knotted stomach. I drove Kairos to the bicycle path we almost daily walked. A pavement wide enough for three abreast ran between a wooded area on one side and well-kept lawns on the other, a few feet of wildness buffering the land-owners from the path-users. The paving followed an easy curve and, after about a thousand feet, bordered a playing field that could accommodate two soccer matches at once and a baseball game as well. Even so, there was room enough for parents and watchers to stand around cheering, to make their way from one contest to another, and still there'd be an unused trapezoid of ground for someone with a dog and a ball.

It was late afternoon by then. Earlier, the wind had moved around to the west, blowing before it the humidity I cannot tolerate, leaving the air fresh, the sky bright blue and cloudless. Kairos trotted ahead of me on the path, and when we reached the playing field I let my eye wander over the groupings of people, idly noting the range of activities that absorbed them.

And then I saw the yellow balloon high in the air. Untethered balloons, no matter their color, rise ever upward, then vanish, but this balloon bobbed and whirled, dipped and soared, all within a visibly circumscribed height. My eye followed the thin white cord angling downward at 45 degrees and connected it to a man on the ground. I crossed the field toward him, and for nearly a quarter of an hour I watched him work the balloon, making it ride each vagrant breeze, while Kairos romped with his female Labrador, the man and I occasionally talking about nothing. After a time I lured Kairos away and we returned home. The yellow balloon against the blue sky tethered to earth by a thin white cord accompanied me for the rest of the evening, until an interval of sleep distanced me from the shattering day.

For its own sake: as I love, as I work. That is the fierceness of the beauty in my collection: that it wrenches me out of the ongoing hour, immersing me in itself. I am in the presence of the thing for no reason other than that the thing is what it is.

Not all beauty is fierce to me. Most of the objects in my household are there because they long ago spoke to me. They are quiet beauty, part of my every day. Any new item joins the company only by harmonizing with or deepening or adding unusual panache to everything else already there. I have arranged, I still arrange, all this: it is the context in which I daily function. Sooner than let some piece of clothing jar my sense of line, some bowl invade the congruence of the other shapes and colors that grace my table, I'll give the thing away. That doesn't mean that everything is always in its place. It means that, wherever it is, it still belongs with everything else.

Beauty is fierce for me when it disconnects me from my ordinary purposes, the great ones and the subsidiary, from even the most wretched circumstances, for the seconds, minutes, hours that I'm in its presence, that it's simply and sheerly present to me. I can almost always arrest the battering of some ugly encounter, some destroyed expectation, by going off in search of fierce beauty: that is its power. When I return to the adversity that had tuned my minded body to full uproar, I have a cleaner purchase on it, I am newly alert to practicable ways of dealing with it, order (or at least calm) tinges what had before been my runaway thinking.

But do I not thereby *use* it? Am I not making it serve a purpose for my sake, in spite of all my talk of being in its presence for its own sake?

Logos first came into my life to serve a certain purpose: to protect me, to let me live without other human beings in an isolated place. To assure his serving that purpose, I took care of him. The taking-caring-of turned into caring-about, and then I was loving Logos for his own sake. He still served that old purpose for me, but it ceased to be my primary reason for having him: he was in my life for no reason. Ousia, too, was to have served a purpose that I could not, in the event, let her serve, because she too became part of my life for her own sake. She nevertheless kept Logos company when deadlines demanded uninterrupted days at my desk. And I do not doubt that the presence of two German shepherds dissuaded anyone from forcibly entering my various secluded dwellings. From having come to me to serve a purpose, Kairos too now occupies that same domain of freedom, even though one of the things he does in the course of existing for his own sake is to warn off those who might be considering intruding.

Writing, I do the only work I'm willing to do for its own sake. That it now supports me is a purpose I had in mind for it when I undertook it, but that purpose was not primary. Indeed, if I had written only to earn money, I think that no part of my life would be what it is today. Except perhaps for collecting beauty.

I am unshakably certain about loving and working. That other purposes attach to them is incidental, has no bearing on their true status.

The case is the same with beauty.

Luthiers construct lutes so that lutenists can play them, but no lute was ever made for the express purpose of impassioning me by its sound, its look, its feel. Horticulturists grow jasmine because they know that people will buy it (they do not grow dandelions), but no jasmine was ever grown to purposely dizzy me by its fragrance. "Mister Lincoln," the hybrid tea whose black buds open into urn-shaped roses of deep blood red, their old rose fragrance luring you to inhale it again and again, was developed by rosiers to have just that unfolding of colors (they did not cloak in mourning the rose they named "Peace"), but those who planted it in dozens in the gardens at Dumbarton Oaks did not intend that every June I'd shove my chair back from my desk in Virginia, drive into Washington, and kneel on the grass to them, as close as decency allowed, until the linings of my nostrils were saturated and my eyes had to look away. White-throated sparrows are perching birds that also sing, have been singing since the late Pleistocene. No single white-throat ever had in mind that I should stand motionless and mute each time I hear its achingly pure song. Nor does the male cardinal design his coloring so that my eyes can never drink their fill of him, the brilliant velvety red of his feathers, the reddish-yellow beak set into the black square whose corners form right angles so perfect that you think a protractor must have laid them down.

That all these things and uncountable others are fierce beauty to me is simply a coming together of them and me. A painstaking combing through of the minutiae of my whole life might explain why this and not that, but even then most thises might remain inexplicable. I am not interested in that piecing together: even with infinite time I would not do it. I am content to say that chance first brought the thing of beauty into my presence or me into its, that I at once knew it to be fierce beauty, and that thereafter, as a rational person, I sought out its presence again whenever I could.

They are not within my control, these things of beauty. Except for my own bit of jasmine sunning itself in my southeasterly windows, I must go to them. I must stop what I'm doing and begin some new doing that will eventuate in my being in the presence of Bellini's *St. Francis* or the four copper beeches radiant in the center of the town of Greenfield Hill. I disrupt my usual doings in order to engage in the peculiar activity that is a doing for its own sake.

When I am in acute physical pain, I bring before my mind's eye the image of a male cardinal. Sometimes the image of a newly opening rose, any species, any color, will lift me out of the present anguish. I call on them because they do in fact have that power for me, but they are no less perfect instances of fierce beauty when I come upon them where they naturally abide.

By parity of reasoning, it makes no difference whether on Tuesday I plan to go to the Fogg Museum on Saturday, or whether on Tuesday, after fruitless hours of trying to think out a difficult paragraph, I fling on my coat and drive through the lunchtime traffic of Cambridge to see the Fogg's original of Rembrandt's *A Winter Landscape*. In advance, I know that the drawing will transfix me in the present by its presence: an imperfect and slightly reduced reproduction of it rests directly in my line of vision whenever I raise my eyes from the sheets of paper on my desk. It is the same reason people spend millions of private and public dollars to build and maintain museums, preserving for their own and all generations to the end of time the human legacy in which such a drawing can exist.

That I from time to time seek out fierce beauty in order to replace a noxious present with a perfect one no more alters the status of that beauty as existing for its own sake than my relying on Kairos to frighten off some sound in the night that awakens me alters the status of my loving him for his own sake. Neither does my having been able to live for two years on the royalty income from *An Unknown Woman* alter its status as work I did for the sake of the doing.

I shall be told that my collecting fierce beauty is a substitute for the God the proofs for whose existence do not exist, or for the human beings who are not at the heart of my life, or for one or another of the pharmacopoeia of drugs that others use to banish the pain they will not confront.

But it matters not at all to me how you interpret what I do. By the time you reach these final words, if I have not made clear to you the idea of doing something for its own sake, the fault is in me or in your understanding, not in the idea. If, on the other hand,

I have clarified the idea but you have not yet woven it into the fabric of your days because you need an exemplar from your own experience, this is the station at which you can find it.

Even understanding the idea, you may choose not to let it pattern your doings. Your circuit of the stations of solitude will thereby differ from mine. Not only in detail, as is to be expected, but in principle as well.

Each station of solitude is a choosing, the whole circuit a collocation of choosings. It is up to you to choose whether even to begin.